The Templars
History & Myth

To Jon Buller and Susan Schade
les châtelains de Mont Becket

The Templars
History & Myth

Michael Haag

P
PROFILE BOOKS

This paperback edition published in 2009
First published in Great Britain in 2008 by
PROFILE BOOKS LTD
3A Exmouth House
Pine Street
Exmouth Market
London EC1R 0JH
www.profilebooks.com

With acknowledgment – and thanks – to Paul Simpson for his
contribution to the chapter, *Born Again Templars: Templars in Popular Culture.*

9 10 8

The moral right of the author has been asserted

Printed and bound in the UK by Clays, Bungay, Suffolk

Typeset in Garamold & Sabon

A CIP catalogue record for this book is available
from the British Library

ISBN 978 1 84668 153 0
eISBN 978 1 84765 251 5

The paper this book is printed on is certified by the © 1996 Forest Stewardship
Council A.C. (FSC). It is ancient-forest friendly. The printer
holds FSC chain of custody SGS-COC-2061

FSC
Mixed Sources
Product group from well-managed
forests and other controlled sources
Cert no. SGS-COC-2061
www.fsc.org
© 1996 Forest Stewardship Council

Contents

The Rise (1099 to 1150)   87

The Power (1150–1291)   125

The Aftermath   239

SURVIVALS   241

CONSPIRACIES   251

Locations   283

OUTREMER   285

Israel   286

Templarism   327

CONTENTS

Introduction

The Templars were founded in Jerusalem on Christmas Day 1119 at the Church of the Holy Sepulchre, on the spot which marks the crucifixion, burial and resurrection of Jesus Christ. A religious order of fighting knights, their headquarters was on the Temple Mount, that vast platform rising above the city where King Solomon had built his Temple two thousand years before. Surrounded by these potent historical and sacred associations, the Templars assumed their responsibility to protect pilgrims visiting the holy shrines and to defend the Holy Land.

The Templars soon became a formidable international organisation. Vast donations of properties were made in Europe to maintain this elite taskforce overseas, and special rights and privileges were granted by popes and kings. Dressed in their white tunics emblazoned with a red cross, they became the West's first uniformed standing army and also pioneered an extensive financial network that reached from London and Paris to the Euphrates and the Nile. As an order they became powerful and wealthy, but as individuals their existence was simple and austere. Their bravery was legendary, their dedication was absolute and their attrition rate was high; at least twenty thousand Templars were killed, either on the battlefield or after being taken captive and refusing to renounce their faith to save their lives.

Yet in the end the Templars were destroyed not by the Muslims in the East but by their fellow Christians in the West. On Friday 13 October 1307 the Templars were arrested throughout France and soon elsewhere throughout Europe. They were charged with heinous heresies, obscenities, homosexual practises and idol worship; many were tortured and confessed. The end came in 1314 when the Templars' last Grand Master was burnt alive at the stake.

The shock and mystery of their downfall has excited interest in the Templars for seven centuries since. Some historians have conjectured that the Templars' sojourn in the East brought them into contact with Gnosticism, the ancient heresy embraced by the Cathars of France, while the Freemasons have drawn a line of occult knowledge transmitted from the Temple of Solomon via the Templars to themselves.

Never has speculation about the Templars been more feverish than today. Did the Templars carry out excavations beneath the Temple Mount and find something extraordinary that explains their rise to power and wealth and, according to some, their continued but clandestine existence to this day? Was it some vast treasure? Or the Ark of the Covenant? The Holy Grail? The secret to the life of Christ and his message? And where did this secret travel when the Templars were suppressed? To Scotland, to America?

What is certainly true is that the rise and fall of the Templars exactly corresponded to the two centuries of the crusading venture in the East, where after a series of outrages against Western pilgrims and Eastern Christians, and in the face of renewed aggression which threatened all of Europe, the First Crusade was launched in 1095 to recover Asia Minor, Syria and Palestine from Muslim occupation. Simultaneously, the struggle was being fought in the Iberian peninsula where the Templars eventually helped liberate Spain and Portugal. But the crusading effort in the East, with the Templars at its heart, was never enough to withstand the overwhelming Muslim forces that could be brought into the field when they were united by the likes of Saladin or the Mamelukes. In 1291 when the Mamelukes drove the last Frankish settlers out of the Holy Land, the Templars lost the main purpose of their existence, and soon they fell victim to the rapacious greed and tyrannical ambitions of the King of France.

One of the great Templar mysteries has always been the role played by the Papacy in the downfall of the order. The Pope was meant to be their protector and to the Pope alone the Templars owed obedience, yet to judge from the apparently supine acquiescence of the Papacy to the demands of the King of France, the Pope either betrayed the Templars or believed them guilty of terrible crimes. These conjectures took a dramatic turn in 2007, when the Vatican published a facsimile edition of a parchment recording the Templar leaders' testimony to Papal investigators at Chinon in 1308. This document had been discovered in the Vatican Secret Archives and revealed – seven hundred years too late to save the lives of James of Molay and countless other knights – that the Pope believed the Templars innocent of heresy.

About this book

There are seven parts to this book. The first four cover the historical narrative. They begin with the origins of Solomon's Temple in Jerusalem – from which the Templars took their name. And they continue with the rise of Christianity and the challenge of Islam – the context for pilgrimages and the Crusades which became the raison d'être for the Templars. The narrative then proceeds through the foundation of the Templars, their rise to power and their dramatic fall as the Holy Land was lost to the Muslims, and it concludes with their trial. Part Five deals with the aftermath of the Templars' dissolution, their various survivals, and their co-optation by Freemasons and conspiracy theorists.

The books' last two parts include guides to the most interesting Templar sites and buildings to be seen today in the Middle East and Europe, and to the emergence of Templarism – the adoption of Templar history and myth in popular culture, from fiction to computer games, as well as reviews of the best Templar books and websites.

MAP OF OUTREMER – CRUSADER TERRITORY IN THE HOLY LAND

CILICIA

Tarsus

COUNTY OF EDESSA

Edessa

Seyhan

Ayas

Baghras

Antioch

Aleppo

Euphrates

PRINCIPALITY OF ANTIOCH

Latakia

Kyrenia

Famagusta

CYPRUS

Kolossi

Limassol

ASSASSINS

Hama

Margat

Masyaf

Tortosa

Ruad

Safita (Chastel Blanc)

Krak des Chevaliers

Homs

MEDITERRANEAN SEA

Tripoli

Gibelet

COUNTY OF TRIPOLI

Beirut

Sidon

Litani

Damascus

Château de Mer

Beaufort

Tyre

Banyas

Saphet

Le Chastellet

Acre

Tiberias

Castel Pèlerin (Athlit)

Hattin

Sea of Galilee

Jordan

La Feve

Caesarea

Nablus

KINGDOM OF JERUSALEM

Jaffa

Ascalon

Ibelin

Jerusalem

Gaza

Ahamant (Amman)

Beth Gibelin

Dead Sea

Kerak

Damietta

Montreal

EGYPT

Petra

Gulf of Suez

Ile de Graye

Aqaba

Gulf of Aqaba

Crusader territory
Lost in 1144
X   Battlefield
Castle
•   Town / city

Part I

The Contexts

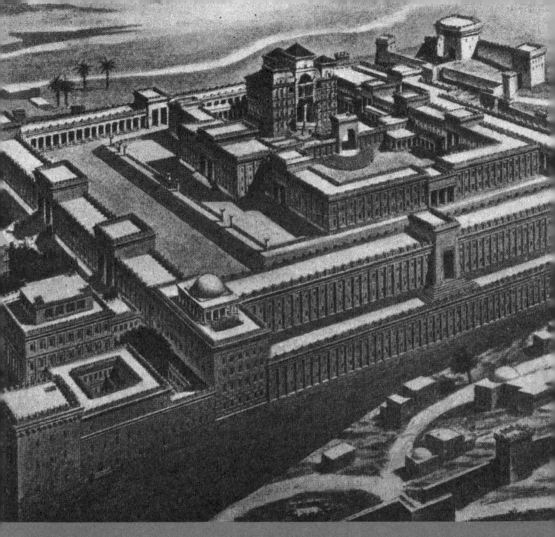

A fanciful early twentieth-century reconstruction of the Temple of Solomon on the Temple Mount

The Temple of Solomon

Three Temples and a Vision

The story of the Templars must begin with that of the Temple Mount in Jerusalem, where the Dome of the Rock stands today. For it was here that Solomon's Temple was built – the legendary, lost temple of the Jews, from which the Templars, as guardians of the Holy Land, took their name, and on whose site they created their military and spiritual headquarters. Sacred to Judaism, Christianity and Islam, no world site has greater resonance; nor, as home of the Ark of the Covenant, such enduring myth.

Physically, the Temple Mount takes the form of a vast platform, which was constructed over a natural hill by Herod the Great to support his gigantic temple – built around 25–10 BC on the site of Solomon's original temple of a thousand years earlier. It is Herod's Temple that is referred to in the *Gospel of Mark 13:1–2*, when a disciple says to Jesus,

'Master, see what manner of stones and what buildings are here!', to which Jesus replies, 'Seest thou these great buildings? There shall not be left one stone upon another, that shall not be thrown down.' And it was this temple that, duly bearing out the prophecy, was destroyed by the Roman emperor Titus in AD 70 in the course of putting down a Jewish rebellion.

The Temple of Solomon

Though nothing survives of Herod's Temple, the exposed western retaining wall of the Temple Mount platform, famously known as the Wailing Wall, has come to symbolise not only the lost Temple of Herod but the first temple built on this same spot three thousand years ago, the Temple of Solomon.

King Solomon is visited by the Queen of Sheba

Solomon, the son of David and Bathsheba, became King of Israel in about 962 BC and died in about 922 BC. During the forty years of his reign, he expanded trade and political contacts, centralised the authority of the crown against tribal fragmentation, and engaged in an elaborate building programme. His principal building works were the royal palace and the Temple in Jerusalem.

Almost all that we know about the planning and building of Solomon's Temple comes from the Old Testament, in particular the books *2 Samuel*, *1 Kings* and *1 Chronicles*. We also know from *2 Kings* about the Assyrians' capture of Jerusalem in 586 BC, and how they destroyed the city, burnt down Solomon's Temple, and sent the population into exile at Babylon where their lament is recorded in *Psalms 137:1*: 'By the rivers of Babylon, there we sat down, yea, we wept, when we remembered Zion.'

We are told by the later *Book of Ezra* that after the Assyrians were overthrown by the Persians, the Persian King Cyrus the Great gave permission for the Jews to return home from their captivity in Babylon and to rebuild their temple. Begun in 520 BC and completed five years later, this Second Temple, also known as the Temple of Zerubbabel, stood on the same spot as the Temple of Solomon and probably followed its plan, but owing to the reduced condition of the Jews at the time it was not possible to reproduce the magnificence of Solomon's decorations.

Jerusalem remained part of the Persian Empire for two hundred years. But when Alexander the Great defeated the Persian King Darius III at the battle of Issus in 333 BC the entire Middle East came under the rule and cultural influence of the Greeks. In time the Greeks were superseded by the Romans, though much of Greek culture remained. Palestine, as the Romans called it, became part of the Roman Empire in 63 BC, but it was given complete autonomy under Herod the Great, a Jew who had proved himself loyal to Roman interests and was installed as King of the Jews in 37 BC.

By Herod's time the Second Temple had suffered five centuries of wear and decay, but it would have been sacrilege for him to have torn it down. Instead he incorporated the Second Temple in his plans, enlarging and refurbishing it on a grandiose scale; in effect it was a third temple, though it still counted as the second. But in less than a century Herod's Temple too was destroyed.

There was yet another temple, and though it never really existed it was described in great detail in the Old Testament *Book of Ezekiel*. The prophet Ezekiel was among those deported to Babylon where he had a vision that Israel was restored to its former glory and that Solomon's Temple had risen again from its ruins. Ezekiel's Temple was the expression of a yearning for the Temple of Solomon, a symbol of a lost ideal. In that sense, and not only for Jews, but for all peoples, the Temple of Solomon has become one of the great legendary buildings of the world, a monument that has inspired imaginations for thousands of years.

The New Testament adds another dimension to Ezekiel's symbolism of the Temple. After prophesying the destruction of the Temple, Jesus announces in the *Gospel of John 2:16*, 'Destroy this temple, and in three days I will raise it up', words which are taken as referring to his own death and resurrection, so that in place of the destroyed earthly Temple, Jesus becomes an everlasting divine Temple. For Christians the resurrection, the cornerstone of their faith, was expressed in this vision of Jesus as the new Temple, and of Paradise as the new Jerusalem.

The Bible and History

Everything we know about the First Temple at Jerusalem comes from the Old Testament, and the same applies even to the existence of the Kingdom of David and Solomon. There are no accounts by outsiders, nor is there any material evidence – not helped by present-day religious and political sensitivities about archaeological digs at the Temple Mount. This has led some to argue that there is no historical basis for the ancient kingdom or the original Temple. But there is too much circumstantial evidence – political, economic and cultural – to dismiss the biblical account. For example there are the details of the complex commercial relationships between Solomon and King Hiram of Tyre (also called Huram in some parts of the Bible), who is an independently attested historical figure.

The existence of Israel as a people and a place was already mentioned by the ancient Egyptians as early as c1209 BC, during the reign of Merneptah, son of Ramses II. And within a century of Solomon's reign (c962–c922 BC), events and figures in the Bible find corroboration in Assyrian inscriptions, and thereafter in contemporary Persian, Greek and Roman texts.

But it is also true that the books of the Old Testament were often written much later than the events they describe. For example four centuries had elapsed before an account of the construction of the First Temple was given in *1 Kings*, and indeed by then it had already been destroyed and its most sacred object, the Ark of the Covenant, had long since disappeared. When *1 Kings* was written, the Jews were a broken and oppressed people who seemed to have somehow lost the favour of God, and at least part of its purpose was to remind them of a time when they had been powerful and united in the presence of God, who had dwelt among them in the splendour of the Temple. More than a historical account, *1 Kings* was a book of desire and hope, an injunction to return to pious ways to restore what had been lost.

Here are the dates of composition, as generally agreed by biblical scholars, of those Old Testament books which describe the reigns of David and Solomon and the period of the First Temple.

2 Samuel: written during the Babylonian exile, sixth century BC, but working with earlier sources.

1 and 2 Kings: as *2 Samuel*.

1 and 2 Chronicles: written in the latter half of the fourth century BC, ie 350–300 BC.

Ezra: Ezra himself arrived in Jerusalem in 397 BC, but the book was written a half century later by the same authors or compilers as *Chronicles*.

Psalms: though ascribed to David by tradition, in fact they were composed and collected over six centuries, with some in their original form perhaps dating to the First Temple period and all of them collected after the Babylonian exile.

Ezekiel: Ezekiel went to Babylon in 597 BC, and he may have written all or part of his book while there, but it is also possible that it is a third century pseudepigrapha, that is a fake written to look three hundred years older.

The books of the New Testament: Often written long after the event, these likewise have purposes beyond the historical. For example, the *Gospel of Mark* was written in tumultuous times, during or immediately after a Jewish rebellion against Rome which was put down by the Emperor Titus in AD 70 when he also razed the Second Temple to the ground, and so the words ascribed to Jesus probably owe less to prophecy than to hindsight. The same is true of the words uttered by Jesus in the *Gospel of John 2:16*, 'Destroy this temple, and in three days I will raise it up.' These are taken as referring to the death and resurrection of Jesus, which occurred in about AD 30, whereas John's Gospel was written no earlier than AD 85.

Sacred Origins of Jerusalem

Long before there was a Temple, and before Jerusalem, there was the Ophel hill. Tombs dating to 3200 BC have been found on the Ophel hill, which was to become David's city, but no traces of habitations have been discovered, no signs of urban life. To the west the land of Canaan fell away to the Mediterranean coastal plain, an avenue of trade, and to the east was the Jordan river valley, where even then stood Jericho, one of the oldest cities in the world. But few people lived in these highlands of Judah in the region of the Ophel hill. Jerusalem, which was to assume such significance for the Jewish, Christian and Muslim worlds, began as a remote mountain site off the beaten track.

Nevertheless, some settlers were attracted to the Ophel hill for the natural protection that it offered and because of the Gihon Spring, which flowed from its eastern flank, so that by the end of the nineteenth century BC the hill was encircled by a defensive wall, a fortress was constructed at its northern end, and houses built on artificial terraces climbing up the slopes of the citadel. By now the Egyptians knew of its existence; among the names of nineteen Canaanite cities which have been found inscribed on Twelfth Dynasty potsherds is one called Rushalimum, meaning 'founded by Shalem'. Hills and mountains in the ancient Middle East were associated with the divine because they reached into the sky, and Shalem, who was a Syrian god identified with the setting sun or with the evening star, had chosen to manifest himself on the Ophel hill. From the moment of its foundation, Jerusalem was a sacred place.

Six hundred years later, in about 1200 BC, Jerusalem was in the hands of the Jebusites, a people who had recently settled in Canaan. These were turbulent times, marked by dramatic climate change and the vast migration of the Sea Peoples who originated somewhere beyond the Black Sea and irrupted southwards through Asia Minor, the Middle East, the Mediterranean and even as far as the shores of Libya and Egypt. In the course of the Sea People's disruptive wanderings entire civilisations were overthrown, including the Mycenaeans of Greece and the Hittites, whose empire had extended over Asia Minor and most of Syria. The Jebusites were probably remnants of the Hittite empire who sought refuge in the highlands of Judah, even as the Philistines, who were probably Sea Peoples beaten back from Egypt, settled along the coastal lowlands of Canaan. But at the same time another people were establishing themselves in the highlands of Canaan: the Israelites, whose tribes soon encircled Jebusite Jerusalem.

The Promised Land

According to the Bible, the Israelites came from Mesopotamia and for a time settled in Canaan. But then in about 1750 BC famine drove the twelve tribes of Israel to Egypt where they were reduced to slavery. Their famous Exodus from Egypt began in about 1250 BC when under the leadership of Moses they escaped into the wilderness of Sinai, from where they were directed by their god Yahweh to the fertile lands of Canaan. Moses did not live to see his people enter the Promised Land, an event dated to about 1200 BC; instead under Joshua, his successor, the tribes of Israel stormed into Canaan, taking the entire country by the sword, all except the walled hill city of the Jebusites, Jerusalem.

But modern scholarship is sceptical about the biblical account of the Exodus. In a stele dating to the reign of the Nineteenth Dynasty pharaoh Ramses II, mention is made of a people called the Apiru who are employed as labourers in the building of his new capital, Pi-Ramesse. There used to be speculation that Apiru (or Habiru/Hapiru) referred to the Hebrews whom the Old Testament describes as engaged in building works immediately before the Exodus. The scholarly view nowadays, however, is that Apiru does not describe an ethnic group but was a term used in both Syria and Mesopotamia to describe mercenaries, raiders, bandits, outcasts and the like, while in Egypt the term Apiru, from the verb *hpr*, meaning 'to bind' or 'to make captive', probably referred to the Asiatic prisoners employed in state building and quarrying projects.

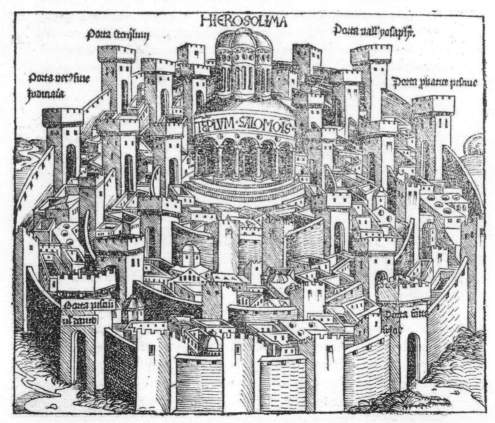

Jerusalem with the Temple of Solomon at the centre in a 1493 German woodcut

In a stele dating to 1209 BC during the reign of Ramses' son Merneptah, there is a brief entry reading, 'Israel is laid waste, his seed is not'. This is the only non-biblical reference to Israel at this time and refers to Merneptah's successful campaign against the allied tribes of Ephraim, Benjamin, Manasseh and Gilead, collectively known as Israel, in the hill country north of Jerusalem. Nothing in these Egyptian records supports the story of an Exodus, which in any case was only written down sometime between the ninth and fifth centuries BC. Indeed, except for a few scholars of a generally fundamentalist kind, the broadly accepted view is that there was no Exodus from Egypt, though a few Israelites who were also Apiru may have escaped to Canaan where their account added drama to a more pedestrian reality – namely that the Israelites were a disruptive outsider caste of mercenaries, bandits or whatever, already living in the mountainous parts of Canaan, who gradually took over the whole of what they called their Promised Land.

King David's City

At a later date, around 1020 BC, the biblical figure of Saul became the first king of the loosely organised group of northern tribes called Israel. After Saul's death, in about 1000 BC, the elders of Israel went to David, who had first served under Saul but then later rebelled against him. David, born the son of a Bethlehem farmer, had since established his own kingship over the tribes of Judah to the south, and the elders of Israel now asked him to be their king also. Entirely encircled by the united Kingdom of Israel and Judah was the alien Jebusite enclave of Jerusalem.

The capital of the Kingdom of Judah was at Hebron, twenty miles south of Jerusalem. Hebron had powerful associations as it was believed to be the burial place of Abraham and other ancestors of the Israelites. David was thirty when the elders came to him at Hebron and made him king of both Judah and Israel, and for seven years he remained there before conquering Jerusalem. For all the symbolism of Hebron, David made Jerusalem his new capital, from where he ruled over 'all Israel', as the Bible puts it, for another thirty-three years.

If Jerusalem's citadel and walls, and its sacred origins, played some part in David's decision to make the city the capital of his united kingdom, it is likely that the overriding reason was that it belonged to neither Judah nor Israel, and that none of the twelve Israelite tribes had any historical or religious claims on the city. In fact Jerusalem after the conquest was a mixed city; instead of expelling the original Canaanite and Hittite inhabitants, the Israelites dwelled among them. Jerusalem was the perfect choice for an independent capital from where the king could bring the tribes of Israel and Judah under his central control.

The Ark of the Covenant

God had told Moses on the mountain in Sinai that the Israelites must build an Ark, a covered chest of acacia wood overlaid with gold, to serve as a mobile container for the Ten Commandments. Carried by the Israelites throughout their wanderings in the desert and over the river Jordan into the Promised Land, the Ark was the most sacred embodiment of their beliefs and represented the presence of God. When at rest, the Ark was housed in an elaborate tent, the Tabernacle, which served as a gathering place for worship. Now that David had conquered Jerusalem, he thought that the Ark of the Covenant should be brought into the city and given a permanent home.

Not only would Jerusalem be the centre of David's political authority; he would also make it the centre of his people's religious life. And so dressed in the linen loincloth of a priest and 'leaping and dancing before the Lord' (*2 Samuel 6:14*), David led the Ark of the Covenant to the Gihon Spring just outside the walls of Jerusalem where it was placed within a tent-like shrine and received the allegiance of all the tribes.

But David's proposal that the Ark should have a permanent home within the walls met with an unexpected rejection when the prophet Nathan announced that God had not needed a temple when the tribes were wandering in the desert and he did not want one now. Instead of David building a house to God, continued Nathan, God would establish a house of David, that is a dynasty, from which the Messiah would come. In any case God's refusal was only temporary; David was not a suitable person to build the Temple because he was a warrior king with blood on his hands, but he was permitted to choose the Temple site, to collect the materials and to draw up the plans, while the honour of building the Temple would go to Solomon, his son.

The Threshing Floor of Zion

Just north of David's city, which stood on the Ophel hill, there was a yet higher summit named Zion where a Jebusite called Araunah had his estate (*2 Samuel 24:15–25*; *1 Chronicles 21:15–28*). When a plague struck David's kingdom, killing seventy thousand people in three days, an angel appeared to him; it was standing on the threshing floor of Araunah at the summit of the mount. There, decided David, he must build an altar and sacrifice to God to avert the plague. Araunah, who may have been Jerusalem's last Jebusite king, offered to give up the threshing floor for nothing, but David insisted on making payment. And when Araunah wanted to give the oxen for the first burnt sacrifice, David paid for them as well. It is likely that David recognised the sacredness of the site, for as well as separating the chaff from the wheat, the Jebusites used their threshing floors for prophetic divination and for the fertility cult of their storm god Baal. But by paying Araunah for his land and oxen, David was ensuring that the sacrifice would be made without obligation to anyone but Yahweh, his god.

From the moment of David's sacrifice the future site of the Temple was marked out. Scholars debate the exact plan and position of the Temple, but Orthodox Jews place the holy of holies, the innermost sanctum of the Temple, on that great rock which can still be seen today behind the grille in the Dome of the Rock on the Temple Mount, the spot where Muslims say Mohammed ascended on his Night Journey to Paradise, and where once the Jebusites had likely made sacrifices to their own gods. As if to bind the place more closely to Jewish tradition, it was also identified in something of a biblical afterthought as the Mount Moriah where Abraham was commanded to sacrifice his son Isaac (*2 Chronicles 3:1*). But for the time being the Ark of the Covenant remained where David had left it when he brought it to the city, just outside the walls, down by the Gihon Spring.

The Empire of David and Solomon

While David was bringing the Ark into Jerusalem and acquiring the future site of the Temple atop Mount Zion, he was also creating a small empire. Already the combined kingdoms of Judah and Israel were greater in extent than the state of Israel today, for they covered both banks of the river Jordan and extended northwards well beyond the Golan Heights. At about the time that he conquered Jerusalem, David defeated the Philistines who lived on the coast in the region round Gaza and became his vassals. In his later years he subdued the kingdoms of Edom and Moab in the east, while in the north he brought Damascus under his control, so that what is today western Jordan, southern Lebanon and central Syria were all part of David's empire.

The main threat to David's empire came from within. As David lay dying, his son Adonijah, backed by disgruntled senior military and religious figures from Hebron who wanted to assert Judah's dominance within the united kingdom, had himself crowned just outside Jerusalem. But in one of his last acts, David gave his support to a faction led by Bathsheba, his Jebusite wife, and by Nathan the prophet and Zadok the high priest. They led Solomon, David's son by Bathsheba, down to the Gihon Spring where in the potent presence of the Ark of the Covenant he was crowned king, and Adonijah's attempted usurpation immediately collapsed.

During Solomon's reign the empire of the Israelites reached its apogee of power and wealth. He continued David's centralising policy of weakening the old tribal ties and further assimilating the Canaanite population. He equipped his powerful army with a corps of chariots and cavalry that operated out of chariot cities in the realm, and he established a fleet at Ezion-geber at the head of the Gulf of Aqaba which ventured throughout the Red Sea. He traded horses with Egypt and Cilicia, obtained timber from Lebanon, and his ships sailed in search of spices, metals and precious stones as far as Yemen, home of

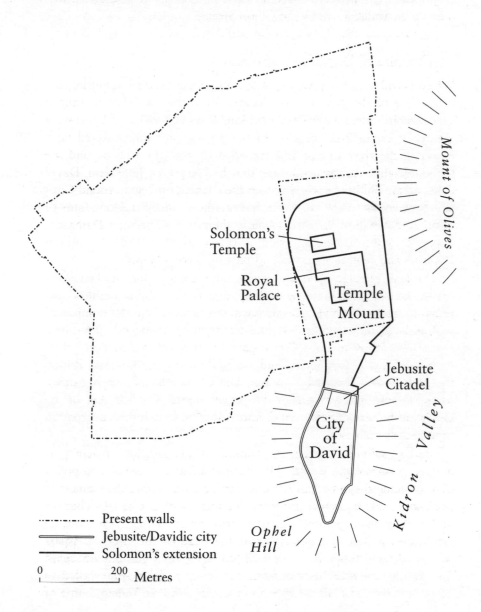

Solomon's
Temple

Royal
Palace

Temple
Mount

Mount of Olives

Jebusite
Citadel

City
of
David

Kidron Valley

Ophel
Hill

·····—·····— Present walls
══════ Jebusite/Davidic city
────── Solomon's extension

0   200
└─────────┘ Metres

the Queen of Sheba, who visited Jerusalem and lavished gifts upon the city and the King. And so eager were the Egyptians to seal an alliance with Solomon that he was granted the rare favour of marriage to the pharaoh's daughter (I Kings 9:16).

Solomon: Wise Man, Mystic and Magician

When Solomon, whose name means peace, was raised to the throne of Israel and Judah, he was asked by God what he desired, and Solomon answered, 'Give thy servant an understanding heart to judge thy people, that I may discern between good and bad'. God was pleased that Solomon had asked for understanding and not for riches nor for a long life, and he answered him saying, 'Lo, I have given thee a wise and an understanding heart; so that there was none like thee before thee, neither after thee shall any arise like unto thee. And I have also given thee that which thou has not asked, both riches and honour: so that there shall not be any among the kings like unto thee all thy days' (1 Kings 3:5–14). Indeed, according to the Bible, Solomon's reign was marked by prosperity and prestige, and his wisdom was said to excel even all the wisdom of Egypt (1 Kings 4:30), and he has come down to us as the wise man par excellence.

In Islam Solomon is also the paragon of wisdom; he is the author of the saying that 'the beginning of wisdom is the fear of God', and he is also accounted wise for his knowledge of the unseen. As Suleiman and as a Muslim he is portrayed in the Koran as being in communion with the natural world and speaks 'the language of the birds' (Koran 27:17). God has also given him dominion over the spirit world: 'We subjected the wind to him, so that it blew softly at his bidding wherever he directed it; and the devils, too, among whom were builders and divers and others bound with chains' (Koran 38:35–36). Among those builders were the jinn, or spirits, whom Solomon commanded to build the Temple for him.

Solomon is also the epitome of the mystical love of women as in the Songs of Solomon in the Old Testament. In Islam this mystical love is expressed in the story of Belkis, the Queen of Sheba, who was converted from paganism by Solomon. He taught her the difference between illusion and the One Reality as expressed in the *shahadah*, 'there is no God but God', and thus became his consort. The Queen of Sheba was the expression of cosmic infinitude complementing Solomon who was the expression of wisdom or self.

In both Jewish and the Islamic traditons, Solomon is associated with stories of the marvellous. He became the subject of rabbinic and kabbalistic lore in which he is portrayed as a fabulous figure, a master magician possessing occult powers. In one kabbalistic legend Solomon orders a demon to convey Hiram, the King of Tyre, down to the seven compartments of hell so that on his return he can reveal to Solomon all he has seen in the underworld. Solomon also appears in *The Thousand and One Nights*, where in the *Tale of the Fisherman and the Jinn* he has used his seal-ring to imprison an evil spirit in a jar for 1800 years.

The Seal of Solomon, the device adorning his seal-ring, is said to have come down to Solomon from heaven. The design consisted of two interlaced or intersecting triangles, one pointing up, the other down, and these were placed within two concentric circles between which was engraved the words 'the most greatest name of God'. In alchemy the upward- and downward-pointing triangles represent fire and water, and they symbolise the combination of opposites and hence transmutation. There are some who see a sexual symbolism in these triangles, and indeed in Egyptian hieroglyphs the V-shape

The Seal of Solomon

does seem to be taken from the shape of the female pubis, while if the upward-pointing triangle is taken to be a phallus, then the fusion of the two can symbolise harmony in the universe and between the sexes. Be that as it may, the device has been a frequent motif used on coins in the Islamic world and as a decoration. Also known as the Star of David, it is the six-pointed star on the flag of the modern state of Israel.

Solomon Builds the Temple

Solomon doubled the size of Jerusalem by extending the city northwards from the Ophel hill to include Mount Zion where he embarked on an ambitious construction programme on Araunah's old estate. He built a vast palace complex (*1 Kings 7–8*) which included a massive palace for himself complete with a huge harem for the 700 princesses and 300 concubines who were the gifts of foreign rulers, and he built a grand palace for his Egyptian wife. He also built a cedar-panelled armoury called the House of the Forest of Lebanon, a treasury, a judgement hall containing his magnificent ivory throne, and on the ancient threshing floor he built the Temple.

Building the Temple was a fantastic undertaking, according to the Bible (*1 Kings 5–8*). It tells of Solomon raising a levy of 30,000 Israelites who were divided into groups of 10,000, each group working in shifts, cutting wood in Lebanon for a month then working for two months in Jerusalem. Additionally 80,000 men were sent into the mountains to quarry stone for the foundations of the Temple and another 70,000 porters carried it down to Jerusalem, with 3300 supervisors overseeing operations. There is no need to take these numbers literally; they are meant to express the magnificence of Solomon and his works.

Construction of the Temple began in the fourth year of Solomon's reign and took seven years and five months in all, that is from the spring of about 958 BC to the autumn of about 951 BC before the rainy season set in. We are told in the *Book of Kings* that in plan the Temple was a rectangle oriented east and west and measuring 60 cubits in length, 20 cubits in width, and 30 cubits in height (*2 Chronicles 3:4* says it was 120 cubits high, but that is an impossible figure probably indicating a corrupt text). A cubit is the length of a man's arm from the elbow to the tip of the middle finger, which is generally taken to be about half a yard or half a metre, so the Temple of Solomon was about 30 yards long, 10 yards wide and 15 yards high.

The purpose of temples in the ancient world was to provide a dwelling place for the god, and so just like all other temples in the East the architectural plan of Solomon's Temple was based on that of an ordinary house. The Temple was divided into three chambers which became more private, more intimate, more holy the farther inwards one progressed. The outermost chamber was the *ulam* or the porch, an entrance hall rather like the porch or narthex of a church. Beyond this was the *hekal* where cult objects were kept, including a gold altar, ten candelabra, various lamps, goblets, cups, knives, basins and braziers. The *hekal* led directly into the *debir*, a windowless chamber 20 cubits long, wide and high, that is a perfect cube. This was the Holy of Holies, closed by folding doors, where Yahweh, who had declared that he would 'dwell in the thick darkness' (*1 Kings 8:12*) was symbolised by the Ark of the Covenant. Flanked by two huge statues of golden cherubim, the Ark resided at this spot untouched by human hands for over three hundred years, as contact with such a powerfully sacred object without taking the proper precautions caused immediate death (1 Chronicles 13:10).

Yet for such a celebrated building the Temple was hardly of any size at all, being only about a third as long and half as wide as the Parthenon built atop the Acropolis in Athens five hundred years later. Indeed Solomon's own palace, at 100 cubits long, 50 cubits wide and 30 cubits high, was four times the size of the Temple and took a good deal longer to build. But then what was most impressive about the Temple, apart from its sanctity, were its costly and finely worked materials and decorations, and for these Solomon relied on his friend and ally King Hiram of Tyre.

King Hiram of Tyre

Tyre on the Mediterranean coast of Lebanon was already a very ancient place, its origins going back to the early centuries of the third millennium BC. From about 1500 BC it came into the sphere of influence of New Kingdom Egypt with which it carried on a lucrative trade. But its moment of greatest prosperity and power coincided with the rule of King Hiram I, a contemporary of Kings David and Solomon.

By Hiram's time, at the beginning of the first millennium, the powerful centralised authority of the New Kingdom had broken down, and Egypt was divided between rule by the high priests of Amun in the south of the country at Thebes and by the pharaohs of the Twenty-First Dynasty in the north at Tanis in the Delta. Asserting Tyre's economic independence against a weakened Egypt, Hiram developed Tyre's harbours, created a formidable merchant marine, established commercial colonies in Sicily and North Africa, and in cooperation with Solomon sent a combined trading fleet to Arabia and East Africa. But the lifeblood of Tanis was also maritime trade, and though Egypt had long ago lost its influence to Lebanon, the pharaoh Siamun (c978–c959) was at least able to engage in limited military actions against his commercial rivals the Canaanites and to consolidate his position in the region by marrying off one of his daughters to Hiram's friend King Solomon at Jerusalem.

Though King David had been prevented from building the Temple himself, he had amassed a great amount of treasure to pay for its construction, he had collected materials, and he had given Solomon detailed plans to follow (*1 Chronicles 22:2–5, 28:11–19*). What is more, when building his own palace, David had received help from Hiram, and now Solomon turned to Hiram too (*1 Kings 5; 9:11; 10:11; 2 Chronicles 2*). The highlands of Solomon's kingdom were barely forested, but the slopes of the mountains of Lebanon were covered with pine, juniper and cedar, all tall trees valuable in construction. Similarly Egypt was a treeless country, and it was the forests of Lebanon that had made that country so attractive to the Egyptians for the last two thousand years. Indeed the Pyramids of Giza were built with the aid of cedar beams from Lebanon, and the pharaoh Cheops' magnificent solar boats buried at the base of his Great Pyramid were also made of Lebanese timber. Now Hiram provided Solomon with the cedar for his Temple, and he also provided the craftsmen who panelled the interior of the Temple with cedar, lined the Holy of Holies with pure gold, and then overlaid the entire exterior with more gold.

Mystery of the Lost Ark

During the nearly four centuries following the construction of the First Temple, the Ark remained untouched in the Holy of Holies. Yet these were often times of trouble and crisis, when the kings at Jerusalem were obliged to reach into their storehouse of treasures in order to meet the exactions of foreign conquerors – the pharaoh Sheshonk I (Shishak in the Bible) who ruled from Tanis in the Egyptian Delta (*1 Kings 14:26*); Ben-hadad, King of Damascus (*1 Kings 15:18*); and Tiglathpileser the

Assyrian (2 *Kings 16:8*). Nevertheless, and though covered in valuable gold, the Ark survived these depredations and is mentioned in the Bible (2 *Chronicles 35:3*) on the occasion of the reform of Yahweh worship during the reign of Josiah (640–609 BC). That is its last appearance; there is no mention of the Ark at the sack of the Temple by the Babylonians in 586 BC (2 *Kings 25:13–15*), though the view generally taken by historians is that the Ark was probably destroyed at this time.

But according to 2 *Maccabees 2:4–8*, which is consigned to the Apocrypha by the Hebrew and Protestant Bibles though included in the Roman Catholic and Orthodox Bibles, the Ark was saved by the prophet Jeremiah on a signal from God. Jeremiah went to the top of Mount Nebo, from which Moses glimpsed the Promised Land, and placed the Ark, the Tabernacle and an incense altar within a dwelling–cave, then blocked up the entrance, refusing to mark the spot. 'The place shall remain unknown until God finally gathers his people together and shows mercy to them. Then the Lord will bring these things to light again, and the glory of the Lord will appear with the cloud, as it was seen

This carving depicting the Ark of the Covenant was found among the ruins of a synagogue of the Graeco-Roman period

both in the time of Moses and when Solomon prayed that the shrine might be worthily consecrated.' If something like this did happen, it is not impossible that the Ark still survives, for recent archaeological discoveries in the Judaean desert have provided remarkable evidence of how perishable materials thousands of years old may be preserved in certain conditions.

The belief that the Ark was hidden before the destruction of the First Temple by the Babylonians gains support from other sources. Among these is the *Mishnah*, ancient oral traditions set down in writing by rabbis around 200 BC, which mentions the Ark and other items from the First Temple being hidden by Jeremiah but not stating where. This is given support and amplification by the discovery in 1952 of the Copper Scroll among the Dead Sea scrolls at Qumran. Etched on the Copper Scroll is what is thought to be an inventory of treasures from the First Temple which are described as having been hidden in a desolate valley, under a hill on its east side, forty stones deep.

This 'desolate valley' has been identified by some as the Valley of the Kings in Egypt, a theory that allows the identification of the Ark of the Covenant and other objects from the Temple with treasures discovered in the tomb of Tutankhamun. (Another fanciful version of this Egyptian theme was presented in the hugely popular 1981 film *Raiders of the Lost Ark*, the first of the Indiana Jones series, directed by Steven Spielberg.) But for those still looking, the most persistent belief is that the Ark of the Covenant lies somewhere within the Temple Mount.

According to one rabbinic legend Solomon foresaw the destruction of his Temple by the Babylonians and so had an underground chamber built below the Temple in which the Ark was eventually hidden. This is supported by some rabbis today who believe on the basis of *midrash*, an esoteric interpretation of biblical texts, that the Ark was hidden directly below its original position in the Holy of Holies. Indeed the chief rabbi of the Ashkenazi community in Israel objected to excavations at the Mount in the late 1960s because he feared that the archaeologists might actually uncover the Ark – with dangerous results, because neither they nor anyone else would be able to handle it with safety as only the long-dead priests of the vanished Temple possessed the ritual purity to touch the Ark and not defile it nor be destroyed by the contact.

The Widow's Son

The most remarkable of all the work done at Solomon's Temple was the casting of the enormous basin known as the Sea of Bronze and both of the huge bronze pillars known as Jachin and Boaz. This large-scale casting was difficult and technologically advanced, and the man sent by King Hiram to undertake the work is singled out in the Bible by name. A man 'filled with wisdom and understanding', he too was called Hiram, and he is described as 'a widow's son' (*1 Kings 7:13–14*).

The Sea of Bronze, an ablutions basin used by the priests, rested on twelve bronze oxen and stood near the southeast corner of the Temple. At 10 cubits in diameter and 5 cubits high, it held 10,000 gallons of water, sufficient for over 2000 baths. The oxen were in groups of three and faced the cardinal points; possibly they suggested fertility, as they did in the Canaanite and Egyptian worlds, and the basin was meant to suggest the sacred lakes of Egyptian temples.

The two hollow bronze pillars, each 18 cubits (nine yards) high, were placed on either side of the entrance porch. The pillars were free-standing and supported nothing, but they were surmounted with capitals five cubits high and of elaborate design, opening out into lotus or lily forms adorned with garlands of pomegranates. Hiram the widow's son gave them each a name, calling the one on the south side of the porch Jachin, meaning 'He shall establish', and the one on the north side Boaz, 'In it is strength'. Most likely the names were meant to be read together, as something like 'He (Yahweh) shall establish (the Temple) in its strength', or perhaps the message was that both God and David's dynasty would endure, 'Yahweh will establish his throne forever. Let the king rejoice in the strength of Yahweh'. The pillars themselves may have served as incense burners or torch holders; or they may have been symbolic, pointing godwards like the Egyptian obelisks raised to the sun god, or representing the tree of life.

These gigantic bronze objects were cast in the Jordan river valley where there was suitable earth to make the moulds, water in abundance and wind to operate the draught of the furnaces. Then with great difficulty they had to be transported to Jerusalem. These things we know

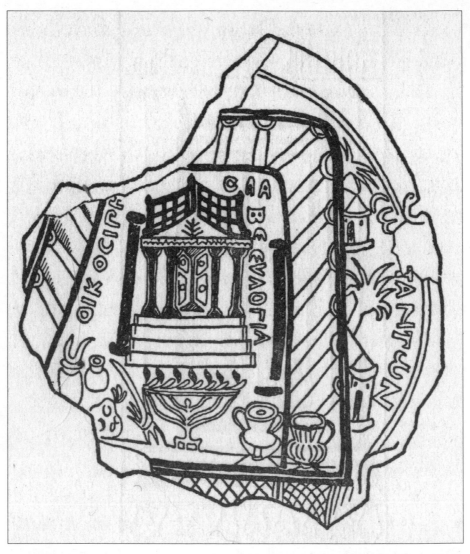

*The huge bronze pillars of Jachin and Boaz
are shown on either side of the Temple of
Solomon in this drawing on a fragment of
glass dating from the Byzantine period*

about Hiram the widow's son, but with the completion of the Temple the Bible lets him quietly leave the scene and tells us nothing more – though the widow's son and Jachin and Boaz would capture imaginations and appear in legends for thousands of years to come.

A House for the Name of God

When the Temple was finished it was dedicated by Solomon, who said he had 'built the house for the name of the Lord God' (2 Chronicles 6:10). The Temple did not contain God, for God was without bodily form; he was everywhere and could not be contained. For the same reason the God of the Jews could have no image, and so the Temple possessed no image of God. This was unheard of in the ancient world, where every shrine contained an image to be worshipped. But at Jerusalem the only thing residing in the Temple was the name of God.

At first the presence of God was symbolised by the Ark, which was kept in the Temple's innermost and holiest recess, but by the time the Assyrians destroyed the First Temple in 586 BC the Ark had disappeared, therefore the Second Temple, begun in 520 BC and later vastly enlarged by Herod, was entirely empty. Instead it had become the house of a completely spiritualised deity, a God beyond all form and description, a place where God's presence was perceived and acknowledged only through the utterance of his name.

The End of the Temple

The Second Temple was destroyed during the First Jewish Revolt against the Romans, which broke out in AD 66. When Titus, the Roman emperor, finally put down the insurrection in AD 70, the Temple was accidentally destroyed by fire, and the prayers and sacrifices practised there came to an end.

During the Second Jewish Revolt the rebels occupied Jerusalem in AD 132 and intended to rebuild the Temple, even striking coins bearing its image. But the Romans returned in force and crushed the revolt completely. Jerusalem became a pagan city, Colonia Aelia Capitolina.

All traces of the Temple were obliterated in AD 135 and statues of Hadrian the conqueror and of Jupiter were erected on the site. This was the final end of Yahweh's Temple. Thereafter Jews were forbidden by official Roman decree to enter Jerusalem, though from time to time tacit permission was given for them to enter the precincts of the former Temple. Nothing remained, only the desolate rock, and here the Jews poured libations of oil, offered their prayers, and tore their clothes in lamentation.

The New Christian Empire

East and West

By the onset of the first century AD the Roman Empire included all the lands around the Mediterranean. Throughout this territory, whether in Europe, North Africa or the Middle East, early Christians endured terrible persecutions for their faith until in 313, during the reign of the emperor Constantine, the Edict of Toleration made Christian worship legal throughout the empire. By the end of the century Christianity had become the almost universal religion of the Roman world.

The word 'catholic' means universal and all-embracing and was the word used to describe the original Christian Church. It was a universal Church, and the faithful travelled freely from one end of Christendom to the other. Tens of thousands of pilgrims travelled to the East to visit the holy sites and to obtain the blessings of monks and other holy ascetics there. 'Not only do the inhabitants of our part of the world flock together', wrote the Syrian monk Theodoret of Cyrrhus (393–466) in his *Religious History*, 'but also Ishmaelites, Persians, Armenians subject to them, Iberians, Homerites, and men even more distant than these; and there came many inhabitants of the extreme west, Spaniards, Britons, and the Gauls who live between them. Of Italy it is superfluous to speak.'

In what had already been the universal Roman Empire, Christianity added a new dimension of unity between the diversity of local cultures. Christian ideas and images were shared from the Thames to the Euphrates, from the Rhone to the Nile. Nor was the past forgotten; memories of the pagan gods still haunted the temples turned into churches, and the tombs and other places of pilgrimage often preserved, in Christian form, the immemorial beliefs and practises of a region. In those early days the only hint of a breach between the East and the West came in the arguments over the divine nature of Jesus Christ.

Pilgrimages to the Holy Land

Pilgrimages are practised among all the world's religions, yet in Christianity there has always been an undercurrent of criticism against the idea of attaching faith to any place or thing. This was expressed by Jesus himself to the woman of Samaria who wanted to know where she should pray: 'The hour cometh when ye shall neither in this mountain nor yet in Jerusalem worship the Father. ... God is a spirit and they that worship him must worship him in spirit and truth' (*John 4: 19–24*). Moreover, during its first three centuries Christianity was a persecuted faith, and it was not safe or practical to go on a pilgrimage.

Yet despite the danger to their lives, Christians did go on pilgrimages from an early date. Already by the early second century a 'cave of the Nativity' was being shown in the Holy Land; people wanted to see sites associated with the life and death of Jesus. There was something like this in Judaism where heroes and holy people had their memorials. But a peculiarity of Christians was their interest in graves and corpses, unclean to Jews but to Christians the focus of hope, for the dead were merely sleeping until the resurrection. Meanwhile there was good reason to treasure the bones or dust of martyrs who had died for their faith and were already in heaven. When Saint Polycarp was burnt alive at Smyrna in 155 his relics were eagerly sought, and the last sight seen by Saint Cyprian at Carthage in 258 would have been a shower of rags thrown at him by the faithful to soak up his martyr's blood the moment he was decapitated.

The era of pilgrimages really got under way with the end of persecutions following Constantine's Edict of Toleration in 313. The pace was set by the Emperor's own mother, the empress Helena, who visited the Holy Land in 326–8. That she was a woman was typical of pilgrimages, for the truth about women in pagan societies was that their worth was judged almost exclusively on their success as sexual and reproductive beings, whereas Christianity, once it had been legitimised by Constantine, was liberating for women in numerous ways, not least in providing them with an excuse for going on long journeys away from home.

As his mother travelled from site to site, Constantine ordered and financed the construction of churches to celebrate the central events of Christian belief. In Bethlehem Constantine built the Church of the Nativity, and in Jerusalem he built the Church of the Holy Sepulchre on the spot, discovered by Helena herself, where Jesus was entombed and then rose again on the third day.

This eighth-century fresco depicts Helena and Constantine with the True Cross

But neither Constantine nor Helena, nor the pilgrims who followed, took any interest in the Jewish monuments of Jerusalem, none of which were restored. In 333, after Helena's visit, a pilgrim noted that two statues of the Emperor Hadrian stood in the Temple area, and not far away was a stone where Jews came to pray. But the Temple Mount had little significance for Christians, and though a chapel or church was built at the southern end of the platform, the Mount was not densely built up during Christian times.

The Search for Relics: from the Holy Prepuce to the Holy Grail

For the collector of relics, Jesus and his mother the Virgin Mary were disappointing; unlike burnt or beheaded saints, they had both bodily ascended to heaven, leaving nothing behind. Though not quite. Neither milk expressed from Mary's breasts nor bodily hair that had come loose had joined her in the ascent, and soon these were identified and enshrined as relics. Also it was discovered that Jesus had ascended without his foreskin. According to Jewish practise he had been circumcised when he was eight days old, and somehow the foreskin had found its way into the hands of Mary Magdalene, who gave it to John the Baptist. To cut a long story short, the foreskin, or Holy Prepuce, is now in the possession of the Vatican, or at one of seventeen churches around Europe which make the same claim.

But if there has been a scarcity of bodily parts left behind by Jesus, the gap has been filled by relics which are said to have had an association with him. Once again it was the empress Helena who got in there first when she turned up the True Cross on which Jesus had been crucified. Other relics include the Holy Lance which pierced the side of Jesus while he hung on the Cross, the Turin Shroud in which his body was wrapped when he was taken down from the Cross, and the Holy Chalice from which he drank at the Last Supper and which is sometimes referred to as the Holy Grail.

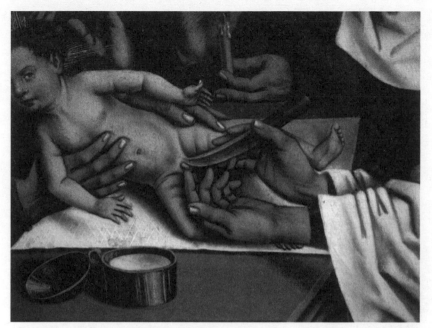

The Circumcision of Jesus by the German painter Friedrich Herlin, 1466

Constantine and Arianism

The great size and diversity of the Roman Empire, and the separate military threats it faced across the Rhine-Danube frontier in the West and the Euphrates in the East, made its governance unwieldy. Constantine's solution was to establish a new imperial capital at the ancient city of Byzantium on the Bosphorus, the strategic meeting point of Europe and Asia. Beautifying the city and enlarging the circuit of its walls, in 330 he dedicated Nova Roma, as he called Byzantium, to Jesus Christ – though it quickly became known as the city of Constantine, Constantinople.

In 395 a more radical step was taken, and the Roman Empire was formally divided into a western empire ruled from Rome and an eastern empire ruled from Constantinople. Greek culture and language increasingly reasserted themselves in the East Roman Empire, which, taken together with its Christian foundations, has led modern-day historians

ARRIVS BISCHOP.

Arianism, one of the greatest heresies of Early Christianity, originated with Arius, a priest of Alexandria in the early fourth century

to give it a different name, the Byzantine Empire. But long after Rome fell to the barbarians in 476, and throughout its struggle in the Middle Ages against Islam, and indeed right up to the last when Constantinople fell to the Ottoman Turks in 1453, the emperors and their subjects in the East called themselves Romans and spoke of their empire as the Roman Empire.

It is to Constantine, too, that the Christian empires owed their sense of orthodoxy. For no sooner was Christianity tolerated than it was threatened by doctrinal splits. The arguments were not over whether Jesus was divine – his divinity was almost universally agreed. Rather they concerned the nature of that divinity. And during Constantine's reign, the first great heresy emerged – Arianism, so named after a priest of Alexandria.

Arius argued that as Jesus was the Son of God, then surely he was younger than God: an appealing notion that brought Jesus closer to mankind and emphasised his human nature. But another Alexandrian, a bishop called Athanasius, saw a danger. If Jesus was younger than God, so there must have been a time when Jesus was not. This challenged the unity of the godhead – the Father, the Son and the Holy Spirit – and opened the way to regarding the nature of Jesus as being not of the same substance as God's. Indeed in time Jesus might be seen merely as a good man, as Unitarians and Muslims see him today, while God would become less accessible and more remote. The counter-argument of Athanasius was that no distinction could be made between Christ and God, for they were of the same substance.

Seeing the Christians within his empire divided between the arguments of Arius and Athanasius, in 325 Constantine summoned the First General Council of the Church at Nicaea, not far from his future capital of Nova Roma. Two hundred and twenty bishops were in attendance, from Egypt and Syria in the East to Italy and Spain in the West. The divine nature of Jesus Christ was argued from both the Arian and Athanasian points of view, and when the bishops balloted on the issue, it was decided in favour of Athanasius by 218 votes to two. This Nicene Creed became the official position of the universal Church and remains the creed of both the Roman and Orthodox Churches to this day.

The Nicene Creed

Here is the text of the Creed as originally passed by the Council of Nicaea in 325. The final paragraph is specifically directed against the Arians.

We believe in one God, the Father Almighty, maker of all things, both visible and invisible.

And in one Lord, Jesus Christ, the Son of God, begotten of the Father God of God and Light of Light, very God of very God, begotten and not made, being of one substance with the Father, by whom all things were made; who for us men and for our salvation came down and was made flesh, made man, suffered and rose again on the third day, went up into the heavens and is to come again to judge the quick and the dead; And in the Holy Spirit.

But the Holy Catholic and Apostolic Church anathematises those who say that there was a time when the Son of God was not, and that he was not before he was begotten, and that he was made from that which did not exist; or who assert that he is of other substance or essence than the Father, or is susceptible of change.

Byzantines, Persians and Jihad

It was during the reign of the Byzantine Emperor Heraclius (610–41) that the pivotal event of Islamic history took place – when a former caravan merchant called Mohammed took refuge in Medina after being driven out of Mecca. The event is called the *Hegira* or migration and its date, 622 AD, marks the beginning of the Muslim calendar. But Heraclius was distracted by what seemed far greater matters. During the first ten years of his reign the Persians had made frightening advances against his empire.

The Persian state religion was Zoroastrianism and wherever it spread, Christianity was persecuted. Antioch fell to the Persians in 611, Damascus in 613, Jerusalem in 614 and Alexandria in 619. Moreover, after slaughtering Jerusalem's 67,000 Christian inhabitants the Persians made off with the True Cross, Christendom's holiest relic – and it was this which turned Heraclius' 622 campaign against the Persians into something new, as it included a crusading zeal. In 627 as Heraclius advanced deep into Persia, its king was overthrown by revolution and his successor sued for peace. Byzantium's eastern provinces were restored to the empire and the True Cross was returned to Jerusalem.

But the Byzantines in their victory and the Persians in defeat both lay exhausted when the sounds of war were heard again. This time it was the army of Umar – Arab followers of the new religion of Islam – who in 633 declared a jihad, a holy Islamic war, against the Byzantine Empire. Mohammed had died the previous year, and the Byzantines, to the extent that they knew anything about Islam at all, mistook it for a revival of Arianism, a familiar Christian heresy which depreciated the divinity of Jesus, and did not feel greatly threatened, failing to recognise the approaching Bedouins as a significant military force.

The Muslim Conquests

The Arab Occupation of Jerusalem

In AD 636 the Arabs invaded Palestine, and by the summer of the following year their army was encamped outside the walls of Jerusalem. The defence of the city was organised by its Patriarch Sophronius with the help of the Byzantine garrison, but in February 638 after a seven-month siege the Christians were forced to surrender to caliph Umar, the Muslim commander, though not before the True Cross was safely removed to Constantinople. According to a traditional account, Sophronius rode out to escort Umar back through the gates of the city, but instead the caliph humbly dismounted from his camel and entered Jerusalem on foot. This was Umar's homage to the city which the Muslims called al-Quds, 'the Holy', from *al-bayt al-muqaddas*, 'the Holy House' – that is the Temple of Solomon.

Once inside Jerusalem, Umar asked Sophronius to take him to the Temple Mount, called the Haram al-Sharif by the Muslims, the Noble Sanctuary, where his purpose was to search for relics, among them what he called the mihrab, or prayer niche, of David, of which Umar had heard the Prophet Mohammed speak. As Jesus had foreseen, not a stone was left standing on the Temple Mount, and now it was covered with refuse. The caliph ordered it cleared and was the first to carry away a load of debris in the fold of his cloak. Umar also had a temporary mosque built at the southern end of the Mount, on the spot where the al-Aqsa mosque, begun sixty years later, stands today.

Al-Aqsa means 'the farthest' and was originally applied to the entire Temple Mount, as though it marked the horizon of Muslim ambition, for Mohammed had had a vision of ascending into Paradise from this spot (Koran 17:1). But by the time the al-Aqsa mosque was completed in 715 the Arab armies had established a vast Islamic empire extending five thousand miles from east to west, from the borders of China to the Atlantic coast of Spain, and Christendom had lost more than half its territory.

Al-Aqsa mosque in a nineteenth-century engraving

From Revelation to Jihad

This story of conquest, one of the most far-reaching and rapid in history, had its beginnings in Arabia in 622 when Mohammed began to unite the Arab tribes into a powerful fighting force through his preaching of a single god – though his activities went entirely unnoticed by the Byzantine and Persian empires, the great powers of the time.

Arabia, despite being largely barren and uninhabited, occupied an important position between Egypt, Abyssinia, Persia, Syria, Palestine and Mesopotamia, whose trade with one another relied to some considerable extent on the Arab caravans that carried their goods across the perilous wastes. Mecca stood at an important crossroads of this desert trade, and the authority of the Arab nomadic tribal sheikhs was in some measure supplanted at Mecca by a kind of oligarchy of ruling commercial families whose religious beliefs and practises transcended narrow tribal allegiances.

The Meccans ensured that their rock-shrine, the Kaaba, contained not one but several venerated tribal stones, each symbolising a local god, so that tribesmen visiting the market fairs could worship their favourite deity during their stay in the city. The Meccans also worshipped Manat, Uzza and Allat, goddesses of fertility and fate, who in turn were subordinate to a yet higher god called Allah.

Such material as we have about the early days of Islam comes mainly from the Koran and from the *hadith*, the oral traditions relating to the actions of Mohammed. Born in about 570, Mohammed was the son of a poor merchant of Mecca who was nevertheless a member of the powerful Quraysh tribe, the hereditary guardians of the Kaaba. While working as a trader he was exposed not only to the flow of foreign goods but to the currents of Jewish and Christian ideas. In particular, through conversing with Jews and Christians he met in Mecca and elsewhere in Arabia, Mohammed had become acquainted with the stories of the Old and New Testaments, with the main elements of Jewish and Christian popular custom and belief, and above all with the concept of monotheism. Drawn into a life of religious contemplation, in about 610 he began to receive revelations via the angel Gabriel of the word of

Allah, who announced himself to Mohammed as the one and only God. Other gods were mere inventions, announced the revelation, and their idols at the Kaaba were to be destroyed.

This message provoked a great deal of antagonism among the Meccans, but slowly Mohammed began making some converts among pilgrims from Yathrib, an agricultural community about 250 miles to the north which had a mixed population of Arabs, Jews and Judaised Arabs and was therefore already familiar with monotheism and other features of his teaching. In 622 the hostility of the pagan Meccans towards Mohammed reached such a pitch that he and his small band of followers accepted an invitation to settle in Yathrib. This migration, or *Hegira*, marked the beginning of the Muslim era, and in time Yathrib was renamed Medinat al-Nabi – 'City of the Prophet' – or Medina for short.

Mohammed's understanding of Jewish and Christian concepts led him to believe that they were basically identical to the revelations, known as the Koran, that he had received, and therefore he expected that Jews and Christians would agree with his teaching and recognise him as a prophet standing in the line of Abraham, Moses, David, Solomon, Jesus and others. But whereas remnants of the heresy known as Arianism may have allowed Mohammed to believe that Christianity could dispense with the divinity of Jesus, the Jews were uncompromising: they told him that his revelations were a distortion and a misunderstanding of their tradition, and they drew attention to the numerous contradictions in his revelations on Old Testament themes.

Mohammed's answer was to turn against the Jews, saying they had deliberately falsified their traditions, while he presented himself as the restorer of the religion of Abraham, whom he said was the founder of the Kaaba and its cult. He abandoned the Muslim fast corresponding to the Jewish Day of Atonement, Yom Kippur, the one day of the year when the High Priest at the Temple in Jerusalem entered the Holy of Holies where he made atonement for all the Jews in the world. In place of a day of fasting, Mohammed instituted the month-long fast of Ramadan. And at the same time, according to tradition, he instructed Muslims to pray towards the Kaaba in Mecca; until then Muslims had prayed towards Jerusalem.

But Mohammed's most important act during his early years in Medina was to set down the revelation giving permission to his followers to go to war against those identified as their enemies. 'Permission to take up arms is hereby given to those who are attacked, because they have been wronged. God has power to grant them victory: those who have been unjustly driven from their homes, only because they said: "Our Lord is God"' (*Koran 22:39–40*).

According to Muslim scholars this concept of *jihad*, or holy war, can legitimately be applied against injustice and oppression, or against the rejectors of the truth, that is the truth of Islam, after it has been made evident to them. In the immediate circumstances it was used against the Meccans. After provoking several clashes with the Meccans, including raids on their caravans which provided the Muslims with considerable booty, Mohammed conquered Mecca in 629. Extending his wars against the Bedouin tribes, Mohammed gained control over the whole of Arabia the following year.

By the time of Mohammed's death in 632 he had unified the Arabs under the banner of Islam, at once a religion, a social, legal and political institution, and a justification in the name of Allah for war and conquest – or as one historian has put it, arguing that Arab expansion was due to excessive population and lack of resources in Arabia, to free themselves 'from the hot prison of the desert'. The first forays were in Mesopotamia (Iraq), to which the raiding Arabs were attracted by booty, ransom and abundant pasturage, and over the next ten years Mohammed's successors, known as caliphs (from Khalifat rasul-Allah, Successor to the Apostle of God), destroyed Persia's Sassanian empire, and in their jihad against the Byzantine Empire overran Syria, Palestine and Egypt.

Problems with Islamic History

From the point of view of Western scholarship there are serious problems with Muslim history. For example, there are no contemporary Muslim sources for Umar's conquest of Jerusalem. The first Muslim account of Umar being shocked at the rubbish on the Temple Mount and making a start at clearing it away comes from Mujir al-Din al-Hanbali towards the end of the fifteenth century, more than 800 years after the events he describes. In fact the earliest Muslim histories appeared only 150 years or so after the death of Mohammed, and according to the oldest history relating the conquest of Jerusalem, the caliph Umar was not there at the surrender at all. Though the Temple Mount had little significance for Christians, it is unlikely that in so well-organised and prosperous a city it was left in a ruinous state. The acts of Constantine and the visit of his mother had the effect of magnifying the importance of Jerusalem and promoting its reconstruction, while sometime no later than the mid-fifth century Jews were again permitted to live within the city. An ancient map, and the testimony of a pilgrim, suggest that at the very least there was a church or chapel on the Temple Mount, probably at the southeast corner adjacent to where the al-Aqsa mosque stands today.

The Dome of the Rock stands on the site of Solomon's Temple. The Muslim shrine is said to mark the spot from where Mohammed ascended for a glimpse of Paradise.

Until about 800 there is an almost total lack of contemporary Islamic sources. Islamic history appears to have been transmitted primarily orally until that date, when Muslim scholars began collecting, editing and recording the traditions, their aim to create a coherent scriptural basis for Islam and to provide an historical underpinning for their now sophisticated world empire.

In fact the earliest date for a written Islamic source is 692: it is the founder's inscription which appears in gold mosaic along the arcade inside the Dome of the Rock. It corresponds to Sura 4:171 in the Koran and is an emphatic warning to the Christians: 'People of the Book, do not transgress the bounds of your religion. Speak nothing but the truth about God. The Messiah, Jesus the son of Mary, was no more than God's apostle and His Word which he cast to Mary: a spirit from Him. So believe in God and his apostles and do not say: "Three". Forebear, and it shall be better for you. God is but one God. God forbid that he should have a son! His is all that the heavens and the earth contain. God is the all-sufficient protector.'

The traditional view is that the Koran consists of passages associated with (or revealed to) Mohammed in Mecca and Medina in the early decades of the seventh century, that it had been committed to writing by about 650, and that it was the most important element in Islam from the time of Mohammed onwards. But a discovery made in 1972 of a cache of ancient Korans in the Great Mosque at Sanaa in Yemen seems to show that even as the Dome of the Rock was being built, Islam was still in flux. The Sanaa cache of Korans have been dated to the early part of the eighth century, and examination of the manuscripts reveals that there are two versions of the text, one written over the other, suggesting that the Koran, and therefore Islam itself, was evolving for at least a century following the death of Mohammed.

By applying the same approaches to the Koran as have long been applied to the Old and New Testaments, various Western scholars based at such institutions as Oxford, Princeton and London's School of Oriental and African Studies (SOAS) have arrived at the view that the Koran, in the form that it survives, was compiled, if not written, decades after the lifetime of Mohammed, probably by converts to Islam in the

Middle East, who introduced elements from Christianity and Judaism, and that it was elevated to the position of Islam's definitive scripture only towards the end of the eighth century.

These scholars conclude that Islam's own accounts of its origins are religiously inspired interpretations of history rather than objective records of events. They say that Islam's history of that period, including accounts of Mohammed and the formation of the Koran, is in fact a back-projection of views that were formed as the culture and religion of Islam emerged in an atmosphere of intense debate between different groups of monotheists influenced by rabbinical Judaism and heretical Christianity.

Defenders of the traditional account of the history of Islam argue that these criticisms, though they come from serious scholars, are overly speculative and lack sufficient evidence. Furthermore they claim that in the light of the most up to date studies these same scholars would not arrive at the same conclusions if they were writing today. As for the Sanaa manuscripts, they say the differences are not significant and can be explained away as copyists' errors.

The Night Journey

Jerusalem is the third holiest place in Islam after Mecca and Medina. In fact the Temple Mount was the original direction for Muslim prayer. The holiness of Jerusalem derives from its association with the Old Testament prophets whom Mohammed also made the prophets of Islam, and from Jesus whom Mohammed also regarded as a prophet but not the son of God. But above all the sacred nature of Jerusalem is confirmed for Muslims by the story in the Koran (17:1) of the Night Journey in which the angel Gabriel brings Mohammed to the Temple Mount from where they ascend heavenwards for a brief glimpse of Paradise.

Nothing in the Koran directly identifies the Farthest Mosque with the Temple Mount; nor is there any mention of Jerusalem: 'Glory be to him who made his servant go by night from the Sacred Temple to the farther Temple whose surroundings we have blessed.' In the view of non-Muslim scholars, and some Muslims too, the identification with the site of

The interior of the Dome of the Rock contains the earliest known Islamic inscription. It warns Christians of their error in believing that God had a son: 'Forebear, and it shall be better for you. God is but one God.'

Solomon's Temple was a later interpretation, probably made generations after the death of Mohammed, some arguing that 'the farther Temple' really refers to Medina and that the Night Journey was Mohammed's *Hegira* to that city. Islam had already appropriated the prophets of Judaism and Christianity, but by means of reinterpreting the Koran it could be made to appropriate their sacred places as well.

The Dome of the Rock illustrates that appropriation. Built on the site of Solomon's Temple, decorated inside and out with inscriptions composed of all the Koranic references to Jesus, and marking the spot where Mohammed was given a glimpse of Paradise awaiting all true believers, the triple associations of the Dome of the Rock confirm the ascendancy of Islam.

Islamic Imperialism and Flourishing Christian Heresies

Though the rapidly expanding Muslim empire was first ruled from Medina in Arabia, from 661 it was governed from Damascus in Syria by caliphs of the Umayyad dynasty. But after a violent transfer of power to the Abbasid dynasty in 750, the caliphate was moved to Baghdad in Iraq.

Throughout these changes, however, Arab policy remained the same, namely to extract the maximum revenue from its conquered territories and its subject peoples. Proud and independent in attitude and nomadic by background, the occupying Arabs were disinclined to become farmers; instead the Muslim Arab warrior caste lived off the poll tax (*jizyah*) and the land tax (*kharaj*), which was paid by the conquered peoples in return for the protection of their lives and property and for the right to practise their own religion.

Because the *jizyah* could be imposed only on non-Muslims, there was little interest in making converts to Islam, and for centuries longer Syria, Palestine and Egypt would remain overwhelmingly Christian. Indeed during its first century under Muslim rule Syria gave the world five Popes. Nor did Arabisation come quickly. Only towards the end of the seventh century was Greek replaced by Arabic as the official language of administration in Aramaic-speaking Syria and Coptic-speaking Egypt.

Nevertheless, the Muslim conquerors imposed restrictions on their subjects to keep them firmly in place. The building of new churches and synagogues was prohibited, the ringing of church bells was forbidden, and festivals and public expressions of faith were curtailed. Further, Christians and Jews stood outside the community; they were not allowed to carry weapons, nor bear witness against Muslims in courts of law, nor marry Muslim women. Also Jews and Christians had to distinguish themselves by their clothing from Muslims, they could not ride horses, only asses, and any who attempted to convert Muslims to their own religion paid with the death penalty, as did any Muslim who apostasised.

If the triumph of Islam had been enabled by the Byzantine Empire's long and exhausting conflict with Persia, it had also been helped by the fierce theological disputes that for hundreds of years had torn apart the unity of the Christian world. And so it is fitting if ironic that an effect of the Muslim conquests was to protect and preserve a considerable variety of Christian heresies. To the Muslims these controversies were of little account; Islam was the revealed and perfected faith, and as for the Christians, and also the Jews, as long as they submitted to Muslim rule and paid their taxes they were permitted to conduct their own affairs according to their own laws, customs and beliefs.

Christian heresy flourished in the Middle East under Muslim rule, or rather what was regarded as heresy by the authorities in Constantinople and by the Popes in Rome. But here in the Middle East all Christian sects were treated alike, so that heterodox and heretic Christians were now freed from persecution by rival Christians or the state. For example, at the Council of Chalcedon in 451 a majority decided that Jesus had two natures, the human and the divine, adding that these were unmixed and unchangeable but at the same time indistinguishable and inseparable.

This is the view of almost all Christian churches to this day, but members of the Syrian Church, known as the Jacobites, and of the Egyptian Church, known as the Copts, while not denying the two natures, put emphasis on their unity at the Incarnation. For this the Syrians and Egyptians were called monophysites (*monophysis*, Greek for single nature), and were charged with the heretical belief that Jesus' human nature had been entirely absorbed in the divine.

What exactly the parties to these disputes meant when they talked of the nature of Jesus Christ was affected by shades of language and culture, but certainly they had a divisive effect within the Byzantine Empire and helped prepare the way for the coming of Islam. As one figure of the Jacobite Church said of the Muslim conquest: 'The God of vengeance delivered us out of the hands of the Romans by means of the Arabs. It profited us not a little to be saved from the cruelty of the Romans and their bitter hatred towards us.'

Heretics, the Antichrist and the Last Days

For a long time the Byzantines viewed Islam as a kind of Arianism, the fourth–century Christian heresy which opened the way to regarding the nature of Jesus as being not of the same substance as God's and even being inferior to God's. Taken to its extreme extent, Arianism could amount to denying entirely the divinity of Jesus and reducing him to merely a good man. Even someone who saw things from up close, such as John of Damascus (c676–749), a Syrian Christian theologian who lived entirely under Muslim rule and served as counsellor in the court of the Umayyad caliphs, did not regard Islam as a new religion but considered it a deviation from orthodox Christianity similar to other early heresies.

Likewise medieval Western Europe conceived of Islam in the same way, as a version of Arianism, and mistook it for just one more aberrant Christian sect. If Islam was still evolving at this time, as some modern scholars believe, then this may have been a reasonable enough estimation of the situation. Or it may be that observers in both the Byzantine Empire and the West could see Islam only through the lens of Christian history and were unable to recognise it as something completely new. Certainly it is remarkable that even in the late Middle Ages Dante (1265–1321) in his *Inferno* (XXVIII, 31–36) should have considered Mohammed as a heretic and placed him in the ninth circle of hell for being 'a sower of schism and discord'.

But the coming of Islam also found its way into Christian prophetic literature, which after the Bible and the works of the Church Fathers was the most influential body of writing circulating in Europe during the Middle Ages. Uncanonical, unorthodox and infinitely adaptable to the preoccupations of the moment, these concoctions followed a common theme derived from the New Testament's *Book of Revelation* – that of the divine warrior who will come and save the world. An early candidate for this role was the Emperor Constantine, who had legalised Christianity and was then expected to bring about the Second Coming. In prophecy after prophecy that role passed from one emperor or king or prince to another while the story took on fantastical dimensions in relating the final triumph of Christianity.

One famous example that would reverberate throughout the Middle Ages was the *Apocalypse of Pseudo-Methodius*. It was written in the seventh century but made to look as though it had been written in the fourth century as a prediction of the Muslim invasion of the Middle East by Bishop Methodius of Patara, who was martyred in 311 at Tyre in Lebanon during the Roman persecutions. It relates how the Ishmaelites, that is the Arabs, emerge from the desert and ravage the land from the Nile to the Euphrates. The Christians are punished for their sins by being subjected for a time to the Ishmaelites, who kill Christian priests, desecrate the holy places, take the Christians' land and force or seduce many Christians from the true faith.

But just when all seems lost a mighty emperor, whom many had thought long dead, rises up and defeats the Ishmaelites, lays waste their lands with fire and sword, and rages against those Christians who had denied Jesus as their lord. Now under this great emperor a golden age begins, a time of peace and joy, when the world flourishes as never before.

This is shattered, however, when fearsome peoples known collectively as Gog and Magog, whom Alexander the Great had imprisoned in the far north, break out and bring universal terror and destruction until God sends a captain of the heavenly host who destroys them in a flash.

St John the Divine's apocalypic vision of the Dragon with the Seven Heads in the New Testament's Book of Revelation as depicted in a woodcut by Albrecht Dürer

The emperor journeys to Jerusalem where he hands over Christendom to the care of God by going to Golgotha and placing his crown upon the Cross, which soars up to heaven. But the emperor dies and the Antichrist appears, installing himself in the Temple in Jerusalem where he inaugurates a reign of trials and tribulations, deceiving people with his miracles and persecuting those he cannot deceive. However, before long the Cross reappears in the heavens and Jesus Christ himself comes on clouds in power and glory to kill the Antichrist with the breath of his mouth and to carry out the Last Judgement.

For medieval people, especially the poor, the oppressed, the disoriented and the unbalanced, the tremendous drama of the Last Days was not a fantasy about some remote and indefinite future but a prophecy which was infallible and which at almost any given moment was felt to be on the point of fulfilment. The coming of the Last Emperor followed by the reign of the Antichrist were tensely awaited, as the lawless chaos of the age was seen as the expected prelude to the universal salvation of the Second Coming.

The First Crusade

Counterstrokes in the West and the East

Though the First Crusade was proclaimed in 1095, Muslim historians think of the Crusades as beginning ten years earlier with the fall of Toledo in Spain. In fact the reaction against Arab imperialism had begun long before that; just as Muslim armies had occupied the Middle East, North Africa and Europe, so the Christian counterattack was on several fronts.

In the West the Arabs had overrun Spain and struck deep into France, to within a hundred and fifty miles of the English Channel, before they were beaten back by Charles Martel between Poitiers and Tours in 732, though that did not prevent the Muslims from holding positions on the coasts of Languedoc and Provence for several decades to come. Throughout the eleventh century Pisa, Genoa and Catalonia fought campaigns in the Western Mediterranean to free Sicily, Sardinia and Majorca from Arab rule. In 1063 Pope Alexander II gave his Papal blessing to Iberian Christians in their wars against the Muslims, granting a remission of sins to those who were killed in battle. The recovery of Toledo from the Arabs in 1085 was a major victory; the northern third of Spain was now back in Christian hands, though not until the fall of Granada in 1492 would the Reconquista succeed in driving the Muslims out of the Iberian peninsula altogether.

In the East the Byzantines were scoring victories in the Eastern Mediterranean already in the tenth century, recapturing Crete from the Muslims in 961 and Cyprus four years later. The Byzantines also recovered great swathes of territory in the Middle East. In 969 they captured Antioch, and shortly afterwards they took Aleppo and Latakia along with a coastal strip extending clear down through Syria nearly to Tripoli in northern Lebanon. The Muslim inhabitants were

Jerusalem seen from the north in a nineteenth-century engraving

left undisturbed and the local Muslim leaders were made vassals of the Byzantine Empire, but now they were made to pay taxes from which the Christians were exempted, while destroyed churches were rebuilt and the freedom to convert from Islam to Christianity or vice versa was guaranteed.

In 975, under the Emperor John Tzimiskes, the Byzantines launched a crusade with the intention of recovering Jerusalem, which was still an overwhelmingly Christian city. Marching out with his army from Antioch, Tzimiskes took Damascus, then advanced into Palestine where Nazareth and Caesarea opened their gates to him and the Muslim authorities at Jerusalem pleaded for terms. But first the Emperor turned towards the Mediterranean to clear the enemy from coastal castles – only to die suddenly in 976 before he could return his attention to Jerusalem. For the next century the Byzantines remained in control of northern Syria but got no closer to the Holy Land.

Arab Divisions and Decline

Until the middle of the eighth century Damascus, the seat of the Umayyad dynasty, had been the capital of a vast and complex empire which stretched from the Atlantic to Central Asia. It was an empire largely administered by Syrians, Christians as well as Muslims. The Arabs were the ruling class, but in turn the Umayyads were deeply influenced by the Graeco-Aramaic civilisation they found in Syria with its many links, intellectual, cultural and mercantile, to the Mediterranean world. The replacement of the Umayyad by the Abbasid caliphs and the shift from Damascus to Baghdad marked a rejection of these influences.

The advance of Christian forces against the Muslim empire from both the West and the East came as evidence of the decay and division in the Arab world. The empire had become a rapacious tax-gathering machine run by provincial governors who paid kickbacks to Baghdad but otherwise offered the caliph no more than the barest homage and granted their subjects even less than that. With the triumph of an authoritarian and incurious religious dogma, with the failure to develop resources or technological advances, and with civil administrations replaced by local military autocrats, the empire of the Arabs fell into intellectual, political and economic decline.

There were uprisings against the Arabs throughout their empire. In Egypt, where the population had been three million at the time of the Arab conquest, the mismanagement of the country's resources was so appalling that there were not many more than one and a half million Egyptians by AD 1000. Muslim discrimination and oppressive taxation stoked up resentment among the Copts, that is the native Egyptians. Their national pride was already wounded by the coming of the Arabs and the continuing infiltration of Egypt by nomadic tribes and led to repeated Coptic revolts, which were only suppressed with much bloodshed. Many Copts converted to Islam after the ferocious repression of 832; being unable to meet taxation demands, partly because the irrigation system was falling into further disrepair, they migrated into the towns, leaving large areas of land uncultivated. Even so, not until the eleventh century, four hundred years after the Arab occupation, did the majority of Egyptians finally adopt Islam.

Similarly the prosperity of Syria declined along with its population. Marginalised and oppressed by their new rulers in Baghdad the Syrians more than once rose up in revolt. Yet under the Abbasids the Arabic language became virtually universal in Syria, and Islam became the religion of the majority of its inhabitants – partly because of fresh immigration from Arabia, and partly from persecutions, pressures and inducements. Many Christians moved to the safety of the Lebanese mountains, among them the Maronites, who established themselves there in the ninth century.

Apart from the tensions between the Arab elite and their eventually Arabised subjects, Islam itself was split between the orthodox Sunni, who controlled the Baghdad caliphate, and the Shia, that is the partisans of Ali, so that religious dissensions added to the original cultural, ethnic and political differences. The Fatimids, who were Arabs originally from Syria but had settled in North Africa, returned eastwards to Egypt where they established a Shiite caliphate in 969, and by the end of the century they had extended their empire over Palestine and southern Syria.

Islam Divided: Shia versus Sunni

In 656 after insurgent Arab troops murdered Uthman, the third caliph, who was a member of the powerful Umayyad family of Mecca, Ali put himself forward as the natural inheritor of the caliphate, basing his claim on his marriage to Mohammed's daughter Fatima, as well as on his considerable religious learning. But Ali was opposed by Aisha, who had been Mohammed's favourite wife, along with her Umayyad family and many of Mohammed's surviving companions. He took to arms and won his first battle, but later saw his authority dissolve when rebels advanced on his army with copies of the Koran fixed to the points of their spears and his troops refused to fight.

Ali was assassinated and the Umayyads were installed once again in the caliphate. But the real wound to Islam occurred when Hussein, Ali's son by Fatima, and therefore of Mohammed's blood, led a revolt against the Umayyads and after a fanatical struggle was killed with all his men. In a sense the Prophet's own blood had been shed, so that for the partisans, or Shia, of Ali, Hussein's death was a martyrdom and also a stain on the Sunni, that is on orthodox Muslims who then as now constituted the greater part of Islam.

From then on the Shia refused to accept as caliph any but Ali's descendants, while the Sunni barred the caliphate to the Prophet's descendants for all time. Shiism took hold in Persia and in much of Iraq, but also, almost three centuries after the death of Ali, his followers in the form of the Fatimids would invade Egypt with the intention of using it as a base from where to oppose the Sunni Abbasid caliphate in Baghdad and to impose Shia dominance throughout the entire Islamic world.

Perilous Pilgrimages

Initially the Muslim presence in Syria and Palestine interfered little with pilgrimage to Christian holy sites, nor did it affect the security of monasteries and Christian communities there. The Muslims were no strangers to the concept of pilgrimage, for they themselves had made the pilgrimage to Mecca one of the pillars of their faith; moreover the

Christian pilgrims were a considerable source of revenue to Muslims at Jerusalem and other holy sites. For Christians, the Holy Land was unique in providing a tangible link with the life and death of Jesus, and throughout the Muslim occupation the numbers of pilgrims continued to grow.

To reach the river Jordan was a special aim of pilgrims, for there they could re-enact the baptism of Jesus by John the Baptist (*Matthew 3:16–17*). The afflicted were particularly attracted, for they recalled that one of Jesus' grievances against the Temple priests in Jerusalem was their rejection of the lame, blind, deformed and sick as imperfect and unworthy, for the belief was that outer illness signified a corruption of the soul. Reacting against the Temple priests, Jesus performed baptisms at which everyone was welcome, for the core of his preaching was that salvation was for all. Pilgrims to the Holy Land sought baptism in the waters of the Jordan in order to undergo a spiritual cleansing, and among them were many afflicted people for whom the purification of their souls might also bring about a physical cure.

But the most popular object of pilgrimage was the Church of the Holy Sepulchre in Jerusalem, built on the traditional sites of the crucifixion, burial and resurrection of Jesus. The Gospels place the hill of Calvary, or Golgotha, and the tomb offered for the burial of Jesus by Joseph of Arimathea, outside the walls of Jerusalem, yet the Church of the Holy Sepulchre stands within the very heart of the city. In fact the city was enlarged and rebuilt by the Emperor Hadrian, and in 135 he had a temple of Venus built upon the spot where the tomb was said to be.

Still, the old tradition remained strong enough to justify the Emperor Constantine in pulling down the temple in 326 in order to search for the tomb reputed to be beneath it. A rock-cut tomb was duly found and pronounced to be that of Jesus, and the outcrop of Golgotha was identified nearby. Constantine immediately ordered the construction of the Church of the Holy Sepulchre, in fact a vast complex consisting of two elements, the Basilica or Martyrium at the site of Golgotha, which was dedicated in 335, and the Church of the Anastasis, meaning 'resurrection', built in the form of a rotunda and surmounted by a great dome over the tomb of Jesus and dedicated in 340. Circulating within

According to tradition, the Church of the Holy Sepulchre stands upon Golgotha, where Jesus was crucified, and over his nearby tomb from which he rose on the third day

the Church of the Holy Sepulchre, which enclosed the most sacred sites in Christendom, pilgrims vividly relived the drama of that first Easter when Jesus died upon the Cross and rose again on the third day.

Following the Arab conquest of Jerusalem in 638 the city's largely Christian population enjoyed a long period of good relations with the Muslims. But by the tenth century the Muslims had become more aggressive, and in 938 they attacked Jerusalem's Christians during the Palm Sunday procession, set fire to the Martyrium and badly damaged the Anastasis church. In 966 a Muslim mob again attacked the Anastasis and set alight the roof of the Martyrium. The Patriarch who had hidden in a vat of oil was set alight and burnt alive. The Muslims set their seal on these acts by seizing part of the east entrance to the Church of the Holy Sepulchre where they constructed a new mosque.

Worse was to come. Starting in 1004 the Fatimid caliph al-Hakim, who ruled over Egypt, North Africa, Palestine and southern Syria, launched a campaign of anti-Christian fanaticism. Christians suffered persecution and had ordinances passed against them; church property was confiscated, crosses were seized and burnt, little mosques were built on church roofs, and finally the churches themselves were set ablaze. By 1014 over thirty thousand churches had been destroyed, and many Christians had been forced to convert to Islam, at least outwardly, to save their lives, while others fled into Byzantine territory. But the critical turning point in Western attitudes towards the Muslim East came in 1009, for in that year al-Hakim ordered the complete destruction of the Church of the Holy Sepulchre, which was carried out with such violence that even the tomb of Jesus, though cut deep into the bedrock, was demolished with pickaxes and all but obliterated.

After the death of al-Hakim in 1021 his successor permitted the Byzantine emperor, under stringent conditions and at his own expense, to rebuild the Church of the Holy Sepulchre. Pilgrimage, too, was again permitted, though sojourns in the Holy Land proved unpredictable and often dangerous. For a while during 1056 the Muslims forbade pilgrims entry to Jerusalem and expelled three hundred from the city..In 1064 a large German pilgrimage led by Gunther, bishop of Bamberg, came under Muslim attack; the party was plundered and hundreds were massacred within sight of Jerusalem. Muslim pirates operated against pilgrims at sea, either attacking them outright or exacting charges, bargains and gifts. Pilgrims were obliged to pay protection money, known as *khafara*, along the roads. Also the sensibilities and prejudices of the Muslims had to be borne in mind: pilgrims could not enter mosques, they could not enter towns or cities except on foot, they could not dress in certain ways, they should not look at Muslim women, and they should not make merry or laugh lest the Muslims thought the Christians' behaviour was directed at them.

Pilgrimage depended on the Muslim authorities maintaining orderly conditions so that the defenceless Christian traveller could move about and worship in safety, but the Middle East was wracked by misgovernment, division, exploitation, fanaticism and aggression, which undermined that guarantee. And now in the last third of the eleventh century a new threat arose – not only to pilgrims but to Byzantium and the Arabs – in the form of a Turkish invasion from the East.

The Turkish Invasion: Byzantium Appeals to the West

Migrating tribes of Turks known as Seljuks began arriving from the East in the territories of the Abbasid caliphate in about 970. They were soon converted to Sunni Islam and became invaluable to the Arabs for their martial qualities, especially for their mounted bowmen and the nomadic speed of their cavalry. But the caliphate was no longer a unified entity. Spain, Africa and Egypt had long since led a political life independent of the caliph in Baghdad. Indeed the enfeebled state of Arab rule stood as an open invitation, and in 1055 the Seljuks took Baghdad and established their hegemony over the caliphate. Under the Seljuks there was an immediate resurgence in the fortunes of Sunni Islam in Iran, Iraq and Syria. In 1071 the Seljuks defeated the Byzantine army at Manzikert in eastern Anatolia, opening the whole of Asia Minor to conquest by the Turks and threatening Constantinople itself. In that same year the Seljuks also turned south, taking northern Syria from the Byzantines and Jerusalem from the Fatimids.

With Byzantium suddenly reduced to hardly more than its capital, Constantinople, and the adjacent regions, in 1074 the Byzantine emperor Michael VII appealed to Pope Gregory VII for help, his desperation all the more evident in his willingness to overlook the Great Schism of 1054, which was the culmination of centuries of often violent doctrinal differences between the Latin and Orthodox Churches. Despite the schism, the appeal fell on ready ears, for already in 1063 the Papacy had given its blessing to a crusade against the Muslims in Spain and it might have done the same now. But this was not the moment when Gregory could call upon the secular powers of Europe to head eastwards on a crusade, as he was embroiled in the Investiture Controversy with many of those same secular authorities over whether it was they or the Church who had the right to appoint high church officials and thereby control the great wealth and powers such officials could command.

Meanwhile the Seljuks tightened their grip on Syria and Palestine. In 1076 they took Damascus from the Fatimids, and when the Fatimids briefly regained Jerusalem that year, the Seljuks recaptured the city after a siege of several months and massacred the entire Muslim population, about three thousand, as well as a large number of Jews who had supported the Fatimids, though the Christians were spared.

Throughout these convulsive events the pilgrim traffic had never entirely ceased, but the journey was now far more difficult than it had been before. Not only was there fighting between Turks and Egyptians in Palestine and Syria, but Asia Minor, which had offered secure passage when it was in the hands of the Byzantine Empire, could no longer be traversed without an armed escort owing to marauding Turkish tribesmen, and even then it was not safe. Everywhere throughout Anatolia and the Middle East there were brigands on the roads, and at every small town along the way the local petty headman tried to extort money from passers-by. The pilgrims who succeeded in overcoming all these harassments and dangers returned impoverished and weary to the West with tales to tell of the appalling conditions in the East.

The Byzantine Emperor Alexius I Comnenus began the fightback against the Seljuks, reclaiming territory along the Black Sea and round the shores of the Sea of Marmara during the 1080s. But in order to press harder against the Turks he sought mercenaries from the West, and in March 1095 he sent an appeal to Pope Urban II. In response Alexius got something wholly unexpected and astonishing. Alexius' daughter, the historian Anna Comnena, described how a multitude from the West approached Constantinople in 1096 on their way to the East: 'They assembled from all parts, one after another, with arms and horses and all the other equipment for war. Full of enthusiasm and ardour they thronged every highway, and with these warriors came a host of civilians, outnumbering the sand of the seashore or the stars of heaven, carrying palms and bearing crosses on their shoulders. There were women and children, too, who had left their own countries. Like tributaries joining a river from all directions they streamed towards us in full force.'

Pope Urban's Call

The Council of Clermont in central France was convened by Pope Urban II during the second half of November 1095. It was largely concerned with the Truce of God, the device by which the Church had for half a century been trying to limit feudal warfare, which was having a devastating effect upon the land. Population growth, shortage of land and petty civil wars had contributed to a feeling of insecurity and desperation at all levels of society. There had been floods and plague in 1094, followed by drought and famine in 1095. A shower of meteorites in April 1095 presaged a great movement of peoples, it was said, and lent an apocalyptic note to the social and economic problems.

Fifteenth-century illustration of Urban at Clermont, proclaiming the First Crusade

Meanwhile Pope Urban had been formulating a policy in response to the appeal from the Emperor Alexius Comnenus. Urban's aim was to provide the Byzantine Empire with the reinforcements it needed in order to drive the Seljuk Turks from Asia Minor, for he hoped that in return the Orthodox Church would acknowledge the supremacy of Rome and that the unity of Christendom would be restored. He was also concerned to give the aggressive nobility, especially that of his native France, an alternative outlet for their martial energies. The Papacy had gained strength through the Investiture Controversy, and not only had it established its authority over Church appointments, but in marshalling public opinion it had also intensified popular piety, so it seemed a propitious moment to inaugurate a new era of religious energy in the West and also to win the prize of Jerusalem. Urban let it be known that in response to the appeal from Eastern Christendom for help, he would make a speech on the penultimate day of the council, Tuesday 27 November. He expected that in addition to churchmen his audience would comprise members of the French nobility, for he envisioned the expedition to the East as an armed pilgrimage of knights.

Three hundred clerics had been attending the council within the cathedral at Clermont, but the crowds, both clerical and lay, that assembled on that Tuesday were huge, and so the Papal throne was set up on a platform in an open field outside the eastern gate of the city, and there, when the multitudes were gathered, Urban rose to address them. The reports of four contemporary chroniclers survive, but all were written years later, were coloured by subsequent events, and differ greatly from one another, so that we can have only a very approximate idea of what Urban actually said.

He began, it seems, by telling his listeners that the Seljuks were advancing into the heart of Christian lands, maltreating the population and desecrating their shrines and churches. The Emperor of Byzantium had called for help, and it was the duty of the West to respond. But he spoke not only about recovering Byzantine territory. He emphasised the special holiness of Jerusalem and told how pilgrims had suffered on their journeys there. Then he made his great appeal. Let the West go to the rescue of the East. The nobility should stop fighting one another and instead fight a righteous war. For those who died in battle there would be remission of sins. Let this armed pilgrimage (the word 'crusade' did not come into use until the thirteenth century when the Crusades were over) set out in the summer, at the Feast of the Assumption, 15 August, after the harvest had been gathered; and the armies should assemble at Constantinople.

Cries of *Deus le volt!* – God wills it! – interrupted Pope Urban's speech and filled the air again when it was over. Adhemar, the bishop of Le Puy, immediately knelt before the throne and begged permission to join the holy expedition. This apparently spontaneous gesture was probably prearranged, as Urban had stayed at Le Puy in August. Yet the enthusiasm was greater than Urban had expected. Knights and peasants, rich and poor, pressed forward to follow the bishop's example. Many burst into tears and many were seized with convulsive trembling. Everyone who listened was swept with emotions of overwhelming power.

Spinning the Pope's Speech

Four contemporary chroniclers – Fulcher of Chartres, Baldric of Dol, Robert the Monk and Guibert de Nogent – wrote accounts of the First Crusade which contained versions of Pope Urban II's speech at Clermont. None set down their accounts of what the Pope said until years after the event, nor did any pretend to standards of accurate and objective history; rather each used the Pope's speech to put forward a point of view reflecting the different ways people looked at the crusade.

The earliest account was by Fulcher of Chartres. He was the only chronicler to actually take part in the crusade and wrote about it immediately afterwards, in 1100–01. His account gives the impression that he was at Clermont. Fulcher presents the Pope as a pragmatic strategist who speaks of the Arabs and the Turks as a threat not only to the East but ultimately to the West: 'If you permit them to continue thus for awhile with impunity, the faithful of God will be much more widely attacked by them.'

Baldric of Dol wrote his account soon after the First Crusade, but he was not a participant, though he does give the impression that he was at Clermont. In this version, references to the Old and New Testaments underline the Pope's call for a holy war of liberation, with Jerusalem itself as the very image of heaven: 'Let us bewail the most monstrous devastation of the Holy Land! This land we have deservedly called holy in which there is not even a footstep that the body or spirit of the Saviour did not render glorious and blessed which embraced the holy presence of the mother of God, and the meetings of the apostles, and drank up the blood of the martyrs shed there. How blessed are the stones which crowned you Stephen, the first martyr! How happy, O John the Baptist, the waters of the Jordan which served you in baptising the Saviour! The children of Israel, who were led out of Egypt; they have driven out the Jebusites and other inhabitants and have themselves inhabited earthly Jerusalem, the image of celestial Jerusalem. You should shudder at raising a violent hand against Christians; it is less wicked to brandish your sword against Saracens.'

Robert the Monk was not on the First Crusade, and though he is the one chronicler to explicitly claim that he was at Clermont, that is questionable. Certainly he was slow to produce his account, completing it only in 1106, eleven years after Pope Urban's speech, which Robert presents in the most lurid terms. Although Urban certainly spoke of the persecution of Christians in the East, the inflammatory atrocities of which Robert accuses the Muslims are not recorded in other versions of the speech:

'They circumcise the Christians, and the blood of the circumcision they either spread upon the altars or pour into the vases of the baptismal font. When they wish to torture people by a base death, they perforate their navels, and dragging forth the extremity of the intestines, bind it to a stake; then with flogging they lead the victim around until the viscera having gushed forth the victim falls prostrate upon the ground. Others they bind to a post and pierce with arrows. Others they compel to extend their necks and then, attacking them with naked swords, attempt to cut through the neck with a single blow. What shall I say of the abominable rape of the women? To speak of it is worse than to be silent.'

Guibert de Nogent, who was neither at Clermont nor went on the crusade, finished his account in 1108. His tone is apocalyptic, and he has Pope Urban playing to the popular medieval drama of the Antichrist and the Last Days. 'With the end of the world already near, it is first necessary, according to the prophecy, that the Christian sway be renewed in those regions either through you, or others, whom it shall please God to send before the coming of Antichrist, so that the head of all evil, who is to occupy there the throne of the kingdom, shall find some support of the faith to fight against him.'

Strategic war, holy war, hysterical war, or the war of the Last Days according to one or another of the chroniclers. But it is most unlikely that Pope Urban would have seen the issue in apocalyptic terms, nor is it likely that he would have stooped to lurid rabble rousing. He never intended to whip up a mass movement of peasants and exhort them to march eastwards. His chosen instrument was the knighthood, and it was to them that he offered his rewards, remission of sins for death in battle and the unstated prospect of carving out estates for themselves in the reconquered Holy Land, just as had been happening in Spain.

Perhaps the best indication of what Urban said that late November day in a field outside Clermont comes in the form of a sober letter of instruction written a month later, at Christmas 1095, by the Pope himself to the gathering knights. 'Your brotherhood, we believe, has long since learned from many accounts that a barbaric fury has deplorably afflicted and laid waste the churches of God in the regions of the East. More than this, blasphemous to say, it has even grasped in intolerable servitude its churches and the Holy City of Christ, glorified by his passion and resurrection. Grieving with pious concern at this calamity, we visited the regions of France and devoted ourselves largely to urging the princes of the land and their subjects to free the churches of the East. We solemnly enjoined upon them at the council of Clermont such an undertaking, as a preparation for the remission of all their sins.'

Taking the Cross

Pope Urban named Adhemar, the bishop of Le Puy, as his representative on the expedition and its spiritual leader. He had been on a pilgrimage to Jerusalem nine years before. Following Adhemar's example, everyone joining the expedition had a cross of red material sewn onto the corner of his coat, symbolising that like Jesus they too carried a cross. Clerics and monks were not to take the cross without the permission of their bishop or abbot. The elderly and infirm were discouraged, the newly married should have the permission of their wives, and no one should go without consulting his spiritual advisor. Otherwise anyone taking the cross was vowing to complete the journey to Jerusalem, and if he failed to set out or turned back too soon he would be punished with excommunication.

The first great secular lord to join the expedition was Count Raymond of Toulouse, who led the knights of Provence, and soon others joined. Robert, the duke of Normandy, who was the son of William the Conqueror, led the knights of northern France; Bohemond, prince of Taranto, led the Norman knights of southern Italy, among them his nephew Tancred; and Godfrey of Bouillon led the knights of Lorraine. Subject in theory to Adhemar, who represented the Pope, these barons became the secular leaders of the campaign, and together with their followers, family and friends, they brought to the expedition many of the most enterprising, experienced and formidable fighting men of Europe.

But Urban had launched a movement greater than he knew, and in the belief that the apocalypse was at hand thousands of peasants, artisans and other ordinary people, often very poor, took the cross for the eastward march to liberate the Holy Land. Yet of all those who set out – the rich, the poor, the humble and the noble – only one in twenty would live to see Jerusalem.

The First Wave: The People's Crusade

Though Pope Urban had asked his bishops to preach the crusade to the Holy Land, the most effective preaching was done by humble evangelicals who inflamed the poor of France and Germany with their version of the Pope's message. Outstanding among these was Peter the Hermit, who had tried to make the pilgrimage some years earlier but had been maltreated by the Turks and forced to turn back. He went about barefoot and his clothes were filthy, but he had the power to move men, and as Guibert de Nogent, who knew him personally, said, 'Whatever he said or did, it seemed like something half-divine.'

*Rabble-rousers like Peter the Hermit
distorted the Pope's call*

While Adhemar and the princely armies of knights were still prepar-
ing for their expedition, Peter's preachings had roused fifteen thousand
French men and women who left their homes to follow him into
Germany where the numbers continued to swell. Already in northern
France this rabble element of the crusade had begun attacking Jewish
communities, giving them the choice between conversion and death –
for according to the apocalyptic prophecy of the Last Days there could

be no Second Coming until all those who had denied Christ repented and were saved or were destroyed.

The worst violence came when Peter's crusade appeared along the Rhine, one of Europe's major trade routes, where Jews had lived for centuries in large numbers, their economic usefulness recognised by the encouragement and protection they had always received from the bishops in the cathedral towns. During May and June 1096 Jewish quarters were attacked, synagogues were sacked, houses were looted and entire communities were massacred. The bishops and the burghers did what they could to protect the Jews but were often overwhelmed. At Worms, for example, the bishop sheltered Jews in his castle, but he could not resist the combined force of the Crusaders and his own poorer townsfolk who demanded their death or conversion; and when the bishop offered to baptise the Jews to save their lives, the entire Jewish community chose suicide instead. During that May and June as many as eight thousand Jews were massacred or took their own lives as the crusading rabble marched through Germany.

Far removed from the spirit and the intentions of Clermont, tributaries of this popular crusade passed across Europe, through France, Germany and Hungary, but only the chaotic stream led by Peter the Hermit and known in history as the People's Crusade got as far as Asia Minor where in October 1096 it was annihilated by the Seljuks, though Peter, who had hung behind in Constantinople, lived to preach another day.

The official crusading army, led by Adhemar and the great secular lords, had no part in these massacres. Assembling their forces in the West, in France especially, they made their preparations and when the harvest was brought in they set out to liberate Jerusalem.

From Pilgrimage to Crusade: The Crux of the Matter

The term 'crusade' is a late one; it came into use only in the thirteenth century after the Holy Land was lost and the Crusades were over. The people we now call Crusaders were known by various names, such as knights of Christ, and they saw themselves as taking a pilgrimage, except that pilgrims were normally forbidden to carry arms. The word 'pilgrim' originally meant a stranger or a traveller, and for Christians life itself was seen as a pilgrimage in an estranged world far from their homeland in heaven.

Before setting out on this expedition to recover the Holy Land, members had a piece of red cloth in the form of a cross (*crux* in Latin) sewn into their clothes in imitation of Jesus, who had said, 'And he that taketh not his cross and followeth after me, is not worthy of me' (Matthew 10:38). This 'taking of the cross' eventually gave the name Crusade to these journeys – *croisade* in French, *crociata* in Italian, *Kreuzzug* in German, and *cruzada* in Spanish and Portuguese. Though crusades were fought in Spain, North Africa and elsewhere, the supreme crusade was to liberate or defend Jerusalem, as that was regarded as Jesus' own territory.

The Second Wave: The Princes Lead the Way East

Setting off in groups after the summer harvest, the official army of Adhemar and the great lords arrived at Constantinople between October 1096 and April 1097. But of the 40,000 Crusaders who approached the city, no more than 4500 were nobles or knights. Travelling in their wake was yet another mass of poor and humble people, artisans and peasants, not unlike the rabble that had caused so much death and devastation the previous year along the Rhine. This untrained and undisciplined horde, which included women and other non-combatants, and a great number of religious fanatics, filled the leaders of the crusade with anxiety, as they did Alexius, the Byzantine emperor, because they were unpredictable and needed to be fed. But as the crusade was also a pilgrimage, there was little that could be done to prevent them joining in the march.

Alexius ferried the Crusaders across the Bosphorus, and in May they had laid siege to Nicaea, the Seljuk capital. Making clear what he saw as their purpose in Asia Minor, the emperor had the Crusader leaders swear an oath that they would 'restore to the Roman Empire whatever towns, countries or forts they took which had formerly belonged to it';

and when Nicaea fell in June 1097, he took care that his imperial forces and not the Crusaders received the surrender. For the Byzantines there was nothing novel in fighting against the infidel; they had been doing so for five hundred years. But their concern now was to secure Asia Minor rather than to rush pell-mell towards Jerusalem, and this made them suspect in the eyes of the zealous Latin knights.

It was in this uneasy atmosphere that Alexius skilfully guided and provisioned the Crusaders across the length of Asia Minor. From Nicaea the First Crusade marched southwards to Dorylaeum (Eskisehir) where with Byzantine help it won a great victory over the Seljuks, and then farther south to Philomelion (Aksehir) and on to Iconium (Konya). A detachment passed through the Cilician Gates to Tarsus, but the main body swung up into Cappadocia, to Caesaria (Kayseri), and the two groups joined up again at Maras before heading southwards along the eastern flanks of the Amanus mountains, so that in the autumn of 1097 they stood before the walls of Antioch. The taking of the city the following year marked the parting of the ways between the Crusaders and the Byzantines, for instead of turning Antioch over to Alexius in keeping with his oath, Bohemond made it a principality of his own.

The Tafurs

The knights and the nobility may have thought that they were leading the crusade, but the poor who marched in their wake regarded themselves as the elite, a people chosen by God. Most of the common people who had joined the first wave of the crusade perished on the long journey across Europe or were cut to ribbons by the Seljuks no sooner than they had crossed the Bosphorus.

Many of those who survived and now joined the second wave of the crusade, the one led by Adhemar, bishop of Le Puy, and the great French, Norman and Provençal lords, were known as Tafurs. Stories describe them as barefoot, wearing sackcloth, being covered in sores and filth, and living on roots and grass and sometimes the roasted corpses of their enemies. Wherever they went they left a trail of devastation. Too poor to afford swords, they fought with clubs, knives, shovels, hatchets, catapults and pointed sticks. Their ferocity was legendary; the leaders of the crusade were unable to control them and never went among them without being armed, while the Muslims were terrified of the Tafurs.

Though the Tafurs made a virtue of their poverty, in fact they were full of greed. The Tafurs looted every city captured by the Crusaders; they also raped the Muslim women and committed indiscriminate massacres. Urban and the princes had intended a campaign with limited objectives, but in reality the crusade tended constantly to become what the common people wanted it to be, a war to exterminate 'the sons of whores', as the Tafurs called the Muslims.

The Reconquest of Jerusalem

After journeying for nearly three years and almost three thousand miles across the known world, on 7 June 1099 the pilgrims arrived within sight of Jerusalem. Many of them wept. It seemed a miracle that any had survived. They had helped restore Asia Minor to the Byzantine Empire. And now before them rose the earthly Jerusalem, which for many was the key to the heavenly Jerusalem.

The Fatimids had lost Jerusalem to the Seljuks in 1076 but in 1098 they had recovered it once more. Now to deny the Crusaders any aid from within the city the Fatimid governor sent away all the Christians, Orthodox and heretic, of whom there were thousands despite the persecutions of al-Hakim and the uneasy times following the Seljuk conquest. Jerusalem was one of the great fortresses of the medieval world, and the governor commanded a sizeable garrison of Arab and Sudanese troops which had recently been reinforced by four hundred cavalrymen from Egypt. He also poisoned all the wells outside the city, secure that within Jerusalem's formidable walls he could rely on its numerous underground cisterns of good water. He knew that the Crusaders were hundreds of miles from any relief from Antioch, and in their haste they had not even attempted to take the nearby port of Jaffa. They were isolated and unsupplied in the midst of an alien land; their complete destruction seemed just a matter of time.

The Crusaders had about 1200 knights and 15,000 able-bodied men; their force was insufficient to effectively surround the city; but they had an unshakeable conviction that under divine protection their moment of victory had come. On 13 June they launched a general attack with great fervour and overran the outer defences, but they had too few ladders to scale the walls in several places simultaneously, and after a long morning of desperate fighting they withdrew. They needed siege engines and more ladders, but the Crusaders lacked the bolts and ropes and mangonels, and the area around Jerusalem had few trees. But then they had a stroke of luck: the Muslims had left Jaffa unprotected and six ships had sailed into the port, two from Genoa, four from England,

Godfrey of Bouillon had a reputation for immense physical strength. He was said to have wrestled a bear in Cilicia and won, and, as depicted in this fourteenth-century miniature, to have beheaded a camel with one blow of his sword.

carrying arms and food supplies and all the equipment necessary for building siege machines.

On the night of 13–14 July the attack resumed, simultaneously from north and south. The fighting continued throughout the day and on into the following night as against terrific resistance the Crusaders managed to move their machines closer to the walls. Around noon on 15 July Godfrey of Bouillon forced his way onto the northern battlements, and soon Tancred and his men surged deep into the city's streets towards the Temple Mount, that is the Haram al-Sharif surmounted by the Dome of the Rock and the al-Aqsa mosque, where the Muslims were retreating, intending it as their last redoubt. To the south the Fatimid governor paid Raymond of Toulouse an immense treasure in return for sparing his life and that of his bodyguard; they were escorted out of the walls and rode off to safety with the Muslim garrison at Ascalon. They were the last Muslims in Jerusalem to be spared their lives. Those on the Temple Mount surrendered to Tancred, who accepted and gave them his banner for protection, but the next morning the Tafurs killed all of them, ten thousand people according to one version, which outraged Tancred when he found out, and they set alight the synagogue where the Jews had taken refuge, burning them all within for having been allies of the Muslims.

Raymond of Aguilers, who was a chronicler attached to Raymond of Toulouse and entered Jerusalem with the Crusaders, gives this often-quoted account: 'Piles of heads, hands, and feet were to be seen in the streets of the city. It was necessary to pick one's way over the bodies of men and horses. But these were small matters compared to what happened at the Temple of Solomon, a place where religious services are ordinarily chanted. What happened there? If I tell the truth, it will exceed your powers of belief. So let it suffice to say this much, at least, that in the Temple and porch of Solomon, men rode in blood up to their knees and bridle reins. Indeed, it was a just and splendid judgment of God that this place should be filled with the blood of the unbelievers, since it had suffered so long from their blasphemies.'

But modern historians do not take Raymond of Aguilers very seriously; he was something of a credulous apocalyptic and described all sorts of visions and miracles, and his accounts of the undoubted slaughter at Jerusalem may be overdrawn. What is more, contemporary letters written by Jews living in the Eastern Mediterranean make it clear that not all Jews and Muslims in the city were killed; and indeed the contemporary Arab writer Ibn al-Arabi estimated the number of Muslim dead at Jerusalem at only three thousand.

When it was over, the knights went 'rejoicing and weeping' to the Church of the Holy Sepulchre to give thanks to God at the site of the death and resurrection of Jesus.

The Tower of David, the last stronghold of the Fatimid governor of Jerusalem

Part 2
The Rise
1099 to 1150

Godfrey of Bouillon at the Holy Sepulchre puts on the crown of thorns

Origins of the Templars

The New Knighthood

Christianity was founded on a pacifist ideal, and strong voices within the Church continued to be raised against the use of violence in any circumstances. But instead of chasing the impossible ideal of the total abolition of violence, the Papacy had spent much of the eleventh century trying to control and channel violence, for example trying to limit feudal warfare by promoting a set of rules called the Truce of God. Part of Pope Urban's thinking in launching the First Crusade was to usefully externalise this aggression by redirecting it against the Muslim threat.

The use of force against a deadly enemy and in the service of Christ had already been justified in the fifth century by no less a figure than Saint Augustine of Hippo, who in *The City of God* described the necessity of repelling the pagan barbarian invasion of Italy. Similarly Christians saw the First Crusade as an entirely just war. But however much the First

Map of Crusader Jerusalem

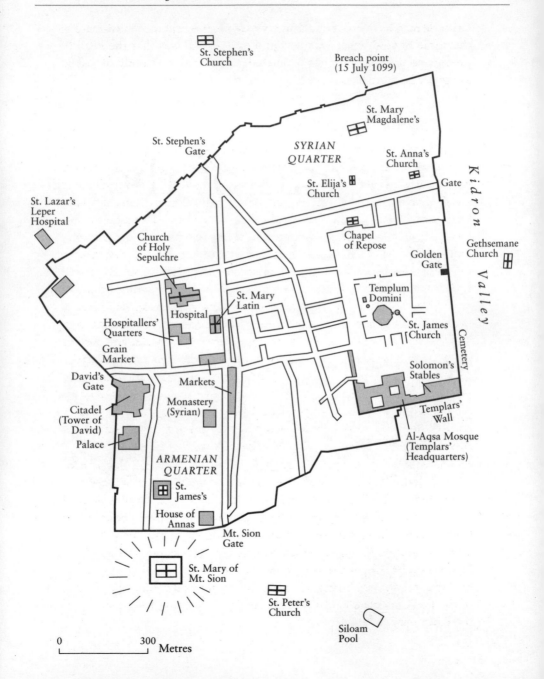

St. Stephen's Church

Breach point (15 July 1099)

St. Stephen's Gate

St. Mary Magdalene's

SYRIAN QUARTER

St. Anna's Church

St. Elija's Church

Gate

Kidron Valley

St. Lazar's Leper Hospital

Chapel of Repose

Golden Gate

Gethsemane Church

Church of Holy Sepulchre

Templum Domini

Hospital

St. Mary Latin

St. James Church

Hospitallers' Quarters

Grain Market

Solomon's Stables

David's Gate

Markets

Cemetery

Citadel (Tower of David)

Monastery (Syrian)

Templars' Wall

Palace

Al-Aqsa Mosque (Templars' Headquarters)

ARMENIAN QUARTER

St. James's

House of Annas

Mt. Sion Gate

St. Mary of Mt. Sion

St. Peter's Church

Siloam Pool

0   300   Metres

Crusade may have brought about a widespread acceptance of warfare in the name of God, what was new and exceptional was that the need to provide security for pilgrims to Jerusalem gave rise to a body of armed knights who were also monks.

The Kingdom of Jerusalem

On 17 July 1099, two days after the reconquest of Jerusalem, the Crusader barons met to choose a leader. This was against the wishes of the Tafurs, who hourly awaited the Second Coming and wanted no government at all. The favourite choice among the barons would have been Adhemar, bishop of Le Puy, but he had died of illness a year earlier at Antioch. In his stead, the crown was offered to Raymond of Toulouse; his age, wealth, experience and his closeness to both Adhemar and the Byzantine Emperor Alexius made him the almost necessary choice. But Raymond knew he was unpopular, and his own soldiers wanted to return home, so reluctantly he refused. Of the other candidates, Bohemond had already made himself prince of Antioch after leading the attack on that city; Tancred was regarded as merely an appendage of his uncle; and Robert of Normandy had let it be known that he wanted to return to Europe. And so on 22 July the crown was offered to Godfrey of Bouillon, who delicately replied that he would wear no crown where Jesus had worn the crown of thorns, nor would he presume to bear the title of King in Christ's holy city, but he would accept kingly powers under the title of *Advocatus Sancti Sepulchri*, the Defender of the Holy Sepulchre.

There were some, and perhaps Godfrey was among them, who wanted Jerusalem to be governed as a theocracy under a patriarch appointed by the Pope in Rome. But within a year Godfrey was dead and the crown passed to his brother, who had no qualms about ruling over a secular Kingdom of Jerusalem as Baldwin I. For his palace he used the al-Aqsa mosque, which was assumed to stand on the site of Solomon's Temple, while the Dome of the Rock, which does occupy that site, became a Christian church, the *Templum Domini*, the Temple of the Lord, surmounted by a cross, and served also as the residence of the Latin patriarch of Jerusalem.

Outremer and Its Muslim Neighbours

The Crusader states, or Outremer as they were collectively called, French for 'overseas', formed a series of contiguous territories that were linked to Europe by Byzantine Asia Minor and reached as far south as Egypt and the Red Sea.

The Kingdom of Jerusalem closely corresponded in extent to the kingdom of David and Solomon, that is all of what is today the state of Israel, plus the east bank of the Jordan river, western Jordan, southern Lebanon and southwestern Syria including the Golan Heights.

Dependent on Jerusalem were the feudal Crusader states of Antioch, Edessa and Tripoli. Bohemond had established the Principality of Antioch in 1098 as the Crusaders were still advancing towards Jerusalem, while Baldwin of Boulogne (the future Baldwin I of Jerusalem) had carved out the inland County of Edessa in that same year. Raymond of Toulouse began the conquest of northern Lebanon and coastal Syria in 1102, which when completed under his successors in 1109 would form the County of Tripoli.

The soldiers and rulers of Outremer were European, largely French in origin, and the commercial class was mainly Italian. During the first decades many of these Franks, as the Westerners were known, conquerors, traders, settlers and pilgrims, mingled with the indigenous inhabitants, adopted their dress and customs, were tolerant towards Muslims and intermarried with local Christians.

Fulcher of Chartres, a chronicler of the First Crusade, who died in Jerusalem in 1127, was a first-hand observer: 'Now we who were Westerners have become Easterners. He who was Italian or French has in this land become a Galilean or a Palestinian. He who was a citizen of Rheims or Chartres is now a Tyrian or an Antiochene. We have already forgotten our birthplaces. Most of us do not know them or even hear of them. One already owns home and household as if by paternal and hereditary right, another has taken as wife not a compatriot, but a Syrian, Armenian, or even a baptised Saracen woman. He who was an alien has become a native, he who was an immigrant is now a resident.'

Divisions in the Islamic world – not only the rivalry between the Fatimids in Egypt and the Baghdad caliphate which had been taken over by the Seljuk Turks, but divisions among the Seljuks themselves – meant that the Middle East was fragmented into numerous Muslim emirates. The Crusader states fitted into this mosaic and, from the Muslim point of view, were no more disturbing than any other emirates. The Franks fought against Muslims, but also made alliances with them; the fighting, which was on a minor scale, was no more than had been taking place in recent centuries among Muslims themselves. The fact that Christians were involved was of no great significance in a region where a large number of Christians had been a factor all along. If anything, Outremer was a source of fruitful interchange of goods and ideas between Latin Europe and the Muslim East.

The Crusaders and Byzantium

With the help of the Crusaders, the Emperor Alexius I Comnenus had recovered Asia Minor for the Byzantine Empire, and in exchange for subsidising the Westerners he assumed that he would get back Syria too. But Antioch, which had been taken from the Byzantines by the Seljuks as recently as 1085, was claimed by Bohemond instead. Bohemond was a Norman, and the Normans had long had designs on Constantinople, wanting to add it to their string of conquests in England, southern Italy and Sicily. Nor were the rest of the Crusaders interested in sharing their conquests in Syria and Palestine.

Behind this was the long-developing rift – religious, political and economic – between Western Europe and the East Roman Empire. This deeply aggrieved Alexius and prevented the formation of a united Christian front against the Muslims such as existed in the West against the Arab occupation of Spain. As previously noted, the Crusaders had arrived in the Middle East at a time when there were deep divisions among the Muslims, not only between Sunni and Shia, but also as the Arabs were being subjected to domination by the newly arrived Turks, who themselves were increasingly at odds with one another. But should that situation ever change, the Crusader states would find themselves alone, dependent on their command of the sea, their supply lines to the West, and what defences they could put in place against a unified Muslim power.

Fear and Massacre on the Roads

Many of those who came on the First Crusade went home when it was over, and few of the pilgrims who followed in their wake chose to settle in the Holy Land. Owing to insufficient Frankish immigration, the Crusader states would always be short of fighting men. The King of Jerusalem, the prince of Antioch and the counts of Edessa and Tripoli could between them raise no more than two thousand knights. The towns were made secure, but travellers along the roads were vulnerable to brigands and sudden enemy raids.

Saewulf of Canterbury, who visited the Holy Land in 1102, described how parties of pilgrims landing at Jaffa were exposed to attack as they journeyed along the mountain road to Jerusalem. Pilgrims who wearied and fell behind, or groups that were vulnerably small, were prey to bands of nomadic Bedouin who lived in the surrounding wilderness. The bandits did not hesitate to kill to get at the money sewn into travellers' clothes. Corpses were left to rot along the route up to Jerusalem because it was too dangerous for their companions to leave their party to give them a proper Christian burial.

There was danger not only from brigands but from Turkish forces in the north and Egyptians in the south. A Russian recounting his pilgrimage in 1106–07 was referring to the Fatimid Egyptians who held Ascalon, south of Jaffa, when he wrote of his visit to the church of Saint George at Lydda on the Jaffa-Jerusalem road: 'There are many springs here; travellers rest by the water but with great fear, for it is a deserted place and nearby is the town of Ascalon from which Saracens sally forth and kill travellers on these roads.'

The Russian's journey to Galilee, which took him near the town of Baisan, was no less hazardous: 'Seven rivers flow from this town and great reeds grow along these rivers and many tall palm trees stand about the town like a dense forest. This place is terrible and difficult of access for here live fierce pagan Saracens who attack travellers at the fords on these rivers.' An especially shocking attack took place at Easter 1019 when a large party of seven hundred unarmed pilgrims, both men and women, set out from Jerusalem for the river Jordan. They were travelling, in the words of a German chronicler, 'in joy and with a cheerful heart' when they were set upon by an Egyptian sortie from Ascalon. Three hundred pilgrims were killed and another sixty were captured to be sold as slaves.

The Poor Fellow-Soldiers of Christ and of the Temple of Solomon

The formation of the Templars arose out of these conditions of insecurity on the roads and the murder, rape, enslavement and robbery of unarmed pilgrims. Only recently a group of nine French knights, most prominently Hugh of Payns, a knight from Champagne who had fought in the First Crusade, and Godfrey of Saint-Omer in Picardy, had proposed to the Patriarch of Jerusalem Warmund of Picquigny and King Baldwin II, who had succeeded his cousin in 1118, that for the salvation of their souls they form a lay community or perhaps even withdraw into the contemplative life of a monastery. Instead Baldwin, alive to the urgent dangers confronting travellers in his kingdom, persuaded Hugh of Payns and his

Hugh of Payns, a founder and first Grand Master of the Knights Templar

companions to save their souls by protecting pilgrims on the roads, or as one chronicler put it, they were to take vows of poverty, chastity and obedience but were also 'to defend pilgrims against brigands and rapists'. The Easter massacre along the road to the river Jordan persuasively drove home the King's view, and on Christmas Day 1119 Hugh and his companions took their vows before the Patriarch in the Church of the Holy Sepulchre, calling themselves in Latin the *Pauperes commilitones Christi*, the Poor Fellow-Soldiers of Christ.

The King and Patriarch probably saw the creation of a permanent guard for travellers as complementary to the work of the Hospitallers who were providing care for pilgrims arriving at Jerusalem. Already in 600 Pope Gregory the Great had commissioned the building of a hospital at Jerusalem to treat and care for pilgrims, and two hundred years later Charlemagne, Emperor of the Holy Roman Empire, enlarged it to include a hostel and a library, but in 1005 it was destroyed as part of the Fatimid caliph Hakim's violent anti-Christian persecutions. In 1170 merchants from Amalfi obtained permission from the Fatimids to rebuild the hospital, which was run by Benedictine monks and dedicated to Saint John the Almsgiver, a charitable seventh-century patriarch of Alexandria. But after the First Crusade the hospital was released from Benedictine control and raised an order of its own, the Hospitallers of Saint John, which was recognised by the Pope in 1113 and came under his sole jurisdiction.

Official acceptance of the new order came at Nablus in January 1120 when the nine members of the Poor Fellow-Soldiers of Christ were formally introduced to an assembly of lay and spiritual leaders from throughout the lands of Outremer. In this year too they first attracted the attention of a powerful visitor to Outremer, Fulk V, count of Anjou, who on his return home granted them an annual revenue, an example that was soon followed by other French nobles, which added to the allowance they were already receiving from the canons of the Church of the Holy Sepulchre. Yet altogether these amounted to only a modest income, and individually the Poor Fellow-Soldiers were genuinely poor and dressed only in donated clothes, meaning they had no distinctive uniform – the white tunic emblazoned with a red cross came later. Their

In this thirteenth-century illustration, King Baldwin II of Jerusalem grants the al-Aqsa mosque on the Temple Mount to the Poor Fellow-Soldiers of Christ, represented by Hugh of Payns and Godfrey of Saint-Omer. Thereafter they became known as Templars.

seal alludes to this brotherhood in poverty by depicting two knights, perhaps Hugh of Payns and Godfrey of Saint-Omer, having to share a single horse.

They were also given the use of another hand-me-down. After the conquest of Jerusalem in 1099, the King had made do with the al-Aqsa mosque for his palace, but now he had built a new palace to the west and he gave what had been the mosque to the Poor Fellow-Soldiers. They made it their headquarters, residing there and using it to store arms, clothing and food, while stabling their horses in a great underground vault at the southeast corner of the Temple Mount. As the vaults were thought to have been Solomon's stables, and the al-Aqsa mosque was known as the mosque of the *Templum Solomonis* because it was

The Templar seal was intended to symbolise brotherhood in poverty through its image of two knights sharing a single horse

believed to have been built on the site of Solomon's Temple, it was not long before the knights had encompassed the association in their name. They became known as the *Pauperes commilitones Christi Templique Solomonici* – the Poor Fellow-Soldiers of Christ and of the Temple of Solomon; or, in a word, the Templars.

Digging Up Secrets

A story much put about these days in books like *The Da Vinci Code* and *The Holy Blood and the Holy Grail* is that the Templars were founded not to protect pilgrims or to defend the Holy Land but to undertake secret excavations beneath the surface of the Temple Mount. This argument takes advantage of gaps and uncertainties in the historical record, and it turns unknowns into mysteries – or into conspiracies. Why were there only nine Templars? Because they had a secret to keep, and so the fewer the better. Why do we know so little about the military activities of the Templars in their early years? Because really they were digging holes in the Temple Mount. Why did the Templars become so powerful? Because they found a huge treasure or discovered an explosive secret beneath the Temple Mount which they used to blackmail the Church. Why were the Templars destroyed? Because they knew too much.

There are indeed numerous holes, cisterns, chambers and tunnels beneath the Temple Mount, some of them very ancient and going back even before the time of Solomon, others dating from the years when the Templars were in residence. Over the centuries pilgrims and travellers have recorded their own explorations and discoveries, and in modern times the Temple Mount has been studied by archaeologists. For more on which, see the Locations section of this book.

Templar Mission to the West

In the autumn of 1127 Baldwin II sent emissaries to the West in an effort to solve two fundamental problems facing the Kingdom of Jerusalem: its military weakness and his lack of a male heir. Baldwin had four daughters but no sons, and to secure the succession he and his barons had decided to offer the hand of Melisende, his oldest daughter, to Fulk V, count of Anjou. In the event the mission to Fulk was a complete success; the count agreed to return to Outremer and marry Melisende, securing the succession and strengthening the kingdom's ties with the West.

Baldwin also sent Hugh of Payns, the Grand Master of the Templars, sailing westwards at the same time, his mission to solicit donations and to raise recruits. The King had prepared the ground for Hugh by writing to Bernard, the abbot of the Cistercian monastery of Clairvaux, explaining that the Templars were seeking approval of their order from the Pope, who they hoped would also initiate a subsidy that would help fund the battle against the enemies of the faith who were threatening the very existence of the Kingdom of Jerusalem. Baldwin knew his man: Bernard had already written to the Pope objecting to a proposal put forward by a fellow abbot to lead a mission of Cistercians to the East, saying that what the Holy Land really needed was 'fighting knights not singing and wailing monks'.

Bernard of Clairvaux, who was made a saint within twenty-years of his death, was one of the most influential and charismatic figures of the medieval Church. A volatile and passionate young man of an aristocratic family, he deliberately sought out the Cistercian order, known for

Sixteenth-century woodcut of Bernard of Clairvaux preaching from the pulpit

its austerity, and in 1113 joined its monastery at Citeaux. Three years later, at the age of twenty-six, he founded a new Cistercian house and became its abbot, calling the monastery Clairvaux, meaning the Valley of Light. By the time Pope Honorius II was elected in 1124, Bernard was already regarded as one of the most outstanding churchmen of France; he attended important ecclesiastical assemblies and his opinion was regularly sought by Papal legates.

Significantly Clairvaux was built on land given to Bernard by Hugh, the count of Champagne, whose vassal was Hugh of Payns, the future founding Grand Master of the Templars. By the time Hugh of Payns sailed westwards in 1127, Bernard was already well informed about the East and what was needed there; his mother's brother was Andre of Montbard, one of the original nine Templars, and Bernard's early patron the count of Champagne had three times gone on pilgrimage to the Holy Land, and on the last occasion, in 1125, he too renounced his worldly possessions and joined the Templars.

Grants of land as well as silver, horses and armour were made to the Templars almost as soon as Hugh of Payns landed in France in the autumn of 1127. The following summer the Grand Master was in England where he was received with great honour by King Henry I, who donated gold and silver to the order. Hugh established the first Templar house in London, at the north end of Chancery Lane, and he was given several other sites around the country. More donations followed when Hugh travelled north to Scotland. In September Hugh of Payns had returned across the Channel where he was met by Godfrey of Saint-Omer and together they received further grants and treasures, all these given for the defence of the Holy Land and for the salvation of their donor's souls.

The climax of Hugh of Payns' tour came in January 1129 at Troyes, the capital of the counts of Champagne, where Theobold, Hugh of Champagne's successor, hosted a convocation of Church leaders dominated by the presence of Bernard of Clairvaux. Hugh addressed the assembly and described the founding of the Templars and presented their Rule, adapted from the precepts followed by the canons of the Church of the Holy Sepulchre. This stipulated attendance at services together with the canons, communal meals, plain clothing, simple appearance and no contact with women. Because their duties carried them away from the church, they could replace attendance with the recitation of paternosters, and they were also allowed a horse and a small number of servants, and while the order was under the jurisdiction of the Patriarch of Jerusalem they owed their individual obedience to the Grand Master. These regulations formed the raw material from which, after considerable discussion and scrutiny by the gathered churchmen, Bernard drew up the Latin Rule of seventy-two clauses.

Bernard's Latin Rule enjoined the Templars to renounce their wills, to hold worldly matters cheap, and not be afraid to fight but always to be prepared for death and for the crown of salvation and eternal life. The knights were to dress in white, symbolising that they had put the dark life behind them and had entered a state of perpetual chastity. The hair on their heads was to be cut short, but all Templar knights wore beards as they were not permitted to shave. Foul language and displays of anger were forbidden, as were reminiscences about past sexual conquests. Property, casual discussion with outsiders, and letters and gifts given or received were subject to the approval of the master. Discipline was enforced by a system of penances with expulsion the punishment in extreme cases.

In all this the Templars were regulated like monks, but when it came to guidance in military matters Bernard offered few practical injunctions, though he did understand that in creating 'a new type of Order in the holy places', one that combined knighthood with religion, the Templars needed to possess land, buildings, serfs and tithes, and was entitled to legal protection against what the Latin Rule called 'the innumerable persecutors of the holy Church'.

Daily Routine of the Knights Templar

For all their reputation as warriors, the Knights Templar were very much monks and lived the monastic life in accordance with the canonical hours as indicated by this outline of their day.

✠ **4am** Rise for Matins and attend to horses, then return to bed.

✠ **6am to noon** Attend services, Prime (around 6am), Tierce (around 9am) and Sext (towards noon). Meanwhile train and groom horses.

✠ **Noon** Dinner of cooked meats. Complete silence throughout the meal while the chaplain reads from the Bible.

✠ **3pm** Attend Nones, the afternoon service.

✠ **6pm** Attend Vespers, followed by supper.

✠ **9pm** Attend Compline, after which the knights receive a glass of wine and water. Then instructions for the following day. Attend to horses.

✠ **Midnight** To bed in complete silence until 4am.

Saviours of the East and Defenders of All Christendom

The endorsement of the Templars by the Council of Troyes was subsequently confirmed by Pope Honorius II. These successes had come largely through the efforts of Bernard of Clairvaux, who was now urged by Hugh of Payn to write a robust defence of the Templars for general distribution.

De Laude Novae Militae was the name of Bernard's panegyric, *In Praise of the New Knighthood*, in which he announced the Templars as the champions of a higher struggle in which homicide, which was evil in Christian eyes, was really malecide, that is the killing of evil itself, which was good. The Holy Land, wrote Bernard, bore the impress of Jesus' life – Bethlehem, Nazareth, the Jordan river, the Temple Mount, and the Church of the Holy Sepulchre, which encompassed the places of Jesus' crucifixion, burial and resurrection. The Templars were the protectors of these holy sites and even acted as pilgrim guides, but by their proximity and daily familiarity with these footsteps in the life of Jesus, the Templars also had the advantage and the duty to search for the deeper

Pilgrims under the escort of Templar knights come within sight of Jerusalem

truth, the inner spiritual meaning of the holy places. The implication of Bernard's *De Laude* was that by understanding the full meaning of their role the Templars would be fortified in their mission, which had gone beyond policing the pilgrimage routes and now embraced the defence of the Holy Land itself.

Following the death of Hugh of Payns in 1136, his successor Robert of Craon, the second Grand Master, consolidated the gains made at Troyes by securing for the Templars a string of Papal bulls (from *bullum*, the Latin for seal, and so meaning an official decree). In 1139 Pope Innocent II issued *Omne Datum Optimum*, which had the effect of establishing the Templars as an independent and permanent order within the Catholic Church answerable to no one but the Pope and sanctioned their role as defenders of the Church and attackers of the enemies of Christ. The Grand Master was to be chosen from among the ranks of the Templar knights free from outside interference. The Templars were also given their own priesthood answerable to the Grand Master even though he was not ordained, which made the order independent of the diocesian bishops in Outremer and the West, and they were allowed their own oratories and cemeteries. The Templars were exempted from all tithes, but they were free to collect tithes on their own properties; all spoils of battle against the infidel were theirs by right; and donations made to the Templars were put under the protection of the Holy See.

These privileges were confirmed and extended by two further bulls, *Milites Templi*, issued by Pope Celestine II in 1144, and *Militia Dei* issued by Pope Eugenius III in 1145, which taken together with *Omne Datum Optimum* put the Templars beyond reproach and formed the foundation for their future wealth and success. It was also under Eugenius III that the Templars were granted the right to wear their famous habit of a red cross over a white tunic, symbolising their readiness to suffer martyrdom in the defence of the Holy Land.

Yet for all the powerful backing the Templars received from the West, it comes as a surprise that there is so little on record to show for their activities in Outremer for the first three decades after their founding in 1119. This is in contrast to their evident importance in the Iberian peninsula.

In Spain King Alfonso I of Aragon had reconquered large territories from the Muslims and was attracted to the concept of military orders as a means to safeguard them. When he died childless in 1134 he willed his entire kingdom to the Templars, the Hospitallers and the Church of the Holy Sepulchre in equal measures. But though the will was contested and adjusted, a settlement was reached with the Templars in 1143 which gave them six major castles in Aragon, a tenth of royal revenues and a fifth of any lands in future conquered from the Muslims, turning the Templars into a major force in the Reconquista against the forces of Islam. The Templars were the first; the Hospitallers followed them into the Iberian peninsula around 1150.

Christian rulers of the Iberian peninsula could call on greater numbers of local Christian troops than their counterparts in Outremer where so much of the population had been converted to Islam or driven out by Muslims. And so the Templars played a less significant role in battle than in the Middle East. Instead the principal task of the Templars

Templars dressed for battle and for prayer, as depicted in an eighteenth-century French history of the order

was to build castles along the frontiers to prevent Muslim incursions. The responsibility for defending Aragon and Catalonia rested largely on the Templars and the Hospitallers, but in the centre of the peninsula the kings of Castille and Leon relied on home-grown military orders established for the most part during the third quarter of the twelfth century. Nevertheless the Templars exercised considerable influence on these Spanish orders which had been founded in direct imitation of their own order. The kings of Castile and Leon also entrusted the Templars with the overlordship of great tracts of underpopulated territory that fell to the Reconquista.

The Templars played a similar role in the west of the Iberian peninsula where in the struggle against the Muslims a new nation was emerging, the independent kingdom of Portugal. The Templars' commitment to the cause of the crusade against Islam made them perfect allies; at no cost to existing Portuguese resources they were given anticipatory grants, so that as the frontier was extended against the Muslims during the 1130s and 1140s the Templars acquired a share in newly recovered lands and were given control of border castles.

Yet in Outremer, where the availability of local Christian troops was more limited than in Iberia, meaning that the military orders might have found a greater battle role, the Templars are reported in medieval sources to have been involved in only three military engagements between 1119 and the arrival of the Second Crusade in 1148. They were at a failed siege of Damascus in 1129, they took part in a campaign to defend an eastern outpost of the County of Tripoli which met with defeat in 1137, and they were worsted in a skirmish at Hebron in 1139. The Templars did take over responsibility for guarding the passes into Antioch from Asia Minor through the Amanus mountains where they were put in charge of Baghras castle in about 1136. Otherwise the surviving record is silent on the early decades of the Templars in the East, though the mystery is probably explained by the loss and destruction of sources than by a lack of Templar activity. Certainly a section of opinion in the West was convinced, according to the chronicler Richard of Poitou, a monk of Cluny writing in 1153, that the Franks would long since have lost Jerusalem had it not been for the Templars.

Templar Origins: Historical Agendas

The Knights Templar would in time become one of the wealthiest and most powerful financial and military organisations in the medieval world, yet there are holes in the historical record about their origins, and there are contradictions too. When were they founded? How many were there? What accounts for their meteoric rise? Part of the problem in finding the answers to these questions lies in the nature of the sources themselves.

The earliest chronicler of Templar history was William, archbishop of Tyre. Born into a French or Italian family at Jerusalem in about 1130, he studied Latin and probably Greek and Arabic there before continuing his education from about 1146 to 1165 in France and Italy. After returning to Outremer he wrote, among other works, a twenty-three volume history of the Middle East from the conquest of Jerusalem by Umar. This *Historia Rerum in Partibus Transmarinis Gestarum*, or *History of Deeds Done Beyond the Sea*, was begun around 1175 and remained unfinished at the time of William of Tyre's death in about 1186. Most of it concentrated on the First Crusade and subsequent political events within the Kingdom of Jerusalem – events from which William was not entirely detached, for he was involved in the highest affairs of both the kingdom and the Church, and as archbishop and contender for the office of Patriarch of Jerusalem he was naturally jealous of any diminution of ecclesiastical authority – and so resentful of the Templars' independence and their rise to wealth and power.

Two other early chroniclers were Michael the Syrian, Jacobite Patriarch of Antioch, who died in 1199, and Walter Map, archdeacon of Oxford, who died in about 1209. But Michael was weak on matters outside his own experience and times, while Walter preferred a good story to sound historical inquiry, and moreover his prejudice against the Templars was fundamental, for he objected to the entire concept of an order of fighting monks. Despite his own bias against the Templars, William of Tyre is considered the most reliable of the three; he diligently sifted through sources to glean the facts about events that occurred before his time, and he made a point of interviewing surviving first-hand witnesses.

All the same, William of Tyre did not even begin writing his history until the mid-1170s, that is fifty-five years after the founding of the Templars,

A manuscript page from William of Tyre's chronicle, depicting Baldwin I of Jerusalem giving an audience to an Armenian delegation

and there is no earlier source. The chroniclers of the First Crusade, men like Fulcher of Chartres, Baldric of Dol, Robert the Monk and Guibert de Nogent, had all completed their works within a decade of the reconquest of Jerusalem in 1099 and long before the foundation of the Templars in 1119 – or was it 1118? According to William of Tyre it was the latter, but he was notoriously poor on dates even if careful in other things, and the balance of scholarly opinion has the Templars established in 1119. In whatever year it was, it does not seem to have occurred to anyone to write a first-hand account of the founding ceremony of the Templars in the Church of the Holy Sepulchre on Christmas Day – at the time it did not register as a significant event.

We do not even know how many founding members there really were. William of Tyre says that there were nine and names the two most prominent as Hugh of Payns and Godfrey of Saint-Omer. Other sources also name Archambaud of Saint-Aignan, Payen of Montdidier, Andre of Montbard, Geoffrey Bissot, a knight called Rossal or possibly

Roland, another called Gondemar, and two more whose names have not survived. Moreover, William of Tyre maintains that even as late as the Council of Troyes in 1129 there were still only nine Knights Templar. But why would only nine men command such attention from the Council and the Pope, and why would Bernard of Clairvaux devote so much effort to praising their worth and propagating their fame? Indeed in this case Michael the Syrian seems to be more reliable, for he says there were thirty founding Templar knights, and most likely there were very many more a decade later.

Just as we owe it to William of Tyre that the Templars comprised only nine members right up to 1129, so we also owe to him the claim that they were a poor and simple order throughout the early decades of their foundation. Certainly the Templars looked back on themselves in this idealistic way, so that in 1167 when they were very rich indeed they adopted as their seal the two knights astride one horse, a self-image perhaps also derived from their ascetic Cistercian promoter in the West, Bernard of Clairvaux. Yet however humble the lives of the individual knights, the order itself was never indigent, not even at the start when already it was receiving an income from the canons of the Church of the Holy Sepulchre as well as significant donations from powerful French barons.

But to portray the Templars as poor and humble and few in numbers in their early years gave William of Tyre a handy stick with which to beat them in his critical history. By the 1170s, according to William of Tyre, the Templars 'are said to have immense possessions both here and overseas, so that there is now not a province in the Christian world which has not bestowed upon the aforesaid brothers a portion of its goods. It is said today that their wealth is equal to the treasures of kings.' William contrasts this state of affairs with the Templars' earlier simplicity, suggesting they have somehow betrayed themselves. But it seems that his real complaint is that their support in the West made them independent of any power in Outremer, particularly that of the Church as represented by William, the archbishop of Tyre, and would-be Patriarch of Jerusalem:

'Although they maintained their establishment honourably for a long time and fulfiled their vocation with sufficient prudence, later, because of the neglect of humility, they withdrew from the Patriarch of Jerusalem, by whom their order was founded and from whom they received their first benefices and to whom they denied the obedience which their predecessors rendered. They have also taken away tithes and first fruits from God's churches, have disturbed their possessions, and have made themselves exceedingly troublesome.'

This was the beginning of the criticism the Templars would receive from sources whose interests they crossed. Some would call them saviours of the East and defenders of all Christendom, others would find them 'troublesome' and accuse them of arrogance, greed, secrecy and deceit. Their destruction lay in their beginning; when there was no more East to save, the Templars would be doomed.

The Second Crusade

The Templars Emerge from the Margins of History

The Christian states of Outremer enjoyed nearly half a century of security after the First Crusade thanks to the divisions among their Muslim neighbours, the Fatimids in Egypt and the numerous Turkish-controlled statelets in Syria and Iraq, who often fought against one another. Occasionally there were clashes between the Franks and Muslims but these were minor affairs and did not threaten the existence of Outremer; indeed Muslim princes made alliances with the Christians against their common enemies.

The most important of these enemies was Zengi, a Seljuk Turk, who began his career in 1127 when on behalf of the moribund Abbasid caliphate in Baghdad he made himself *atabeg*, or governor, of Mosul in northern Iraq. By means of war and intimidation, Zengi soon extended his authority over much of Muslim Syria, and he would have taken Damascus too but for an alliance between its Turkish ruler and King Fulk of Jerusalem.

In the event Zengi's greatest victory was his conquest of the County of Edessa in 1144. The first state founded by the Crusaders, Edessa was the first to fall, and Arab chroniclers later looked back on this triumph as the start of the jihad that would drive the Franks from the East. In the West the loss of Edessa touched off the Second Crusade, a huge campaign by sea and land, this time led by two European kings. But the crusade may never have reached the Holy Land at all had it not been for the Templars, and when unexpectedly it failed they became convenient scapegoats. Yet against the gathering forces of the Muslim jihad Outremer could not have survived as it did for another one hundred and fifty years without the religious conviction and military prowess of the brotherhoods of Christian warriors.

Muslim Friends and Allies

In 1138 the Arab diplomat and chronicler Usamah ibn Munqidh was sent by the Turkish governor of Damascus, Muin al-Din Unur, to Jerusalem to discuss with King Fulk the possibility of an alliance against Zengi, the atabeg of Mosul. The Christian chronicler William of Tyre called Zengi 'a vicious man', and the Muslim inhabitants of Damascus agreed: they had learnt something of his brutality during his unsuccessful siege of their city in 1135, and the mission to Jerusalem was sent with popular support. For two years Usamah travelled back and forth, negotiating an alliance and making friends. Zengi threatened Damascus again in 1140, but his fear of being caught in a pincer movement forced him to withdraw, an event celebrated later that year when Usamah accompanied Muin al-Din Unur on a state visit to the Kingdom of Jerusalem.

During the times he spent in Jerusalem Usamah became a close observer of the Franks and their ways and wrote about them in his chronicle. He regarded the Franks as the enemies of God and attached to almost every account of them some imprecation like 'May Allah's curse be upon them!', but that was more a doctrinaire reaction to their faith than a true expression of his attitude towards them as a people. Of one knight in the army of King Fulk whom Usamah got to know well, he wrote, 'He was of my intimate fellowship and kept such constant company with me that he began to call me "my brother". Between us were mutual bonds of amity and friendship.' He admired Western medicine, and he was struck by the lack of restriction placed on their women by Frankish men: 'The Franks are void of all zeal and jealousy. One of them may be walking along with his wife. He meets another man who takes his wife by the hand and steps aside to converse with her while the husband is standing on one side waiting for his wife to conclude the conversation. If she lingers too long for him, he leaves her alone with the conversant and goes away'.

Usamah came to know the Templars particularly well and tells how they made a point of providing him with a place to pray. 'When I was visiting Jerusalem, I used to go to the al-Aqsa mosque where my Templar friends were staying. Along one side of the building was a small oratory in which the Franks had set up a church. The Templars placed this spot at my disposal that I might say my prayers.' Of course Usamah arranged himself to pray towards Mecca, which is south of Jerusalem, whereas Christian churches, wherever they may be, are oriented to the east. A Frank noticed Usamah's direction of prayer and roughly pointed him towards the east, saying 'Thus do we pray.' Usamah's Templar friends rushed forward and led the man away, but when their attention was diverted the man accosted Usamah again, repeating 'Thus do we pray.' Again the Templars intervened and led the Frank away, apologising to their Muslim friend, saying the man had just arrived from the West and had never seen anyone pray as Usamah had done. Usamah concluded that 'everyone who is a fresh emigrant from the Frankish lands is ruder in character than those who have become acclimatised and have held long association with the Muslims'.

The Fall of Edessa

Unfortunately for the Franks they were often engaged in petty quarrels among themselves, and when Zengi's large and powerful army turned its unwelcome attention upon Edessa in 1144 Outremer was divided. The count of Edessa, Joscelyn II, was at odds with the prince of Antioch; the count of Tripoli was only vaguely interested in events so far to the east; and in Jerusalem King Fulk had just died, leaving the government in the hands of Queen Melisende as regent for Baldwin III, their thirteen-year-old son. Consequently, Zengi found his attack opposed only by the negligible forces of Edessa itself.

The other Crusader states fringed the Mediterranean, but Edessa was landlocked; it lay beyond the Euphrates, a day's ride east of the river. Its population was made up of Christians of the East, Chaldeans and Armenians, who were more devoted to trade than skilled in the use of arms; Westerners rarely visited the city and those Franks who lived there had mostly married the local Christians, so that its defence was entrusted largely to mercenaries. When Zengi laid siege to the city he came up against its formidable walls, but in the words of William of Tyre, 'All these defences could be of use against the enemy only if there were men willing to fight for their freedom, men who would resist the foe valiantly. The defences would be useless, however, if there were none among the besieged who were willing to serve as defenders. Towers, walls, and earthworks are of little value to a city unless there are defenders to man them. Zengi found the town bereft of defenders and was much encouraged.' Help was sent too late from Jerusalem and Tripoli, while Antioch sent no help at all. On Christmas Eve 1144 Zengi's forces breached the walls and rushed into the streets and houses of the city. 'They slew with their swords the citizens whom they encountered, sparing neither age, condition nor sex', wrote William of Tyre, and they enslaved any who survived.

Bernard Launches the Second Crusade

At first the West was slow to react to the fall of Edessa. In autumn 1145 Pope Eugenius III wrote to King Louis VII of France asking him to undertake a new crusade to the East. At Christmas Louis summoned his barons and told them that he was taking the cross and invited them to do the same, but their response was poor. Louis was young, only twenty-five; he was seen as impetuous, weak and greedy; and he had angered his barons by recently seizing land from the count of Champagne. But the barons did agree to convene again at Easter 1146 at Vezelay in Burgundy.

Meanwhile Louis arranged that Bernard of Clairvaux should speak at Vezelay. Not only was Bernard the friend of Popes and kings (Eugenius had been a monk at Clairvaux and the king's brother had recently joined the Cistercians there), but his asceticism, conviction and eloquence combined to make him the most formi-dable spiritual figure of the age. At word that Bernard would speak, such a crowd of aristocrats and admirers from all over France were drawn to Vezelay that, as at Clermont when Pope Urban called for the First Crusade, the cathedral was not big enough to contain the throng and a platform was erected in the fields outside the town.

This was an age like no other, Bernard told the crowd. God had found new ways to save the faithful. The fall of Edessa was a gift from God. It was an opportunity created by God to save men's souls. 'Look at the skill he is using to save you. Consider the depth of his love and be astonished,

King Louis VII kneels before Bernard of Clairvaux at Vezelay, by Gustav Doré

sinners. This is a plan not made by man, but proceeding from the heart of divine love.' Amid the roars of *'Deus le volt!'*, so many came forward to take the cross that Bernard had to tear his own habit into strips. King Louis was the first among them, followed by his barons, many of whom were the sons and grandsons of original Crusaders. Bernard was able to write a few days later to the Pope: 'You ordered; I obeyed. I opened my mouth; I spoke; and at once the Crusaders have multiplied to infinity. Villages and towns are now deserted. You will scarcely find one man for every seven women. Everywhere you see widows whose husbands are still alive.'

Bernard broadcast his message farther, travelling into the north of France and to Flanders, and addressing a letter to the people of England, explaining that Jesus, the Son of God, was losing the land in which he had walked among men for more than thirty years. 'Your land', Bernard told the English, 'is well known to be rich in young and vigorous men. The world is full of their praises, and the renown of their courage is on the lips of all. Do not miss this opportunity. Take the sign of the cross. At once you will have indulgence for all the sins which you confess with a contrite heart. It does not cost you much to buy and if you wear it with humility you will find that it is the kingdom of heaven.'

News of the crusade had also reached Germany where it touched off anti-Semitic pogroms along the Rhine. Bernard hastened to Germany to condemn the atrocities on the spot. 'The Jews', he said, 'are not to be persecuted, killed or even put to flight. The Jews are for us the living words of Scripture, for they remind us always what the Lord suffered.' And then to control and give direction to the popular feeling, Bernard preached the crusade to the reluctant King Conrad III of Germany himself, finally persuading him to take the cross at Christmas 1146.

The following spring, Pope Eugenius gave his blessing to the campaign of Alfonso VII of Castile against the Muslim occupation of Spain, declaring it a crusade, and that autumn a Crusader fleet from northern Europe helped the Portuguese capture Lisbon from the Arabs. Largely through the energy of Bernard, the Second Crusade had rapidly become an international campaign against the forces of Islam on both the eastern and western fronts.

Mary Magdalene at Vezelay

Vezelay was a particularly potent spot from which to launch the Second Crusade for it possessed the bones of Mary Magdalene. The claim was first made by the great abbey church at Vezelay in the 1050s, an assertion quickly supported by a Papal document dated 27 April 1058. The Muslim occupiers in the Middle East had recently been making it difficult for Europeans to undertake pilgrimages to the Holy Land, and this encouraged the development of pilgrimage sites within Europe itself. Various well-known New Testament figures were suddenly discovered to have travelled to the West and died there, their bones unearthed by enterprising churches. Glastonbury had already laid claim to Joseph of Arimathea in this way; in Paris they announced the discovery of the bones of Saint Denis, a convert and student of Saint Paul; while Saint James had turned up in Spain at Compostela to aid the reconquest, and Saint Mark had arrived at Venice. Unfortunately the great ninth-century Romanesque church at Vezelay had been dedicated to the Virgin Mary, and as she had bodily risen to heaven at her assumption, there was no question of finding her relics. But Vezelay lay along the profitable pilgrimage route from Germany to Compostela, and the profits to be gleaned from the passing trade, not to mention the prestige and the protection to be had, made the happy discovery of some suitable remains all but unavoidable, and who better than Mary Magdalene.

In the Gospels Mary Magdalene is present at the most important moments of the Jesus story – his death and his resurrection. At the crucifixion of Jesus his disciples have gone into fearful hiding, but Mary Magdalene is at both the Cross and the tomb, and it is she who carries the news to the disbelieving disciples that Jesus has arisen. Her appearances in the Gospels are brief but telling. It is as if she fulfils the role of those ancient goddesses whose lives embraced the deaths and rebirths of their men.

The shrine of Mary Magdalene at Vezelay became immensely popular, but how, the faithful wondered, had her bones come to Burgundy? A pious fiction was circulated saying that her relics had first been in Provence but were threatened by Saracen raiders, and so they were removed and brought to Vezelay for safekeeping. But how had the bones come to Provence in the first place? Another legend was invented to conveniently explain that Mary Magdalene and her companions had

This sixteenth-century altarpiece shows Mary Magdalene and
her companions setting sail from the Holy Land for France

escaped from the Holy Land by sea and landed, some say, at Marseilles,
or according to others at Les Saintes-Maries-de-la-Mer, from where she
made her way inland and died at St-Maximin-la-Ste-Baume. It was from
there that a monk from Vezelay had dug up her bones and taken them
back to Burgundy.

Meanwhile Mary Magdalene's bones were performing miracles; she
was associated with the liberation of prisoners, assistance with fertility
and childbirth, spectacular cures and even the raising of the dead. Such
wonderful stories demanded yet wider circulation, a challenge taken up
in the thirteenth century by the Dominican writer Jacobus de Voragine.
To his account of Mary Magdalene in his compendium of saints' lives
called the *Legenda Aurea* (the *Golden Legend*), he added the plethora
of new miracles put about by Vezelay and produced what very quickly

became a medieval bestseller that was soon translated from Latin into nearly every European language, including Dutch and Czech.

However, King Charles of Anjou (1226–85) was establishing a Mediterranean empire based on Naples, Sicily and his newly acquired territory of Provence. Learning from the *Legenda Aurea* that Mary Magdalene's bones had been associated with St-Maximin-la-Ste-Baume, he went to have a look for himself. And what did he find? The bones of Mary Magdalene. Clearly the church at Vezelay had been mistaken. Charles installed the Dominican Order as caretakers of Mary's shrine, and they in turn proudly broadcast the importance of their mission by fabricating the *Book of Miracles of Saint Mary Magdalene*, documenting all the miraculous intercessions and cures the saint had wrought at her Provençal sanctuary. The publication's success was measured by the fact that Vezelay as a centre for the miraculous soon went into decline. Indeed, pilgrims still come to Les Saintes-Maries-de-la-Mer to see where Mary Magdalene came ashore and visit St-Maximin-la-Ste-Baume to kneel before her bones.

The Templars' Role in the Crusade

The growing importance of the Templars can be measured by the fact that on 27 April 1147 King Louis VII and Pope Eugenius III came to the Paris Temple – which had become the European headquarters of the order – to discuss plans for the Second Crusade. Also in attendance were four archbishops and 130 Templar knights, with at least as many sergeants and squires.

Here, it was agreed that the Templars would accompany the French army to the East, and it was probably on this occasion that the Pope conferred on the Templars the right to emblazon their white robes with the red cross, symbolising their willingness to die in defence of the Holy Land. The Pope also appointed the Templar treasurer to receive the tax that had been imposed on all Church goods to finance the crusade. It was the start of a fateful relationship, that would last for over a century and a half, with the Paris Temple serving in effect as the treasury of France.

Everard des Barres, the master of the Temple in France, was sent ahead to Constantinople by the king to negotiate with the Byzantine Emperor Manuel I Comnenus for the passage of the French and German armies; this time they had not been invited, and in Constantinople the prospect of their approach was regarded with some scepticism and alarm. Moreover, the Byzantines were at war with Roger II, the Norman king of Sicily, and to cover their backs had recently agreed a treaty with the Seljuks. To the minds of those in the West this accommodation with the infidel seemed treacherous, an attitude that deepened suspicions on both sides.

Nevertheless, everything seemed set fair in September 1147 when Conrad's army arrived in Constantinople and was ferried across the Bosphorus, to be followed by Louis' army a month later. The Second Crusade had two armies marching through Byzantine territory, and a large northern European fleet was heading into the Mediterranean after capturing Lisbon from the Muslims.

The first disaster struck in late October. Conrad led his army on the direct route across Asia Minor and straight up against the border of

Templars in pursuit of the enemy in this detail
from a twelfth-century illustration

Seljuk territory where at Dorylaeum on 25 October the Germans were heavily defeated by the Turks. The survivors, including Conrad himself, retreated to Nicaea where they joined the French who were following the safer coastal route. At Ephesus Conrad fell ill and returned with his forces to Constantinople, while the French, inadequately provisioned by the Byzantines, marched up the Maeander valley and eastwards against the advancing winter. Toiling through the narrow defiles of the Cadmus mountains in early January 1148 the heavily armoured French knights were easy prey for the Seljuks' light cavalry with their talent for firing off arrows at full gallop.

With his army on the verge of disintegration, King Louis surrendered his responsibilities to Everard des Barres, the Templar master, who divided the force into units, each under the command of a Templar knight whom they swore to obey absolutely. Thanks to the boldness and organisational skills of the Templars, the army was led to safety at Attalia (modern Antalya) on the Mediterranean. But their ordeal was not yet over, for the expected Byzantine fleet was too small to take them all to the Holy Land, so only Louis and part of his army sailed east. The rest attempted to march overland through Seljuk lands, and most of them died on the way.

By the time Louis arrived at Antioch early in March the cost of supplies and shipping had been so great that he needed to borrow if he was to continue with the crusade. Abandoning his intention of retaking Edessa, Louis instead led his army southwards via Tripoli to Jerusalem where he fulfiled his pilgrim's vow, meanwhile despatching Everard des Barres to Acre where he raised enough money from Templar resources to cover the cost of the French expedition – a sum that was more than half the annual tax revenue of the French state.

Fiasco at Damascus

Despite the French losses in Asia Minor, the crusading forces that finally arrived in the Holy Land were far from negligible, and added to these were the survivors of the German army which had arrived by sea from Constantinople with Conrad. On 24 June 1148 the lords and military leaders then in Outremer attended a great council at Acre; Baldwin III, the seventeen-year-old King of Jerusalem presided over the gathering, which included the Hospitallers and the Templars and the kings of Germany and France.

Zengi was dead but his son Nur al-Din controlled Aleppo in northern Syria astride the route to Edessa, and Raymond of Antioch wanted to strike in that direction. Others spoke of Egypt, but the road south was blocked by Ascalon, a powerfully fortfied city still in the hands of the Fatimids. The third possibility was Damascus, the one Muslim power in the region willing to ally with the Franks against Nur al-Din, a fact that might have deterred some in Outremer but meant nothing to the new arrivals from the West. In any case, for the Frankish states of Outremer, perilously clinging to the Mediterranean seaboard, it was always a strategic necessity to extend their depth, to conquer Aleppo, Damascus or Cairo. Damascus was a venerable and wealthy city whose capture would give the Franks control over the crossroads of commerce and communications in the East. After vigorous discussion of these various plans of action the assembly finally decided to concentrate all the available forces of the crusade against Damascus.

The Second Crusade marched out from Galilee for Damascus in late July 1148. The army camped in a well-supplied position amid orchards and fresh-flowing water in front of the western walls and prepared for the

The Citadel at Aleppo was the base for Muslim power in northern Syria

siege. But the orchards also served detachments of Damascenes who used their cover to make repeated sorties against the Crusaders. Louis and Conrad responded by switching their attack to the eastern walls where there was open ground and they could deploy their heavy cavalry to greater effect. But the city walls were higher on this waterless desert side, and when the siege dragged on the Crusaders had no choice but to withdraw. Without even fighting a battle the Second Crusade was defeated, ending in a whimpering fiasco. Six years later Damascus fell to Nur al-Din, and the encirclement of Outremer by a united Muslim power began.

The Strategic Importance of Damascus

If the Second Crusade proved a calamity for its failure to capture Damascus, the great error had already been committed half a century before when Damascus was not seized by the First Crusade. Then the momentum was with the Franks, who had the men to do the job, but their ideological fixation on Jerusalem obscured the strategic reality. As it was, the Crusader states formed a long thin line along the Mediterranean coast from the Amanus mountains in the north to the Gulf of Aqaba in the south, but they had no depth: the Crusaders never controlled the hinterland to the east where Damascus sits on the desert fringe. Eastwards of this hinterland lay nothing but barren desert, not easily traversed by large armies. If the First Crusade had taken Damascus it would have cut the Muslim world in two; instead this hinterland became a highway for Muslim forces moving between Baghdad, Aleppo, Damascus and eventually Cairo, who freely harassed Outremer all along its desert flank and kept the Christian forces permanently stretched.

The Bitter Aftertaste

The withdrawal from Damascus caused a bitterness in relations between Outremer and the West that lasted for a generation. Seen from the perspective of the East, Kings Louis and Conrad had neither recovered

Edessa nor offset its loss by taking Damascus or anything else; indeed their bungling placed Outremer in greater peril than before the crusade began.

In the West the failure of the crusade came as a shock because it had been led by the powerful kings of Germany and France and had been preached by Bernard of Clairvaux, the greatest spiritual figure of the age. Some blamed the Franks of the East, who had previously been in alliance with the ruler of Damascus; some German chroniclers, anxious to protect Conrad, blamed the Templars, saying that they had deliberately engineered the retreat; the anonymous Wurzburg chronicler wrote of Templar greed, and of betrayal by taking a massive bribe. The French did not make the same accusations, having been supported by the Templars throughout. And in fact there is no evidence of Templar treachery, but it is significant that they were blamed – it was the first indication that the long history of ambiguous feelings about the foundation of an order of monks who also fought for God might be translated into open and specific complaints.

The problem was that the more the Franks of Outremer relied on Western subsidy and military aid, the more critical the West became if things went wrong; the enthusiasm was there, but only for victories that came easily and cheap. From now on, the defence of the Holy Land would depend on its network of castles, largely built and commanded by the knights of the military orders.

Part 3
The Power
1150–1291

Krak des Chevaliers, a Hospitaller castle, is
the best surviving example of the concentric
system in the military architecture of
Outremer, one defensive wall set within
the other, each wall higher than the one
before. Along with the Templar castle at
Safita and the Templars' fortified city of
Tortosa, it dominated the Homs Gap,
the principle route between the interior
of Syria and the Mediterranean.

Crusader Castles

The Defence of the Holy Land

From the moment that the First Crusade arrived in the Middle East, the Crusaders started building castles. As in Europe, they served as residences and administrative centres, as well as having a military function. But after the Second Crusade the Franks in Outremer found themselves on the defensive and the military nature of castles became more important. Often large and elaborate, and continuously improved by the latest innovations in military science, the Franks built over fifty castles in Outremer. Geography, manpower and the feudal system all explain this considerable investment in stone.

The Crusader states were long and narrow, lacking defence in depth. The Principality of Antioch, the County of Tripoli and the Kingdom of Jerusalem stretched 450 miles from north to south, yet rarely were they more than 50 to 75 miles broad, the County of Tripoli perilously constricting to the width of the coastal plain, only a few miles broad, between Tortosa (present-day Tartus) and Jeble. The inland cities of Aleppo, Hama, Homs and Damascus all remained in Muslim hands, while Mesopotamia and Egypt were recruiting grounds for any Muslim counterthrust, as the campaigns of Saladin and the Mamelukes would show. For the Crusaders the natural defensive line was the mountains, and they built castles to secure the passes.

Stones more than soldiers were pressed to this purpose as Outremer was chronically short of men. After the conquest of Jerusalem in 1099 most of the Crusaders returned to Europe; the Kingdom of Jerusalem was thereafter defended by 300 mounted knights. Despite successive crusades, at no time during the entire history of the Crusader states were they able to put more than 2600 horse in the field. Moreover, though there was still a large local Christian population, these were Orthodox while the Crusaders were a Latin minority.

Outnumbered and insecure, the Franks of necessity housed themselves in fortified towns or in castles. Nevertheless, if the Crusader states were to survive they had to be a going concern, and the Franks set about organising their possessions along familiar European feudal lines. Castles were as much centres of production and administration as they were military outposts – battlemented country houses, containing corn mills and olive presses, and surrounded by gardens, vineyards, orchards and fields. Their lands in some cases encompassed hundreds of villages and a peasantry numbering tens of thousands. Wood to Egypt, herbs, spices and sugar to Europe, were important exports; indeed throughout the twelfth and thirteenth centuries Europe's entire supply of sugar came from the Latin East.

But in times of war, agriculture was always the first victim. Were it not for Western subvention and the taxes imposed on trade between the Muslim East and Europe as it passed through the Crusader states, they would have collapsed sooner than they did. The Latin rulers were always strapped for cash, the bulk of their revenues going towards the upkeep of mercenaries, knights and castles. It was a vicious circle; insufficient land and manpower making castles a necessity; the cost of knights and castles greater than the productivity of the land could justify.

In this situation the military orders came into their own. They had the resources, the independence, the dedication – the elements of their growing power.

Structure of the Templars

THE TOP FIVE OFFICIALS of the Knights Templar were the Grand Master, the Seneschal, the Marshal, the Commander of the Kingdom of Jerusalem, and the Draper. Ultimately, the Order owed its allegiance to the Pope – and to no other authority, spiritual or temporal.

✠ THE GRAND MASTER Ruler of the order, the Grand Master was elected by twelve senior Templar members, the number representing the twelve apostles, plus a chaplain who took the place of Jesus Christ. The master had considerable but not autocratic powers.

✠ GRAND CHAPTER Comprised of senior officials. All major decisions by the Grand Master – such as whether to go to war, agree a truce, alienate lands, or acquire a castle – required that he consult with the chapter.

✠ SENESCHAL Deputy and advisor to the Grand Master.

✠ MARSHAL Responsible for military decisions such as purchase of equipment and horses; he also exercised authority over the regional commanders.

✠ DRAPER The keeper of the robes, the Draper issued clothes and bedlinen, removed items from knights who were thought to have too much, and distributed gifts made to the order.

✠ REGIONAL COMMANDERS These were the COMMANDER OF THE KINGDOM OF JERUSALEM, who acted as the order's treasurer and within the Kingdom had the same powers as the Grand Master; the COMMANDER OF JERUSALEM, who within the city had the same powers as the Grand Master; and the COMMANDERS OF ACRE, TRIPOLI AND ANTIOCH, each with the powers of the Grand Master within their domains.

✠ PROVINCIAL MASTERS France, England, Aragon, Poitou, Portugal, Apulia and Hungary each had a provincial master who was responsible to the Grand Master.

✠ THE KNIGHTS, SERGEANTS and other MEN AT ARMS were subject to these various officers and their deputies.

A Power Unto Themselves

After the Second Crusade both the Hospitallers and the Templars came to provide the backbone of resistance to the Muslims, but the military impetus came from the Templars. The Hospitallers were still an entirely pacific order when the armed order of the Poor Fellow-Soldiers of Christ came into being. But sometime in the 1120s the Hospitallers extended their role from caring for pilgrims to protecting them by force of arms if need be, becoming known as the Knights of the Hospital of Saint John, or Knights Hospitaller, with Saint John no longer the Almsgiver but replaced by the more imposing figure of Saint John the Baptist. The first recorded instance of Hospitallers in combat dates from 1128, eight years or so after the founding of the Templars; it was the example of the Templars that helped turn the Hospitallers into a military order.

In due course the military orders were put in possession of the great castles, a task for which they were perfectly suited. The frontier castles were remote, isolated and lonely places; they did not appeal to the secular knighthood of Outremer. But the monastic vows of the military orders suited them to the dour life of castles where the innermost fortifications served as monasteries for the brothers. Their members were celibate, which made them easy to control, and they had no outside private interests. Superbly trained and highly disciplined, the Hospitallers and the Templars were led by commanders of considerable military ability; the capabilities of the orders generally stood in marked contrast to those of the lay institutions of Outremer.

The orders owed direct responsibility to the Papacy, placing them above not only local feudal quarrels but the antagonisms of nations and their kings. As corporate bodies, the orders were everlasting, their numbers undiminished by disease or death, and they were able to draw on an inexhaustible supply of young men of noble families in Europe seeking to fulfil the moral and religious obligations of knighthood. Also the Templars and the Hospitallers received donations of property in Europe which soon made them wealthy. Each order levied its own taxes, had its own diplomatic service and possessed its own fleet of ships. In effect the Hospitallers and the Templars were states within the state.

Very quickly the under-manned and under-financed Crusader states were selling or giving frontier fortresses to the orders, and by 1166 there were only three castles in the Kingdom of Jerusalem which the military orders did not control.

Costing the Templars

Every Templar was a highly trained and expensive mounted knight. Such a knight in the second half of twelfth-century France required 750 acres to equip and maintain himself as a mounted warrior, and a century later that cost had quintupled to 3750 acres.

For a Templar knight operating overseas in the Holy Land the costs were even greater, as much had to be imported, not least horses. Each Templar knight had three horses, and because they fell victim to warfare and disease, and had a lifespan of only twenty years, they needed to be renewed at a rate greater than local breeding allowed. The cost of horses rose sixfold from the twelfth to the thrteenth centuries. Moreover, horses consumed five or six times as much as a man, and required feeding whether or not they were in use. A bad harvest in the East, and urgent food supplies had to be shipped in for men and horses alike.

Each Templar also had a squire to help look after the horses. And in addition there were sergeants, more lightly armed than knights, who each had a horse but acted as their own squires. Sergeants were often locally recruited and wore a brown or black tunic instead of white. In fact for every Templar knight there were about nine others serving in support, whether as squires, sergeants or other forms of help. This is not much different from modern warfare in which every frontline soldier is backed up by four or five who never see combat, not to mention the many thousands of civilians producing weapons and equipment and providing clothing, food and transport.

Growing responsibilities increased Templar costs immensely. As secular lords found themselves unable to maintain and defend their castles and their fiefs, they handed these responsibilities over to the military orders. According to Benedict of Alignan, a Benedictine abbot visiting the Holy Land in the 1240s, the Templars spent 1,100,000 Saracen besants in two and a half years on rebuilding their castle of Saphet (Safad) – this at a time when a knight in Acre could live well on 500 Saracen besants a year – and continued to spend 40,000 Saracen besants in each following year on the day-to-day running of the castle. Saphet had a complement of 50 Templar knights, 30 mounted sergeants, as well as 50 mounted archers, 300 crossbowmen, 820 engineers and other serving men, plus 400 slaves – 1650 people, which in wartime increased to 2200, all of whom had to be housed, fed, armed and kept supplied in various ways.

Only their vast holdings in Outremer and more especially in the West permitted the Templars to operate on such a scale and recover after losses and setbacks to continue the defence of the Holy Land.

Templar Castles

When the First Crusade marched into the Middle East it came over the Belen Pass, about sixteen miles north of Antioch, that same crossing over the Amanus mountains that Alexander the Great had taken 1400 years before, after crushing the Persian army of Darius III at the battle of Issus. Known also as the Syrian Gates, the Belen Pass was the doorway into Syria and it was also the northern frontier of Outremer. Sometime in the 1130s the task of defending the pass was given to the Templars. Their key fortress was Baghras, built high above the pass itself, and the Templars built several others in the Amanus mountains. These castles formed a screen across the northern frontier where the Templars ruled as virtually autonomous border lords, effectively independent of the Principality of Antioch.

The Templars also took charge of the Kingdom of Jerusalem's southern frontier with Egypt when they were made responsible for Gaza during the winter of 1149–50. Gaza was uninhabited and ruinous at this time, but the Templars rebuilt a fortress atop a low hill and slowly the Franks revived the city around it. This was the first major castle in the Kingdom of Jerusalem that the Templars are recorded as receiving, and its purpose was to complete the blockade of Ascalon ten miles to the north, a small patch of territory on the Mediterranean coast still held by the Fatimids. Ascalon had long been the base for Muslim attacks on pilgrims coming up the road from Jaffa to Jerusalem or descending to the river Jordan, and in 1153 the city finally fell to Baldwin III, the king

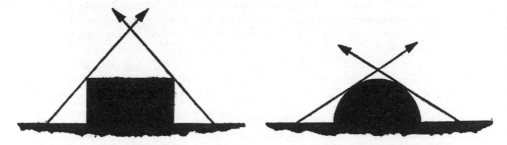

These sketches by T. E. Lawrence show how castle walls were defended by towers and flanking fire. The Byzantines and Arabs generally built square towers, but the Crusaders introduced the superior round tower, which was more solid and defensible. The arrows indicate lines of fire; a round tower offers an approaching enemy hardly any place to avoid the defenders' fire, making it difficult for him to scale the wall or mine it.

of Jerusalem. The Templars played a prominent part in this triumph, for they were first into the breach when a section of the walls came down, yet William of Tyre was predictable in turning this against them when he claimed in his chronicle that their eagerness was due to their greed for spoils. In fact the Templars lost forty or so knights in the attack, and their Grand Master lost his life.

Another vital strategic site as well as an important spot for pilgrims was Tortosa (present-day Tartus) on the Syrian coast. Said to be the place where the apostle Paul gave his first mass, a chapel dedicated to the Virgin Mary was built there in the third century, long before Christianity was officially tolerated within the Roman Empire, and it contained an icon of the Virgin said to have been painted by Saint Luke. To help the pilgrims who came to pray, the Crusaders built upon this history with the construction of Our Lady of Tortosa in 1123, an elegant cathedral which architecturally marks the transition from the Romanesque to the Gothic. But in 1152 Nur al-Din captured and burnt the city, leaving it deserted and destroyed; and as the County of Tripoli lacked the means for its restoration, Tortosa was placed in the care of the Templars, who greatly improved its defences, building a massive keep and halls within a triple circuit of tower-studded walls, and with a postern in the seawall enabling the city to be supplied from sea.

The strategic significance of Tortosa was that it stood at the seaward end of an opening in the range of coastal mountains which runs back into the interior towards the Muslim city of Homs. Towards the eastern end of this Homs Gap, as it is called, and towering high above the route between the interior and the sea, is the great castle of Krak des Chevaliers gained by the Hospitallers in 1144, while in the mountains between Krak and Tortosa is the castle of Chastel Blanc, now known as Safita, already in the hands of the Templars some time before 1152. From the roof of the massive keep at Chastel Blanc can be seen both Krak des Chevaliers to the east and the Templar castle of al-Arimah to the west on the Mediterranean coast just south of Tortosa. In short the Templars, together with the Hospitallers, entirely controlled the one important route between the interior of Syria and the sea. Moreover, they did so with sovereign rights within their territories, having been granted full lordship over the population of their estates, the right to share in the spoils of battle, and the freedom to have independent dealings with neighbouring Muslim powers.

In the 1160s the Templars took over further castles, this time across the Jordan river at Ahamant (present-day Amman) and in Galilee at Saphet (also called Safad) to which was added Chastellet in 1178. Gaza, Ahamant, Saphet and Chastellet were all within the Kingdom of Jerusalem but close to its borders where they served defensive purposes. Chastellet covered Jacob's Ford, the northernmost crossing point of the river Jordan, previously a weak point where Saladin came down out of Damascus and made easy raids against the Christians. So alarmed was Saladin when the Templars installed themselves at Chastellet that he immediately attacked, failing in his first attempt in June 1179 but two months later storming the castle and taking seven hundred prisoners whom he then slaughtered, although the Templar commander threw himself to his death to avoid capture.

More centrally placed was La Feve at the crossroads of the route between Jerusalem and Acre via Galilee. Acquired by the Templars in about 1170, it served as a major depot for arms, tools and food, and it

The Templar keep at Safita. The surrounding houses
follow the pattern of the original concentric walls

housed a large garrison. It was later the launching point for the expedition that led to the disastrous defeat at the Springs of Cresson on 1 May 1187, a foreboding of the catastrophe at Hattin.

As well as fighting in the defence of the Kingdom of Jerusalem, the Templars continued to fulfil their original role of protecting pilgrims coming up to the holy sites at Jerusalem from the ports of Acre, Haifa and Jaffa, or going down from Jerusalem to the Jordan river. One of the duties of the Templar commander in Jerusalem was to keep ten knights in reserve to accompany pilgrims to the Jordan and to provide a string of pack animals to carry food and exhausted travellers. The Templars had a castle overlooking the site at the Jordan river where Jesus had been baptised, to protect not only pilgrims but also the local monks after six of them were gratuitously murdered by Zengi.

The acquisition of castles was accompanied by lands which helped to support them, especially around Baghras, Tortosa and Saphet. In these areas the Templars held many villages, mills and much agricultural land. The details are lacking because of the destruction of the Templar archives on Cyprus by the Ottoman Turks in the sixteenth century. But from what can be pieced together it seems that the orders between them, the Hospitallers and the Templars, may have held nearly a fifth of the lands in Outremer by the middle of the century, and by 1188, the year of the Battle of Hattin, something like a third.

Merchant Bankers

Europe's Original Financiers

The Templars became Europe's first bankers, a development unintended and unforeseen yet one that arose naturally out of their situation. From their inception the Templars were an international organisation. Their purpose was in the Holy Land but their support came from Europe where they held land, collected tithes and received donations from the pious. They organised markets and fairs, managed their estates and traded in everything from wool and timber to olive oil and slaves. In time they built up their own formidable Mediterranean merchant fleet capable of transporting pilgrims, soldiers and supplies between Spain, France, Italy, Greece and Outremer.

Disciplined, honest and independent, the Templars were trusted throughout medieval society, and their experience in commerce and finance made them the ideal bankers to Popes and kings. Yet in their success as bankers and financiers lay a chief cause of their fall. The Templars, like the Church and like the Crusades, were international in conception, but the thirteenth and fourteenth centuries were a time when national states were being constructed by European kings, especially by the kings of France. Just as the Templars raised money to defend the Holy Land with their arms, so they also provided money for the new nationalism arising in the West. But the nation state of France would in turn 'nationalise' the Templars and destroy them.

The Templars' Ports and Mediterranean Trade

Most of the Templars' imports such as horses, iron and wheat came by sea. At first the Templars contracted with commercial shippers and agents, but early in the thirteenth century they began building up a fleet of their own. They had a substantial presence at all the important ports of Outremer – at Caesarea, Tyre, Sidon, Gibelet (ancient Byblos and present-day Jubail), Tripoli, Tortosa, Jeble and Port Bonnel north of Antioch. But their principal port was Acre, a walled city built on a tongue of land offering good protection for its double harbour.

All the major powers of the Kingdom of Jerusalem were represented at Acre, but in 1191, after the fall of Jerusalem to Saladin, the city became the Templars' new headquarters in the Holy Land. According to the thirteenth-century chronicler known as the Templar of Tyre, 'The Temple was the strongest place of the city, largely situated along the seashore, like a castle. At its entrance it had a high and strong tower, the wall of which was 28 feet thick.' He also mentions another tower built so close to the sea that the waves washed up against it, 'in which the Temple kept its treasure'.

After 1218 the Templars supplemented their facilities at Acre with a new fortress of their own thirty miles to the south; known today as Atlit, the Templars called it Chastel Pelerin because it was built on a rocky promontory with the help of pilgrims (*pelerin* in French). This castle, said a German pilgrim who visited in the early 1280s, 'is sited in the heart of the sea, fortifed with walls and ramparts and barbicans so strong and castellated, that the whole world should not be able to conquer it.'

Acre, now the Israeli town of Akko. The Templar quarter occupied much of headland, some of which has since subsided into the sea, forming the harbour in the foreground where the remains of Templar structures can still be seen.

From their ports in Outremer the Templars' ships sailed to the West. Their major port of call in France was Marseilles from where they shipped pilgrims and merchants to the East. Italy's Adriatic ports were also important, especially Brindisi, which had the added advantage of being near Rome. Bari and Brindisi were sources of wheat and horses, armaments and cloth, olive oil and wine, as well as pilgrims. Messina in Sicily acted both as a channel for exports from the island and as an entrepôt for shipping arriving from Catalonia and Provence. The Templars also built ships in European ports, everywhere between Spain and the Dalmatian coast.

The White Slave Trade

Another Templar cargo was white slaves. They were transported in considerable numbers from East to West where they were put to work helping to run Templar houses, especially in southern Italy and Aragon. The Hospitallers also engaged in the trade and the use of slaves; indeed the trade in white slaves was a flourishing business for everyone, including the Italian maritime powers, especially Genoa, and most of all the Muslim states in the East.

The centre of the slave trade in the late thirteenth century was the Mediterranean port of Ayas in the Armenian Kingdom of Cilicia. Marco Polo disembarked at Ayas in 1271 to begin his trip to China at about the same time that the Templars opened a wharf there. The slaves, who were Turkish, Greek, Russian and Circassian, had been acquired as a result of intertribal warfare, or because impoverished parents decided to sell their children, or because they were kidnapped, and they were brought to Ayas by Turkish and Mongol slavers.

The pick of young strong males from the South Russian steppes or the Caucasus generally went to Egypt where they were converted to Islam and served as elite slave soldiers known as Mamelukes. In 1250 the Mamelukes seized power in Egypt for themselves – and led the final jihad that drove the Franks out of Outremer.

The Templar Banking Network

In Outremer and the Iberian peninsula the Templars provided military services, but in England, France and Italy their primary contribution was financial. Individual monasteries had traditionally served as secure depositories for precious documents and objects, but during an age of greater movement owing to the Crusades and the growth of trade and pilgrimages the Templar network in the West of preceptories, that is houses and estates, could offer a better service. The Templars developed a system of credit notes whereby money deposited in one Templar preceptory could be withdrawn at another upon production of the note, a procedure that required the meticulous and scrupulously honest record-keeping at which they excelled.

Whether at Paris or Acre or elsewhere, the Templars kept daily records of transactions, giving details of the name of the depositor, the name of the cashier on duty, the date and nature of the transaction, the amount involved and into whose account the credit was to be made. These daily records were then transferred to a larger register, part of a vast and permanent archive. The Templars also issued statements several times a year, giving details of credits and debits and stating the origin and destination of each item.

With their branch offices, so to speak, at both ends of the Mediterranean, and with major strongholds at the Paris and London Temples, not only could they take deposits but they could also make funds internationally available where and when they were needed.

International Financial Services

An obvious extension to guarding Crusaders' documents and money was to make funds available during the expeditions themselves. The Templars operated treasure ships offshore from which campaigning knights and nobles and kings could make emergency withdrawals. The Templars also provided loans, for example to Louis VII, the king of France, during the Second Crusade. This was the beginning of the Templars' close financial association with the French monarchy, effectively becoming its treasurers.

From financing crusades it was a small step for the Templars to become an integral part of the European financial system. King John of England borrowed from the master of the Temple in London around the time of Magna Carta in 1215. After the Fourth Crusade, in which Latins overthrew the Byzantine emperors and put a Frenchman on the throne instead, the Latin Emperor Baldwin II borrowed an immense sum which was secured against the True Cross. As part of their integral relationship with the European financial system, the Templars also became involved in the web that Italian merchants and bankers had spun across Europe and the Levant.

In return for these services the Templars received various privileges and concessions. By Papal bull and the decrees of French and English kings, the Templars were given full jurisdiction over their estates and their inhabitants. They also obtained royal consent to organise weekly agricultural markets and annual fairs which formed a focus for local trade and brought much income to the order both from the dues paid by those taking part and through boosting the local economy generally. Combining agriculture with capital the Templars were notably successful in the commercial exploitation of their estates, as in sheep-farming in England, for example, which in combination with the Templars' ability to provide credit turned them into major suppliers of wool. Not least among the benefits they obtained was the unimpeded export of goods and funds from the West to Outremer.

Additionally the Templars made profits on currency conversions and imposed charges on their services. Though not always openly stated in documents, they charged interest on loans, sometimes under the name of expenses to get round medieval scruples against interest, though sometimes they felt bold enough to declare that too. In 1274, for example, Edward I of England repaid the Templars the sum of 27,974 livres tournois together with 5333 livres, 6 sous, 8 deniers for 'administration, expenses and interest' – the total cost of the loan approaching 20 per cent.

The Paris and London Temples

The Paris Temple was the Templar headquarters in France. Built on land acquired by the Templars in the 1140s, nothing of it survives today and it is remembered only by a street name in the Quartier du Temple, the northern part of the Marais district of the city. But from the twelfth to the fourteenth century it was one of the key financial centres of northwest Europe.

The Temple was located to the north of the city walls and was fortified with a perimeter wall and towers. Inside there was an impressive array of buildings, and in the late thirteenth century the Templars added a

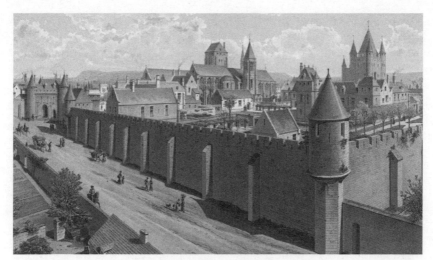

*The enormous complex of the Paris Temple was
one of Europe's major financial centres*

powerful keep about 165 feet high – nearly twice as high as the White
Tower, the keep at the centre of the Tower of London. This Templar keep
in Paris was the heart of the Templar bank, and it was also effectively the
treasury of the kings of France. During the French Revolution it served
as a prison for Louis XVI and Marie Antoinette, and it was from the
keep that the king was led out to his execution.

The London Temple, or the New Temple as it was called, would have
been comparable to that of Paris, but only Temple Church, consecrated
in 1185, remains today, amid the Inns of Court off the south side of Fleet
Street. The nave of Temple Church is round, as was typical with Templar
churches, its plan following that of the Church of the Holy Sepulchre
in Jerusalem. King John was actually resident at the New Temple at
the time of Magna Carta in 1215 and was accompanied to his famous
meeting with the barons at Runnymede by the master of the London
Temple. But while the kings of England entrusted Templars with military,
diplomatic and financial commissions, they were always careful to keep
the royal treasury as part of the royal household where it was run by
royal officials, so that at most the New Temple merely served to provide
additional safe-deposit space.

Vulnerable Relationships with Kings

The Templars' experience made them useful to the French monarchy and to the Papacy, both of which wanted to maximise their revenues from taxation and reform the managing of their finances. For example, during the 33-year reign of Philip II, which extended from the late twelfth century well into the thirteenth, the king's revenues were increased by 120 per cent thanks to Templar management.

Yet Templar holdings were never entirely secure. Only the Paris Temple presented a truly formidable obstacle to a raid; Templar houses elsewhere in France were raided by the king; the London Temple was raided by kings of England in the thirteenth and fourteenth centuries when in desperate need; and in Spain the kings of Aragon did the same. But these were passing events in desperate times of need, and restitution was made. Ultimately the Templars' best protection was not the stone walls of their treasure houses but practical and moral constraints. The kings needed the Templars and their services too much to alienate them, nor could they afford to put themselves on the wrong side of a spiritual cause – at least not until Philip IV of France came up with a rationalisation in October 1307.

Medieval Heresy

Nothing Is What It Seems

Bernard of Clairvaux described the Templars as men whose bodies were protected by iron and whose souls were clothed in the breastplate of faith. Religious orthodoxy was seen as no less a part of their equipment than their swords and armour. This was just as well, for Outremer at this time was a hothouse of heterodox and heretical beliefs, both Christian and Muslim, as was southern France from where the order drew much of its support. The breastplate did its work; for nearly two centuries the Templars were seen as paragons of faith, and there was no suggestion that contamination had touched their souls. Moreover, within a century of their founding the Templars had entered into the Western imagination as the ideal of chivalry – and the guardians of the Holy Grail.

All of which adds to the irony of the Templars' arrest in 1307 on charges of heresy and blasphemy. These charges and the Templars' prosecution and trial are covered later in the book. This chapter looks at the wider context: the Templars' encounter with strange religious systems whose doctrines can be traced back to some of the earliest Christian beliefs in the East. At the root of these beliefs, which spread westwards into Europe during the Crusades, was the radical idea that man inhabits a world of delusion in which nothing is what it seems.

Templars and Cathars

During the twelfth and thirteenth centuries Languedoc in southern France was the centre of a rich and complex religious life in which both Christian orthodoxy and heresy flourished. William of Puylaurens, the thirteenth-century chronicler of the region, reported heretic communities of Arians, Waldensians and Manichaeans. The Arians were the survival of that 900-year-old heresy that began in Alexandria and tended towards undermining the divinity of Jesus Christ, while the Waldensians were a new twelfth-century movement that espoused poverty, called for the distribution of property to the poor, rejected the authority of the clergy and claimed that anyone could preach, saying their literal reading of the Bible was all that was needed for salvation. According to Peter of Les Vauz de Cernay, another thirteenth-century chronicler, the Waldensians 'were evil men, but very much less perverted than other heretics; they agreed with us in many matters, and differed in some'. The 'other heretics' were the Manichaeans, also known as Cathars, meaning 'pure'.

Languedoc was a major source of Templar income and recruits. The Templars partly owed their great expansion in the region to the support of the nobility with whom they were in close alliance, the combination of nobles' land and Templar capital allowing the establishment of new communities and the development of previously uncultivated territories. Some of these Templar patrons were renowned Cathar supporters.

Catharism first appeared in southern France sometime in the years following the First Crusade. Its adherents quickly became numerous and well organised, electing bishops, collecting funds and distributing money to the poor. But they could not accept that if there was only one God, and if God was the creator, and if God was good, that there should be suffering, illness and death in his world. The Cathars' solution

Montségur was the last redoubt of the Cathars. Two hundred of its defenders were burnt as heretics below the castle

to this problem of evil in the world was to say there were really two creators and two worlds. The Cathars were dualists in that they believed in a good and an evil principle, the former the creator of the invisible and spiritual universe, the latter the creator of our material world. All matter was evil because it was the creation of the devil, but the ideal of renouncing the world was impractical for everyone, and so while most Cathars lived outwardly normal lives, pledging to renounce the evil world only on their deathbeds, a few lived the strict life of the *perfecti*.

Because human and animal procreation perpetuated matter, the *perfecti* abstained from eggs, milk, meat and women. But both ordinary Cathars and the *perfecti* actively shared in their belief that Christ was not part of this world of evil. Therefore he was not truly born of the Virgin Mary, nor had he human flesh, nor had he risen from the dead; salvation did not lie in his death and resurrection, which were merely a simulation; instead redemption would be gained by following Jesus' teachings.

By 1200 the Cathar heresy had become so widespread that the Papacy was alarmed. Pope Innocent III said that the Cathars were 'worse than the Saracens', for not only did Catharism challenge the Church but by condemning procreation it threatened the very survival of the human race. In 1209 a crusade was launched against them – the Albigensian Crusade, as so many Cathars lived around Albi – and an inquisition was introduced. In that year the core of Cathar resistance withdrew to the castle of Montségur atop a great domed hill in the eastern Pyrenees, where they withstood assaults and sieges until capitulating in 1244. Some two hundred still refused to abjure their errors, were bound together within a stockade below the castle and were set ablaze on a huge funeral pyre. The Templars played no part in the Albigensian Crusade, which was bound to attack some of their own patrons, who were likewise patrons of the Cathars.

The Gnostics

The origins of Cathar dualism lay in the East where it can be traced back to the Christian Gnostics who flourished in the second and third centuries AD all round the shores of the Eastern Mediterranean, in Egypt, Syria and Palestine, and perhaps also in Asia Minor and Greece. Gnosis is Greek for knowledge, and the Gnostics believed that salvation lay in their understanding of the true nature of creation. They believed that there were two worlds, the material world of evil and decay that had been made by an evil demiurge, the enemy of man, and the world of light where the primal God resides.

One of the most prominent Gnostics was Valentinus, who flourished around AD 140 in Alexandria and Rome. He claimed to possess the true knowledge of how the world had been created and how evil had come into being, a story that he introduced to his followers in terms of a cosmic myth. He conceived of a primal God, the centre of a divine harmony, who sends out manifestations of himself in pairs of male and female. Each pair was inferior to its predecessor, and Sophia, the female of the thirtieth pair, was the least perfect of all. She showed her imperfection not, like the angel Lucifer, by rebelling against God, but by desiring too ardently to be united to him, so that she fell through love, and the universe is formed out of her agony and remorse. As she fell she bore a son, the Demiurge, who rules this world of sadness and confusion, yet is incapable of realising anything beyond it.

Mankind inhabits a catastrophe not of God's making, but the Gnostics said they knew the secret of salvation. At the moment of the cosmic blunder, sparks of the divine light, like slivers of shattered glass, became embedded in a portion of humankind. These people were the elect, and the Gnostic aim was to lead them back to God. Cosmic redemption, however, and not just personal salvation was necessary because the whole of creation had been a mistake; it had nothing to do with God, who had never intended that there should be a universe, indeed never intended man. Creation was a defective work, and so man lived in a meaningless world or in the iron control of evil powers; in any case he was caught in the trap of the material world which was sundered from the spirit of God.

Valentinus taught his followers that they could free themselves by attempting to quell their desires and by practising sexual abstinence. For in the polarity of the male and the female was mirrored the division, the duality, of the universe, so that the Last Judgement and the world's redemption would come – as Jesus says in the Gnostic Gospel of the Egyptians – 'when the two become one, and the male with the female, there being neither male nor female'. Other Gnostics than Valentinus also had their stories, and some, instead of practising abstinence, promoted sexual licence, though the purpose was the same: to join the male and the female in order to achieve the desired oneness of the world. The crucifixion and resurrection has no place in these Gnostic stories; instead the role of Jesus was to descend from the primal God and impart to his disciples the secret tradition of the gnosis.

Islamic Dualism

Dualism was deeply rooted in the East and did not confine itself to Christianity. In fact the term Manichaean, the name some medieval French chroniclers gave to the Cathars, was used by the Byzantines to describe the dualist ideas of Mani, a third-century Persian, who drew on Zoroastrianism, Buddhism and Babylonian Mandaeism, as well as Christianity. And so it was from several sources that dualism made its appearance in Islam. Though dualism is fundamentally incompatible with Islam, which teaches that God is the sole principle and is good, the political unity of the Muslim world had long been in decay, allowing for the manifestation of new religious tendencies.

Just as the Middle East was divided into local dynasties and subject to pressures from the Abbasid caliphate, the Seljuk Turks and the Fatimids of Egypt, not to mention the Byzantines, so it was divided into numerous sects. Among the Christians there were the Jacobites, Maronites, Copts and Orthodox, and among the Muslims the Sunnis and numerous heterodox groups that had evolved out of Shiism, among these the Qarmatian, Alawi, Druze and Ismaili movements, which were not only movements of belief but also initiatory secret societies with political aims tending towards the apocalyptic.

The Ismailis continued certain pre-Muslim beliefs, in particular dualism, in which they saw evil not as the absence of good but as part of the essence of both the world and its creator, who in turn may have been an emanation of an ultimate and unknowable God. Like the Gnostics they believed that man possesses slivers of the divine spark which, given possession of the secret knowledge, can reunite man with the unknown God. The Ismailis claimed to possess this knowledge.

But after Zengi's conquest of Edessa in 1144 and the surrender of Damascus to his son Nur al-Din, the Zengid dynasty imposed Sunni Islam on the entire Muslim population of Syria, driving the Shia sects into inaccessible regions.

The Assassins

The Ismailis withdrew into that region of the coastal mountains, the Jebel al-Sariya, girded by the great Templar and Hospitaller strongholds of Tortosa, Chastel Blanc, Margat and Krak des Chevaliers, where the movement assumed its militant and murderous form known as the Assassins. From such strongholds as al-Ullayqa, Qadmus, Qalaat al-Kahf and especially Masyaf, headquarters of the Assassins' leader, the Sheikh al-Jebel, the Old Man of the Mountain, they employed a strategy of assassination to influence and control anyone, mostly Sunni Muslims but sometimes also Christians, who might threaten their independence.

The Assassins' particular glimpse of divine knowledge was described by Marco Polo, who encountered a branch at Alamut in Persia. The Assassins used drugs (including hashish, from which the word 'assassin' derives) to convince novices destined to become self-destructive feddayin, 'the self-sacrificers', that they had entered a garden of delights where fountains flowed with milk, honey and wine, and where houris, those maidens of Paradise, were likewise on tap. Brought back to their normal state, the initiates were told that they had indeed visited Paradise, which would certainly be forever theirs provided they gave absolute obedience to the commands of the Assassins' imam.

According to the reports of European chroniclers, the Assassin leaders demonstrated their complete domination over their adepts by commanding them to leap from precipices to their deaths. Their willingness to sacrifice their lives made the feddayins' attacks that much more

The castle of Masyaf in the Jebel al-Sariya was the headquarters of the Assassins under the command of the Old Man of the Mountain

disturbing; their mission was to sow fear of the sect and at the same time weaken the resolve of their enemies by the murder of key figures. The Assassins infiltrated the ranks of their adversaries, and when they had won their victim's trust they would kill him, always using a knife. These were suicide attacks, for apparently by design they themselves perished in carrying out their orders.

Among the Assassins' Christian victims were Raymond II, count of Tripoli, in 1152; Conrad of Montferrat, king of Jerusalem, in 1192; and another Raymond, heir to the thrones of Antioch and Tripoli, who in 1213 was stabbed to death outside the door of the Cathedral of Our Lady at Tortosa. But the Assassins' most famous attempt was against Saladin in 1176. As the champion of Sunni orthodoxy and leader of the Muslim resurgence, Saladin had already overthrown the Shia Fatimids in Egypt and was now in full cry against the Crusaders and the Assassins. He entered the Jebel al-Sariya to lay siege to Masyaf, but his soldiers reported mysterious powers about, while Saladin was disturbed by terrible dreams. One night he awoke suddenly to find on his bed some hot cakes of a type that only the Assassins baked and with them a poisoned dagger and a threatening verse. Convinced that Rashid al-Din Sinan, the Old Man of the Mountain, had himself entered his tent, Saladin's nerves gave way. He sent a message to Sinan asking for forgiveness and promised not to pursue his campaign against the Assassins provided he was granted safe conduct. Saladin was pardoned and hastened back to Cairo.

The Templars and the Old Man of the Mountain

The one effective organisation against the Assassins was the Templars. Being an undying corporate body, the Templars could not be intimidated by the death of one of their members. The Assassins themselves admitted that they never killed a Grand Master because they knew that someone equally good would be put in his place.

In their hatred of the Sunni, the Assassins sometimes found themselves in alliance with the Christians, and even under trying circumstances they were tolerated by the Crusader states and the Templars. After the Assassins murdered Raymond II, the count of Tripoli, in 1152 – for no reason that anyone could figure out, unless they had been hired by Raymond's wife – the Templars threatened to go after the Assassins, who readily agreed to pay an annual tribute of two thousand besants as a form of protection money. The Assassins and the Christians shared a common enemy, and it was in their interest to keep the peace with one another.

But on one significant occasion the Templars' distrust of the Assassins led them to oppose the policy of King Amalric of Jerusalem, who had entered into talks with the Old Man of the Mountain. The Ismailis had always seen their leaders as the embodiment of emanations flowing from the unknow-

Hassan ibn Sabbah was the Persian founder of an Ismaili sect that spread to the mountains of Syria where it became known as the Assassins

able God, but in 1164, in an apocalyptic moment, Rashid al-Din Sinan openly renounced Islam and declared that the resurrection had arrived. The contemporary Syrian chronicler Kamal al-Din described scenes of wild frenzy in the Jebel al-Sariya where 'men and women mingled in drinking sessions, no man abstained from his sister or daughter, the women wore men's clothes, and one of them declared that Sinan was God'. In fact the divine status accorded to the Old Man of the Mountain was general, according to the Spanish Muslim traveller Ibn Jubayr, who wrote that all his followers treated him as God.

It was nine years after these events, in 1173, that Amalric attempted to negotiate an alliance with Sinan, one of its conditions being that the Assassins would convert to Christianity. But as Sinan's envoy was returning from Jerusalem to Masyaf, bearing a safe–conduct from Amalric, he was ambushed and killed by some Templar knights. Only with the greatest difficulty was Amalric able to persuade Sinan that the attack was not of his doing. Meanwhile he accused the Templars of treason and of bringing the kingdom to the edge of ruin by destroying the chance of an advantageous alliance. The chronicler William of Tyre implied that the murder was prompted by a financial motive, for peace would have meant an end to the tribute paid by the Assassins to the Templars. Another chronicler, Walter Map, wrote that the Templars killed the envoy 'lest (it is said) the belief of the infidels should be done away and peace and union reign' – in other words war justified the existence of the Templars, who feared the outbreak of peace.

The argument of Templar greed is typical of William of Tyre, for the order did not need the Assassins' tribute. However, the Templars were likely concerned that King Amalric was being duped, for they understood that whatever religion the Assassins professed, it would be no more than an outer garment, just as Islam had been an outer garment, as the Assassins saw this world as mere illusion, and despite any conversion to Christianity their inner and secret beliefs would remain. The Templars controlled important castles adjacent to the Assassin enclave, castles that also controlled the passes to the yet more dangerous Sunni-held interior, and to have let their guard down on the word of such a sect would have been grossly irresponsible and cost the Templars their credibility in the West. In the event, the negotiations were never resumed; after Amalric died in 1174 Raymond III, count of Tripoli, was made regent, and as his own father had been murdered by the Assassins he shared the Templars' distrust.

Saladin and the Templars

The View from the Temple Mount

In the decades following the Second Crusade, visitors to the Temple Mount were impressed with how it was being developed by the Knights Templar. After prayers at the Church of the Holy Sepulchre, with its chapels associated with the crucifixion and burial of Jesus and the discovery of the True Cross, pilgrims walked to the Temple Mount, entering through the western gate near the south side of the Dome of the Rock, the Templum Domini, or Temple of the Lord, a church served by canons of the Augustinian order. On the outer court the canons and Templars had built houses and planted gardens.

According to Theoderich, a German pilgrim who wrote about his visit to the Holy Land in 1172, the Temple of the Lord bore an inscription that read 'The house of the Lord is well built upon a firm rock', but that as pilgrims were in the habit of chipping away bits of the holy rock, its

MAP OF TEMPLE MOUNT (HARAM AL-SHERIF)

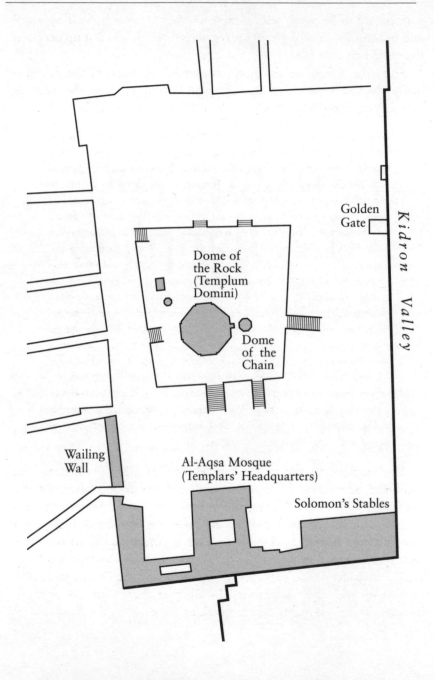

Golden
Gate

Kidron Valley

Dome of
the Rock
(Templum
Domini)

Dome
of the
Chain

Wailing
Wall

Al-Aqsa Mosque
(Templars' Headquarters)

Solomon's Stables

surface had to be paved with marble and it was cordoned off by a tall and beautifully worked wrought-iron screen which was put up between the encircling columns.

From the Temple of the Lord, continued Theoderich, the pilgrims made their way south to the Templar headquarters at the al-Aqsa mosque, or rather what he called the Palace of Solomon:

> *which is oblong, and supported by columns within like a church, and at the end is round like a sanctuary and covered by a great round dome. This building, with all its appurtenances, has passed into the hands of the Knights Templar, who dwell in it and in the other buildings connected with it, having many magazines of arms, clothing, and food in it, and are ever on the watch to guard and protect the country. They have below them stables for horses built by King Solomon himself in the days of old, adjoining the palace, a wondrous and intricate building resting on piers and containing an endless complication of arches and vaults, which stable, we declare, according to our reckoning, could take in ten thousand horses with their grooms. No man could send an arrow from one end of their building to the other, either lengthways or crossways, at one shot with a Balearic bow. Above, it abounds with rooms, solar chambers, and buildings suitable for all manner of uses. Those who walk upon the roof of it find an abundance of gardens, courtyards, ante-chambers, vestibules and rain-water cisterns; while down below it contains a wonderful number of baths, storehouses, granaries, and magazines for the storage of wood and other needful provisions.*

The southern part of the Temple Mount had therefore become the combined administrative, military and religious headquarters of the Templars, with a vast stable underneath. The Grand Master had his chambers there and was attended by his entourage which included a chaplain, two knights, a clerk, a sergeant, a Muslim scribe to act as an interpreter, as well as servants and a cook. The Seneschal, the Marshal, the Commander of the Kingdom of Jerusalem and the Draper were also here along with their attendants. In addition there were about three hundred Templar knights and a thousand sergeants in the Kingdom of

The Stables of Solomon beneath the Templar
headquarters on the Temple Mount

Jerusalem, as well as the native Syrian light cavalry, called Turcopoles, who were employed by the order, and numerous auxiliaries, including grooms, blacksmiths, armourers and stonemasons, and many of these would have been quartered on the Temple Mount.

The Temple Mount was a busy place. Yet at its heart it was as silent as any monastery, for the Templars followed the canonical hours like any Cistercian or Benedictine monk, rising at four for Matins and retiring to bed after Compline, attending regular services and prayers in between, eating their meals in silence while listening to readings from the Bible, and otherwise caring for their horses.

The so-called Stables of Solomon were in fact a substructure of vaults and arches built by Herod to extend the platform of the Mount, and later reconstruction work was undertaken by the Umayyads and the Templars. The Templars indeed used this as a stables, but Theoderich's claim that ten thousand horses could be stabled beneath the Mount is an exaggeration; other travellers estimated the capacity at about two thousand horses, and allowing space for squires, grooms and perhaps even pilgrims sleeping there, the number of horses stabled at any one time was more like five hundred.

These warrior monks were a powerful force in the Holy Land, whose defence since the Second Crusade fell increasingly on their shoulders. Contrary to popular belief the Templars were not fanatics forever in search of battle with the infidel. Generally they were pragmatic and conservative in their approach to politics and warfare, if anything more so than the counts and kings of Outremer who were driven by personal and dynastic ambitions in the here and now. In becoming a Knight Templar each man surrendered his will to the order, as in the words of one recruit: 'I, renouncing secular life and its pomp, relinquishing everything, give myself to the Lord God and to the knighthood of the Temple of Solomon of Jersualem, that, as long as I shall live, in accordance with my strength, I shall serve there a complete pauper for God.'

Self-will was replaced with service to the order and its aims, and the Templars were playing a long game, dedicated to defending the Holy Land for all time. In any case conflict in the Middle Ages tended to be more about sieges of cities and castles than battle in the open field, which was unpredictable and risky even under the most favourable circumstances. And in Outremer patience had its rewards as it was usually only a matter of time before the uneasy Muslim coalitions against the Christians fell apart. And so it was with confidence that the Templars looked out from their headquarters atop the Temple Mount upon Jerusalem and the future that lay beyond.

Tunnels and Chambers Beneath the Dome of the Rock

In his account of the Temple Mount, the twelfth-century pilgrim Theoderich mentioned some strange underground features. After ascending the Mount pilgrims arrived at the lower court of the Templum Domini, the Temple of the Lord, formerly the Dome of the Rock, which was built on the site of Solomon's Temple. 'One mounts from the lower court to the upper one by twenty-two steps', wrote Theoderich, 'and from the upper court one enters the Temple. In front of these same steps in the lower court there are twenty-five steps or more, leading down into a great pool, from which it is said there is a subterranean connection with the Church of the Holy Sepulchre, through which the holy fire which is miraculously lighted in that church on Easter Even is said to be brought underground to the Temple of the Lord.'

The first mention of an aperture in the rock was made in AD 333 by a traveller known as the Bordeaux Pilgrim, but the first documented reference to the cave beneath the rock was made by Ibn al-Faqih in 903: 'Under the rock is a cavern in which the people pray. This cavern is capable of containing 62 persons.' A Persian, Nasir-i Khusraw, who visited the Dome of the Rock in 1047, described the large cavern under the rock 'where they burn tapers', which was perhaps the tradition that led Theoderich to make the connection with the miraculous Easter fire at the Church of the Holy Sepulchre. Ali of Herat, who visited the Temple Mount in 1173 when Jerusalem was under Christian rule, gave this description: 'Underneath the rock is the Cave of the Souls. They say that

The cavern beneath the Dome of the Rock. According to some Jewish traditions this was where the Ark of the Covenant stood.

Allah will bring together the souls of all True Believers to this spot. You descend to this cave by some fourteen steps. The Cave of the Souls is of the height of a man. Its length extends 11 paces from east to west and 13 paces from north to south.'

Muslims say that the souls of the dead can be heard here as they await the Day of Judgement. And according to both Muslim tradition and the Talmud of the Jews the rock lies at the centre of the world. Beneath it is the abyss where Muslims say the waters of Paradise flow, but the Talmud says the waters of the Flood rage.

In some Jewish traditions it is also regarded as the place where the Ark of the Covenant stood – and where, when Solomon's Temple was destroyed in 587 BC, the Ark was concealed and remains hidden.

Amalric's Egyptian Campaigns

The Fatimid garrison at Ascalon had controlled the route into the Nile Delta and to Cairo, the same line of attack taken by the Arabs when they invaded Egypt in 640, after their conquest of Syria and Palestine. When King Baldwin III captured Ascalon with Templar help in 1153 it opened the door to Egypt for the Franks. But the opportunity was only seized after Baldwin died in 1162 and was succeeded by his twenty-five-year-old brother Amalric, who on three occasions, in 1164, 1167 and 1168, entered Egypt to prevent it falling to Nur al-Din.

The Fatimid regime in Cairo had grown weak and unstable, with two viziers vying with one another for control over the enfeebled caliphs. Each of the viziers reached outside Egypt for support, drawing Amalric in Jerusalem and Nur al-Din in Damascus into their quarrel. For the Franks the prize was potentially enormous: by installing a friendly government in Cairo the Kingdom of Jerusalem would not only gain access to the vast resources of Egypt but would also protect its southern flank. But the prize was no less great for Nur al-Din: not only would his acquisition of Egypt give him control over the trade route from Damascus that terminated in Cairo, but he would entirely surround the Christian states.

Each side had grounds for hope. Alaric understood that for the Fatimids, who were both Shia and Arab, their greatest enemy was not his Christian kingdom but Nur al-Din, who was a Sunni and a Seljuk Turk. But though two centuries of Fatimid rule meant that Shia influences were strong in Egypt, Nur al-Din knew that the mass of Egyptians remained Sunni, and he counted on the shared Muslim bond between Cairo and Damascus. For five years this contest was waged between Amalric and Shirkuh, the Kurdish general commanding Nur al-Din's army. If either rival won Egypt to its side, the gain could be decisive.

Amalric had large contingents of Templars in his army when he twice, in 1164 and 1167, forced Shirkuh to withdraw from Egypt and then withdrew himself. A leading Templar also took part in the mission which negotiated the treaty of alliance between Amalric and Shawar, the Fatimid vizier, prior to the Franks' military intervention in 1167. But by then the fundamental weakness of the Fatimid regime was obvious to both Nur al-Din and Amalric, and it was only a matter of time before one of them would strike the *coup de grâce*. Amalric struck first, marching into Egypt in 1168 with the intention of outright annexation – without the support of Templar forces. The Fatimids withdrew within the walls of Cairo and burnt its suburbs to the ground, and they sent for help to Nur al-Din. This time it was Amalric who was forced to withdraw, and Nur al-Din's Kurdish general Shirkuh entered Cairo, decapitated Shawar and installed himself as vizier. His rule was not long; in March 1169 Shirkuh died and was succeeded as vizier by his nephew Salah al-Din, better known in the West as Saladin.

Templar Relations with the Kingdom of Jerusalem

The capture of Egypt by Nur al-Din's forces was a strategic calamity for the Franks. Why the Templars refused to participate in Amalric's 1168 invasion has been a matter of speculation and debate. Again the earliest principal source for these events is William of Tyre, who was commissioned by Amalric to write his history of the Kingdom of Jerusalem and might have been expected to fiercely condemn the Templars. Yet William himself disapproved of the campaign and said that the Templars objected on moral grounds; 'it seemed against their conscience' to break the treaty which they had helped negotiate with Shawar in 1167.

What William did not mention, though it was true, was that the Templars were financially connected with the Muslims and with the Italian merchants, who carried on a greater trade with Egypt than with all the Crusader ports combined. William confined his criticism to the suggestion that the Templars may have been jealous of the Hospitallers, who had taken the lead in urging Amalric to undertake the expedition and had already claimed Pelusium on the edge of the Egyptian Delta for themselves. The perpetual rivalry between the two orders was a problem; it was seldom that they could be induced to campaign together, and each followed its own line regardless of the official policy of the Kingdom of Jerusalem.

For all the strategic importance of Egypt, there were other strategic considerations that the Templars would reasonably have taken into account. In 1164 when the bulk of Templar forces had been with Amalric on campaign in Egypt, Nur al-Din had taken advantage by striking in the north, inflicting heavy losses against the army of the prince of Antioch, which included the deaths of sixty Templar knights and numerous more sergeants and Turcopoles, precisely in the area where the Templars bore responsibility for manning strategically sited castles that were part of the ultimate defence of Outremer. The experience may have impressed upon the Templars the need to husband their resources and concentrate them where they were most needed.

Certainly there were strong differences over military strategy between Amalric and the Templars, with William of Tyre describing a dramatic incident that occurred in 1166. Learning that a Templar garrison was under siege beyond the Jordan, Amalric rode out to relieve them with a large force. But when he reached the river he was told that what William describes as an 'impregnable cave' had already fallen to Nur al-Din's general Shirkuh. The Templars may have thought that their garrison was out on a limb too far. But outraged and confounded by the news, Amalric hanged twelve of the Templars who had surrendered to Shirkuh. Add to this the story of the Assassins' envoy killed by the Templars in 1173, an event, according to William of Tyre, that brought the kingdom to the edge of 'irrevocable ruin' as it cost Jerusalem an ally against encircling Sunni power, and there is a pattern of Templar wilfulness in military, political and religious matters. The Hospitallers could be no less independent of secular authority, but their image was softened by the alms and care they lavished on pilgrims, whereas the image of the Templars rested more exclusively on their military prowess, and then there was their involvement in financial activities. The independence of the orders was liable to provoke resentment, and in the case of the Templars it led increasingly to criticism that the order was primarily concerned with protecting and advancing its own interests.

Excellent Soldiers and Humble Monks

An unknown pilgrim visiting Jerusalem sometime after the middle of the twelfth century described the Templars as follows:

The Templars are most excellent soldiers. They wear white mantles with a red cross, and when they go to the wars a standard of two colours called balzaus is borne before them. They go in silence. Their first attack is the most terrible. In going they are the first, in returning the last. They await the orders of their Master. When they think fit to make war and the trumpet has sounded, they sing in chorus the Psalm of David, 'Not unto us, O Lord', kneeling on the blood and necks of the enemy, unless they have forced the troops of the enemy to retire altogether, or utterly broken them to pieces. Should any of them for any reason turn his back to the enemy, or come forth alive [from a defeat], or bear arms against the Christians, he is severely punished; the white mantle with the red cross, which is the sign of his knighthood, is taken away with ignominy, he is cast from the society of brethren, and eats his food on the floor without a napkin for the space of one year. If the dogs molest him, he does not dare to drive them away. But at the end of the year, if the Master and brethren think his penance to have been sufficient, they restore him the belt of his former knighthood. These Templars live under a strict religious rule, obeying humbly, having no private property, eating sparingly, dressing meanly, and dwelling in tents.

From *Anonymous Pilgrims*, translated by A. Stewart, London 1894.

The Rise of Saladin

In 1171 as the Fatimid caliph al-Adid lay dying, prayers rose from the mosques of Cairo, but not for the last of Egypt's Shia rulers, instead for Nur al-Din's puppet, the Sunni caliph in Baghdad. Notional Abbasid rule was reimposed on Egypt; in reality al-Adid was the last Arab ruler in the Middle East, and the once imperial Arabs were now governed by Turks and Kurds. Saladin continued in the office of vizier, supposedly ruling Egypt on behalf of Nur al-Din, but in effect ruling Egypt for himself. To consolidate his position, Saladin began constructing the Citadel of Cairo and extended the city walls. When Nur al-Din died in 1174 Saladin declared himself sultan in Egypt and rushed to seize Damascus. The Christians were now reaping the consequences of their failure to take Egypt; for the first time they were surrounded by a united Muslim power. Moreover the able Amalric had died in 1174 and was succeeded by his young son Baldwin IV, who suffered from leprosy.

Saladin was admired for his chivalry, but he found the Templars dangerous and he feared them because they were not attached to the things of this world. When he captured Templars he did not hesitate to kill them in cold blood.

By the end of 1177 Saladin was ready to strike, and in November he crossed the frontier from Egypt. The Templars summoned all their available knights to defend Gaza, but Saladin bypassed them for Ascalon. Raising what men at arms he could, Baldwin rushed to block him, and together with the True Cross and the commander of his army, Raynald of Chatillon, he managed to get inside the walls of Ascalon before Saladin arrived. But instead of attacking, Saladin left a small force to besiege Ascalon and marched towards an undefended Jersualem with 30,000 men, though the figure is probably exaggerated. Sending a message to the Templars, Baldwin told them to abandon Gaza and join him. When they came near, Baldwin broke out of Ascalon and chased after Saladin, marching north along the coast and then inland. On 25 November Saladin's army was crossing a ravine at Montgisard near Ramleh close by the Jaffa-Jerusalem road when Baldwin and the Templars fell upon them, taking them by surprise. The king himself was in the vanguard, and Raynald of Chatillon and Balian of Ibelin helped on the victory, and some saw Saint George himself, whose church was nearby at Lydda, fighting by their side.

The Christian force comprised 450 knights, 80 of them Templars, and a few thousand infantry, and they lost about 1100 men. But they inflicted on Saladin's forces an overwhelming defeat, killing 90 per cent of his army, Saladin himself only narrowly managing to escape back to Egypt where to cling to power he spread the lie that the Christians had lost the battle.

The battle of Montgisard had been a great victory and it saved the Kingdom of Jerusalem for the moment, but it did not alter the fundamental situation. Against the vast resources of Egypt on which Saladin could draw, the Franks were short of men and it was dangerous to risk their army on offensive operations. Had Baldwin the forces to pursue the enemy to Cairo or to make a sudden attack on Damascus, he might have destroyed Saladin with a crushing blow. Instead he decided to reinforce his defences along the Syrian frontier, and at the insistence of the Templars he built the castle of Chastellet to control a ford across the upper Jordan where Jacob of the Old Testament was said to have wrestled with the angel (Genesis 32:24). But lacking neither resources nor resolution, Saladin kept up the pressure on the Damascus front, laid siege to Chastellet in June 1179 and again in August 1179, succeeded in mining the castle walls, then executed its 700 defenders and razed it to the ground.

Faced with an extreme drought that was threatening harvests throughout Syria and Outremer, in May 1180 Baldwin and Saladin agreed a two-year truce. For Saladin this was convenient as it allowed him to pursue his siege of Aleppo, which was in the hands of Nur al-Din's son.

For Baldwin it bought time. And for Christian and Muslim traders the truce meant that they could pass freely through each other's territory. But the treaty was broken the following year by Raynald of Chatillon, a bold and able soldier who was lord of Oultrejourdain, which lay astride Saladin's line of communication between Cairo and Damascus. From his castle of Kerak he could see the rich Muslim caravans travelling to Medina and Mecca, and falling upon one of these, he made off with all its goods. Saladin complained to Baldwin and demanded compensation, but Raynald refused to make restitution. In 1182 Raynald took matters further when he launched a fleet of ships into the Gulf of Aqaba and down the Red Sea where they raided Egyptian and Arabian ports, including those of Mecca and Medina, until they were driven back by a naval force under the command of Saladin's brother.

Chivalry and Reality

The concept of chivalry (the word derives from chevalier, the French for knight) arose in Western Europe in the century leading up to the First Crusade. A moral, religious and social code, chivalry emphasised the virtues of courage, service and honour. Combined with piety and faith, it found expression in the Crusades. Godfrey of Bouillon, the leader of the First Crusade, was widely seen as an exemplar of knightly virtues, and the chroniclers celebrated Baldwin, his brother and successor, for the chivalry he showed after capturing the wife of a Muslim prince and upon discovering she was pregnant immediately sending her back to her husband with every mark of respect.

Saladin came to admire the chivalrous code of the Frankish knights, and he acted with courtesy and sometimes clemency in return. There was the famous instance when he laid siege to Raymond of Chatillon's castle of Kerak. A marriage was being celebrated within, and when Raymond's wife sent trays of the festive meal to Saladin outside he tactfully inquired in which chamber the bridal couple were lodged so that he would not bombard them on their wedding night. For gestures such as these Saladin became a legend throughout Christendom, a worthy and honourable adversary – a phenomenon some naively explained by supposing that he must have had an English mother. In fact Saladin was following the precepts of Islam's own version of chivalry called *futuwwa*, which roughly means nobility.

But in reality chivalrous relations were rarely the rule between the Crusaders and the Muslims. The massacre perpetrated by the Crusaders at the fall of Jerusalem in 1099 was disgraceful but it was hardly an exceptional event. Populations that did not surrender were marked down for death or slavery as Zengi showed when he captured Edessa in 1144 or as the Mamelukes would show when they stormed Acre in 1291 and beheaded every last person in the city. Not that surrender was a guarantee: the Mameluke Sultan Baybars, in spite of his oath, murdered nearly a thousand prisoners after the fall of Saphet in 1266.

Saladin could be ruthless, and in the interests of policy he did not shrink from bloodshed. He was a devout Muslim who abhorred free-thinkers, and though he made many friends among the Christians, he never doubted that their souls were doomed to damnation. His famous magnanimity lay partly in his humanity but was also a matter of calculation. He did not shrink from cruelty when it suited his policy of instilling fear and asserting his dominance over his adversaries. In Cairo he ordered the crucifixion of his Shia opponents, and he was not averse to mutilating and executing his captives, as after the battle of Hattin when he slaughtered his Hospitaller and Templar captives in cold blood. It seems to have been only the threat made by the Frankish defenders of Jerusalem in 1187 that they would destroy all the sacred places, everything atop the Temple Mount, that caused Saladin to prefer a negotiated surrender to his original intention of purifying the city with Christian blood.

Factions in Outremer

Behind the scenes of these events was a growing division within Outremer between those who wanted to pursue an aggressive policy towards Saladin and those who sought accommodation. Among the former was Raynald of Chatillon, while among the latter was Count Raymond III of Tripoli and the slowly dying king. But Saladin had his own policy, which was to annihilate the Christian states, and their internal differences only made it easier for Saladin to destroy them. But for the moment the forces of Outremer were able to make a united stand against Saladin, who in May 1182, at the expiry of the truce, rode out with an invasion army from Cairo. Baldwin, who was now almost blind and had to be carried in a litter, was waiting with his army on the west bank of the Jordan, accompanied by Heraclius, the Patriarch of Jerusalem, and the True Cross. Following a fierce battle Saladin was repelled but not defeated, and both sides claimed victory.

The following June, however, Saladin finally captured Aleppo – and with it he gained full control of Syria. Not for two centuries had there been such a powerful Muslim ruler, his territories stretching from North Africa to the Tigris. Now Saladin was ready to unleash his jihad against the Christians. With Outremer encircled, the Templar and Hospitaller Grand Masters set sail in 1184 together with Heraclius to seek help from the West. The kings of France and England and the Holy Roman Emperor received them with honour and discussed plans for a great crusade, but they gave pressing domestic reasons for not going to the East themselves, and instead they paid barely sufficient money to cover the cost of a few hundred knights for a year. While in London early in 1185 Heraclius consecrated the new Temple Church, the one that stands there to this day. But the Templar Grand Master did not get that far; he had fallen ill en route, and died at Verona.

At about the same time as Heraclius was consecrating the new Templar church in London, Gerard of Ridefort was elected the new Grand Master by the Templars in Jerusalem, his elevation coinciding with the culmination of the factional disputes within the kingdom. Baldwin IV died in March 1185 and was buried in the Church of the Holy Sepulchre, and his successor the child-king Baldwin V died in 1186, not yet nine years old. Raymond III of Tripoli, leader of the party seeking accommodation with Saladin, had been the boy's regent according to his father's will, which also stated that if the child died before the age of ten Raymond was to remain as regent until a new king was chosen through the arbitration of the Pope, the Holy Roman Emperor and the kings of France and England.

Instead the boy's mother, Sibylla, who was the sister of the leper king, claimed the throne for herself and her husband Guy of Lusignan. Backed by the party that supported an aggressive policy towards

Saladin – among them Raynald of Chatillon, the lord of Oultrejourdain; Gerard of Ridefort, the Grand Master of the Templars; and Heraclius, the Patriarch of Jerusalem, who had also been the lover of Sibylla's mother – Sibylla and Guy were quickly crowned at Jerusalem. All the barons of Outremer accepted what in effect was a *coup d'état*; all except Raymond of Tripoli, who felt he had been cheated of the kingship, and his close ally Balian of Ibelin.

The Springs of Cresson

Going from factional rivalry to treason, Count Raymond of Tripoli entered into a secret treaty with Saladin. Not only did it apply to Tripoli itself but also to his wife's principality of Galilee, even though it was part of the Kingdom of Jerusalem, which might soon be at war with the Muslims. Saladin also promised his support for Raymond's aim to overthrow Sibylla and Guy of Lusignan and make himself king. In April 1187 Guy responded by summoning his loyal barons and marching north to Galilee to reduce it to submission before the expected Muslim attack began. But Balian of Ibelin, fearing the consequences of civil war, persuaded Guy to let him lead a delegation to Tiberias on the Sea of Galilee and try to negotiate a reconciliation between Raymond and the king. The delegation would include the Grand Masters of the Hospitallers and the Templars, and Balian would meet them at the Templar castle of La Fève on 1 May.

Meanwhile Saladin had asked Raymond's permission to send a reconnaissance party of Mameluke slave troops through Galilee on that day, and though the timing was embarrasing Raymond was obliged to agree under the terms of the secret treaty, stipulating only that the Muslims should traverse his territory within the day and be gone by dark, and do no harm to any town or village. Raymond broadcast the news that the Muslim party would be passing through and urged his people to stay indoors. But Balian had heard nothing of this when he arrived at Le Fève in the middle of the morning on 1 May expecting to join the Grand Masters there. Instead he found the castle empty, and after waiting in the silence for an hour or two, he set out again towards Tiberias, thinking the others had gone ahead, when suddenly a bleeding Templar knight galloped by shouting out news of a great disaster.

Raymond of Tripoli's message about the Muslim party had reached La Fève in the evening of the previous day, 30 April, where Gerard of Ridefort heard the news. At once he summoned the Templars from the surrounding neighbourhood and by nightfall ninety had joined him there. In the morning they rode north through Nazareth where forty secular knights joined the hunt for the enemy's scouting party. But as they passed over the hill behind Nazareth what they saw was a large expedition of perhaps 7000 elite Mameluke horsemen watering their mounts at the Springs of Cresson in the valley below. Both the Templar marshal and the Hospitaller Grand Master advised retreat, but Gerard of Ridefort, the Templar Grand Master, insisted on attack. Charging furiously down the hillside, the 130 knights rode into the mass of the Muslim cavalry and were slaughtered almost to a man, only three Templars, Gerard among them, escaping with their lives.

That at any rate was the account given by an anonymous chronicler who obtained much of his information from the lost chronicle of Ernoul, who was a member of Balian's entourage. But neither Balian nor Ernoul were at the battle, and any account issuing from Balian's camp was likely to paint their factional opponent Gerard of Ridefort in the worst possible light. Another chronicle, the *Itinerarium Regis Ricardi*, apparently based on the lost journal of an English knight writing in about 1191, contradicts the story that Gerard rushed recklessly at the enemy; instead, and much more plausibly, it reports that the Templars were caught unaware and were the victims of a Muslim attack. Even so, Saladin's expedition kept to his agreement with Raymond of Tripoli, for his horsemen rode home long before nightfall, and they had not harmed a town or village in Galilee. But fixed to the lances of the Mameluke vanguard were the heads of the Templar knights.

The Horns of Hattin

Shamed by this tragedy, which was much his doing, Raymond of Tripoli broke his treaty with Saladin and rode to Jerusalem where he made his peace with the king. The peril was far too great for Guy of Lusignan to do anything but welcome Raymond's renewed loyalty to the kingdom, for at that moment Saladin was gathering a great army just over the frontier. Guy called every able-bodied man to arms at Acre, emptying the cities and castles of fighting men; at 12,000 strong, including 1200 mounted knights, the army was all that Outremer had to give. Against this Saladin had drawn on the Turkish and Kurdish occupiers of Egypt, Iraq and Syria, along with their Mameluke slave troops, and some Arabs too, for his invasion force of 18,000 men, and on 1 July 1187 he crossed the Jordan at Senabra where it issues from the southern end of the freshwater lake known as the Sea of Galilee.

On the following day, as Saladin was laying siege to Tiberias, the Crusader army settled in a good defensive position, well watered and with plenty of pasturage for the horses, fifteen miles to the west at Sephoria. The Templars and the Hospitallers were there, also Raymond, the count of Tripoli, and Raynald of Chatillon, Balian of Ibelin and many other lords with all their men, together with the bishop of Acre, who carried the True Cross, and the plan they had all agreed with the king was to wait, confident that Saladin could not hold his large army together in the parched countryside for very long during the heat of summer. But that evening a message arrived from Raymond's wife Eschiva, the countess of Tripoli, telling how she was at Tiberias holding out against Saladin's attack. King Guy held a council in his tent where many of the knights were moved by her desperate situation and wanted the army to march to her rescue. But Raymond rose and spoke, saying it would be foolhardy to abandon their present strong position and make a hazardous march through barren country in the fierce July heat.

'Tiberias is my city and my wife is there', spoke Raymond, according to the chronicle *De Expugnatione Terrae Sanctae per Saladinum*:

> *'None of you is so fiercely attached, save to Christianity, as I am to the city. None of you is so desirous as I am to succour or aid Tiberias. We and the king, however, should not move away from water, food and other necessities to lead such a multitude of men to death from solitude, hunger, thirst and scorching heat. You are well aware that since the heat is searing and the number of people is large, they could not survive half a day without an abundance of water. Furthermore, they could not reach the enemy without suffering a great shortage of water, accompanied by the destruction*

of men and of beasts. Stay, therefore, at this midway point, close to food and water, for certainly the Saracens have risen to such heights of pride that when they have taken the city, they will not turn aside to left or right, but will head straight through the vast solitude to us and challenge us to battle. Then our men, refreshed and filled with bread and water, will cheerfully set out from camp for the fray. We and our horses will be fresh; we will be aided and protected by the Lord's cross. Thus we will fight mightily against an unbelieving people who will be wearied by thirst and who will have no place to refresh themselves. Thus you see that if, in truth, the grace of Jesus Christ remains with us, the enemies of Christ's cross, before they can get to the sea or return to the river, will be taken captive or else killed by sword, by lance, or by thirst.'

By the time the council broke up at midnight it had resolved to remain at Sephoria. But Raymond's earlier treaty with Saladin had created an atmosphere of bitterness and mistrust among some, and his motives were now suspect. Later that same night the Grand Master of the Templars, Gerard of Ridefort, came to the king's tent and said that Raymond was a traitor and that to abandon Tiberias, which lay so close by, would be a stain on Guy's honour, as it would be on the Templars' own if they left unavenged the deaths of so many of their brothers at the Springs of Cresson. At this the king overturned the council's decision and announced that the army would march at dawn.

There were two ways to Tiberias: the one Saladin had taken via Senabra along the shores of the Galilee lake, the other across the parched hill country to the north. Leaving the gardens of Sephoria behind in the morning of 3 July, the Christian army marched across the barren hills towards the climbing sun. The day was hot and airless, and the men and horses suffered terribly for there was no water along the road. Guy was at the centre of the column and the Templars brought up the rear. As Raymond of Tripoli held Galilee in fief from the king it was his prerogative to lead the way. This led some to find treachery in the choice of route, for the choice was his. There may have been treachery from some quarter, for Saladin quickly discovered the line of the Franks' advance, warned, it was said, by several secular knights, and sent skirmishers to harass and weary the vanguard and rearguard with flights of arrows, while he himself marched his army the five miles from Tiberias to Hattin, a well-watered village amid broad pastures situated where the road across the hills descended towards the lake. By the afternoon the Christian army had reached the plateau above Hattin, and here Raymond said they should camp; there was water there, he thought, but the spring turned out to be dry. According to one version it was the Templars who said they could go no further and the king who made the decision to set up camp, causing Raymond to cry out, 'Alas, Lord God, the battle is over! We have been betrayed unto death. The Kingdom is finished!' Between the Franks and the village from where the ground fell away towards the lake rose a hill with two summits. It was called the Horns of Hattin.

There on the waterless plateau the Christian army spent the night, their misery made worse by the smoke and flames from the dry scrub on the hillside that the Muslims had set alight. Under cover of darkness, Saladin's forces crept closer; any Franks who slipped away in search of water were killed; and by dawn the Christian army was surrounded on all sides. Soon after daybreak on 4 July 1187 Saladin attacked. Against him charged the Christian infantry desperate to break through his lines to reach water, but they were killed or driven back; so goes the account in one chronicle, but in another they simply ran away and refused to fight. By all accounts the knights put up a terrific fight and repeatedly checked Saladin's cavalry attacks, but their real enemy was thirst and as their strength failed them their numbers were diminished.

The Templars and the Hospitallers gathered round the king and the True Cross where they were surrounded by the confusion and press of battle, the *Expugnatione* describing how the Christians were 'jumbled together and mingled with the Turks'. It goes on to tell how the king, seeing that all was lost, cried out that those who could escape should do so before it was too late. At this Raymond of Tripoli and Balian of Ibelin with their men charged the enemy line, hoping to break through. 'The speed of their horses in this confined space trampled down the Christians and made a kind of bridge, giving the riders a level path. In this manner they got out of that narrow place by fleeing over their

The battle of Hattin was a disastrous defeat for the Crusaders, but it made the Templars more necessary than ever, as they alone had the single-minded policy of defending and preserving the Holy Land

own men, over the Turks, and over the cross.' As they bore down on Saladin's line, it opened and let them pass through, then closed again; they were the last to get away. Soon the battle was over. The True Cross fell to Muslim hands. King Guy and those around him gave way to exhaustion and were taken.

Saladin's tent was set up on the battlefield, and here the king and his surviving barons were brought before their conqueror. Seating the king next to him, Saladin handed Guy a cup of water to slake his thirst. It also was a sign, for it was the custom that to give food or drink to a captive meant that his life was spared. But when Guy passed the water to Raynald of Chatillon, Saladin told the king, 'You gave the man the drink, not I.' Then he turned angrily on Raynald, reminding him of his brigandage and his raids down the Red Sea coast to the ports of Medina and Mecca, and accused him of blasphemy. When Saladin offered Raynald the choice between conversion to Islam and death, Raynald replied that it was Saladin who should convert to Christianity to avoid the eternal damnation that awaited unbelievers – at which Saladin struck off his head. The others were taken to captivity at Damascus where those who were worth a handsome ransom were treated well, the remainder sold into slavery.

Saladin was not so clement towards the miltary orders. Though Gerard of Ridefort, the Templars' Grand Master, was among the prisoners taken to Damascus, the other monastic knights faced a different fate. Frankish nobles were 'irresponsible, thoughtless, petty and covetous', thought al-Hawari who wrote a military treatise for Saladin, qualities which allowed them to be manipulated to suit Saladin's purposes; but the Templars and Hospitallers were dangerous because 'they have great fervour in religion, paying no attention to the things of this world'. Two days after his victory, wrote his secretary Imad al-Din, who was an eye-witness to the event, Saladin 'sought out the Templars and Hospitallers who had been captured and said: "I shall purify the land of these two impure races." He assigned fifty dinar to every man who had taken one of them prisoner, and immediately the army brought forward at least a hundred of them. He ordered that they should be beheaded, choosing to have them dead rather than in prison. With him was a whole band of scholars and Sufis and a certain number of devout men and ascetics; each begged to be allowed to kill one of them, and drew his sword and rolled back his sleeve. Saladin, his face joyful, was sitting on his dais; the unbelievers showed black despair.'

The Battle of the Chronicles

What really happened at the battles of the Springs of Cresson and of Hattin, and what happened at Saladin's siege of Jerusalem? There are several sources; some are eyewitness accounts, some are worked up after the events they describe; all of them are biased, and they are often flatly contradictory. Reading them, it is possible to portray the Templars as rash and irresponsible or as defiant heroes; to see Raymond of Tripoli as a wise advisor or a traitor to the king; and to imagine Balian of Ibelin not as the bold defender of Jerusalem but as a collaborator with Saladin. Clearly there were two factions as Outremer was confronted by the crisis of Saladin's onslaught, and that fact alone was a serious weakness.

One of the most important documents is the so-called *Chronicle of Ernoul*. In fact the entire chronicle is lost but a number of similar manuscripts seem to derive from a single original account by Ernoul, who was a squire to Balian of Ibelin. Some see Ernoul as an apologist for Balian, for people would wonder how he escaped unscathed from the battle of Hattin. Ernoul blames Raymond for having chosen the camping ground where the well turned out to be dry. But he also defends Raymond, as well as Balian, from breaking through the Muslim lines and escaping from the battlefield at Hattin, saying they were acting under the command of the king. Ernoul directs his strongest criticism at Gerard of Ridefort, the Grand Master of the Templars, for his recklessness at the Springs of Cresson and for urging the army forward across the hot and waterless landscape towards the Horns of Hattin. This description of events puts in the most favourable light that faction in Outremer who opposed the crowning of Guy of Lusignan as king.

In contrast, the anonymous *De Expugnatione Terrae Sanctae per Saladinum* shows admiration for the military orders while describing the flight from the battlefield at Hattin by Balian, Raymond and others in a none too flattering light. Nevertheless it is sympathetic to Raymond and presents him as a wise counsellor on the eve of battle, and it is very likely that its author was an Englishman who was one of Raymond's men. The *Expugnatione* also gives an eyewitness account of the siege of Jerusalem in which it manages to suggest the suspicion that Balian had been sent to the city by Saladin himself, his task to convince its inhabitants to arrive at a negotiated surrender.

Another work, the *Itinerarium Regis Ricardi*, was quite possibly based on a lost journal kept by an English Templar and rejects any criticism of the orders. Far from being rash, the actions of the Templar Grand Master Gerard of Ridefort showed him to be a man consistent in his refusal to compromise with the Muslims, but he was undermined by Raymond of Tripoli whom the *Itinerarium* blames for the disaster at Hattin, saying that he lured the army on because he had a secret deal with Saladin. This accusation of treachery against Raymond clears the king and the faction gathered round him of the blame for subsequently losing Jerusalem. On the Muslim side, an account by Saladin's secretary Imad al-Din is authoritative; he was an eyewitness at the heart of events, but he knew little about the inner workings of the Franks.

Saladin Takes Jerusalem

The towns and cities and castles had been emptied to defend the Holy Land against the Muslim invasion. Now, after the battle of Hattin, Outremer stood almost entirely defenceless against Saladin. Acre surrendered without a fight on 10 July, Sidon followed suit on the 29th, and Beirut capitulated on 6 August. Jaffa refused to yield; in July it was taken by storm and its entire population were killed or sent to the slave markets and harems of Aleppo. Ascalon offered some brief resistance but surrendered on 4 September. A few days later Saladin brought Gerard of Rideford to the walls of Gaza and made him tell the Templars inside to surrender, which obedient to their Grand Master they promptly did. In the south only Tyre resisted capture; in the north there was Tripoli, Tortosa and Antioch, and they could be dealt with later. Saladin's immediate aim was to take Jerusalem.

Refugees were flooding into Jerusalem, but there were few fighters among the men, and for every man there were said to be fifty women and children. The patriarch Heraclius together with officials of the military orders tried to prepare the city's defence, but Jerusalem lacked a leader until Balian of Ibelin appeared. After Hattin his wife and children had sought safety within its walls, and Balian had come to Jerusalem to bring them to the coast at Tyre. But the people of the city clamoured for him to stay, and finally Balian accepted the task of readying Jerusalem against Saladin's attack. His most immediate need was to raise morale; there were only two knights left in the city, so Balian knighted every boy over sixteen of noble birth and also thirty burgesses. To fund the defence he took over the royal treasury and even stripped the silver from the dome of the Church of the Holy Sepulchre. He sent parties out into the areas all around to collect all the food before the Muslims arrived, and he gave arms to every able-bodied man.

On 20 September Saladin was camped outside the city. He inquired about the location of al-Aqsa mosque and asked the shortest route to it, saying that was also the shortest route to heaven. Then he set his sappers to work undermining that section of the northern battlements where Godfrey of Bouillon had forced his way into Jerusalem eighty-eight years before. By 29 September a great breach was made in the wall which was tenaciously defended, but it was only a matter of time before they would be overwhelmed by Saladin's hordes. Balian with the support of the Patriarch decided to seek terms, and on 30 September he went to Saladin's tent.

Saladin was uncompromising. He had been told by his holy men, he said, that Jerusalem could only be cleansed with Christian blood, and so he had vowed to take Jerusalem by the sword; only unconditional surrender would make him stay his hand. But Balian warned that unless they were given honourable terms the defenders in their desperation would destroy everything in the city: 'We shall slay our sons and our daughters, we shall burn the city and overthrow the Temple and all the sanctuaries which are also your sanctuaries.' Saladin consented that Jerusalem's 20,000 Christians could leave the city if they paid him ten dinars for each man, five for each female, and one for each boy up to seven years old. But the poorest would be unable to ransom themselves, and so Balian produced 30,000 dinars from public funds to pay for the release of the poorest 7000 people.

Looking Back at the Temple Mount

On 2 October 1187, the twenty-seventh day of Rajab according to the Islamic calendar, and the anniversary of the Prophet Mohammed's Night Journey, the Muslims reoccupied Jerusalem. The Temple Mount was surrendered to Saladin and the Templars were removed from their headquarters at the al-Aqsa mosque. The cross erected by the Crusaders on the Dome of the Rock was thrown down before the army of Saladin and in the presence of the Frankish population. A great cry went up when it fell, of anguish from the Christians, and of 'Allah is Great' from the Muslims, who dragged it round the streets of the city for two days, beating it with clubs.

The initial euphoria of the victory was followed by a busy week during which the many structures built by the Templars on the Temple Mount and the modifications they made within the al-Aqsa mosque were demolished. Saladin himself oversaw these works, ensuring that the al-Aqsa mosque and the Dome of the Rock were restored to their earlier Islamic character. Finally both buildings were sprinkled with rose-water to cleanse them of Christian pollution. Saladin joined the vast congregation that gathered for Friday prayers on 9 October at the al-Aqsa mosque where the cadi of Aleppo gave the sermon in which he compared Saladin's victory to Umar's conquest of the city and other Muslim triumphs going back to Mohammed's battles at Badr against the Meccans and at Khaybar which led to the expulsion of the Jews from the Arabian peninsula. 'Jerusalem', he continued to the Muslims, 'is the residence of your father Abraham, the place of ascension of your prophet, the burial ground of the messengers and the place of the descent of revelations. It is in the land where men will be resurrected and it is in the Holy Land to which Allah has referred in the Koran.'

Two great lines of Christian refugees were led out from Jerusalem, one bound for slavery, the other freedom. The ransomed refugees were then assembled in three groups. Balian and the Patriarch Heraclius took charge of one group, another was placed in the custody of the Hospitallers, and the third in that of the Templars. After one last look back at Jerusalem and the brow of the Temple Mount, the refugees were led to the coast where they were distributed between Antioch, Tyre and Tripoli.

The Kingdom of Jerusalem had suffered a comprehensive defeat from which no feudal monarchy could have emerged with its powers unimpaired. But the military orders, because of their military functions and their external financing, became yet more important and independent than before. This was particularly true of the Templars, whose single-minded policy and purpose was to preserve, to defend and now to regain Jerusalem and the Holy Land.

Holding On

Power in Adversity

Defeat at Hattin and the loss of Jerusalem did not diminish the crusading cause; indeed, crusading thrived on disaster and was fuelled by a new enthusiasm. After capturing the Christian coastal ports and Jerusalem in 1187, Saladin turned his attention to northern Syria where during his campaign of 1188 he stormed one castle after another and took the city of Latakia. But he baulked at the key Hospitaller castles of Margat and Krak des Chevaliers and at the Templars' fortified city of Tortosa and their castle at Safita called Chastel Blanc. More than ever Outremer relied on castles and on the military orders who manned them, and the power of the orders grew. In fact at no point in their history would the Templars be more powerful than in the century after nearly everything in the Holy Land was lost to Saladin.

The West reacted with shock to the loss of Jerusalem and responded by launching the Third Crusade in 1190. In a remarkable series of victories first Philip II of France and Richard I of England, known as 'the

Lionheart', recovered Acre in July 1191, and then Richard went on to take Jaffa and Ascalon as well, after defeating Saladin in a great battle at Arsuf in September 1191 in which the military orders played a leading role. Richard the Lionheart marched to within sight of Jerusalem but was advised by both the Templar and the Hospitaller grand masters that even if he took the city it could not be held without also controlling the hinterland, especially once his army had left Outremer. Richard took their advice and instead came to an agreement with Saladin. The Franks would demolish the walls of Ascalon while Saladin would recognise the Christian positions along the coast; free movement would be allowed to Christians and Muslims across each other's territory; and Christian pilgrims would be permitted to visit Jerusalem and the other holy places.

In name and number the revived Crusader states were as before, but their outlines were diminished. There was the Kingdom of Jerusalem, though its capital was at Acre, which the Templars made their new headquarters. To the north was the County of Tripoli. But the Muslims retained control of the Syrian coast around Latakia for some time, and so the Principality of Antioch further to the north was now no longer contiguous to the other Crusader states. Nevertheless the Third Crusade, in which Richard relied heavily on the Templars, had saved the Holy Land for the Christians and went a long way towards restoring Frankish fortunes. Accompanied by a Templar escort, Richard left the Holy Land in 1192, and in the following year Saladin died. Peace settled over Outremer and its immediate future looked secure.

Richard the Lionheart and the Templars

The Templar Grand Master Gerard of Ridefort, who had been captured by Saladin and then released in 1187, received a last acclaim from the anonymous English knight on whose lost journal the *Itinerarium Regis Ricardi* was based. The chronicle records Gerard's death in 1189, during an abortive attempt to retake Acre, and says that the Grand Master was crowned with the laurel of martyrdom 'which he had merited in so many wars'. The lost journal may well have been written by a Templar serving with Richard I of England during the Third Crusade. In any case the new crusade certainly marked the close association of the Templars with the English king.

Robert of Sablé became Grand Master of the Templars in 1191, almost certainly through the influence of King Richard, whose vassal he had been. On his way to the Holy Land, Richard paused to capture Cyprus from the Byzantines, but lacking the means to control the island he sold it to the Templars, a transaction that probably owed something to the already close link between Robert of Sablé and the king. The entire future of the Templars might have been different had they devoted more resources to the island, but they placed only twenty knights on Cyprus and another hundred men at arms, insufficient to secure it, and so they gave it back to Richard. Possessing a territory

A victorious Richard the Lionheart sets sail from the Holy Land. With the Templars, who were his allies, he inflicted a great defeat on Saladin at Arsuf and restored the Crusaders' fortunes in Outremer.

of their own, the Templars would have anticipated the achievement of the Knights Hospitaller, who established their own independent state on Rhodes in 1309. Instead Templar fortunes remained tied to the Holy Land, and when it fell the Templars fell soon after.

Meanwhile, the Templars were invaluable to Richard the Lionheart, never more so than when he relied on their steadiness and discipline to help him win his great victory over Saladin in the battle of Arsuf on 7 September 1191. As Richard marched south along the coast from Acre his army was vulnerable to flank attacks by Saladin's Turkish cavalry, and it was thanks to the Templars and the Hospitallers that the Turks were beaten off and the coherence of the Christian column was maintained – much as the Templars had done for Louis VII during his march across Asia Minor during the Second Crusade.

On the battlefield itself Richard placed the Templars at the front rank of his army, the Hospitallers at the rear. Richard's plan was for his army to stand firm while Saladin's forces wore themselves out in attack. And so it went, beginning with wave after wave of lightly armed black and Bedouin infantry rushing against the Christian lines, followed by charging Turkish horsemen swinging their scimitars and axes. And still the knights held their ground, Richard waiting for the moment when the Muslim charges showed signs of weakening. The Templars withstood everything thrown at them. The Hospitallers broke ranks first; unwilling to endure the assaults any longer, they rode out against the enemy, and then the whole army followed suit. Saladin's secretary Imad al-Din, who watched the battle from a nearby hill, gasped at the splendour of the spectacle as Richard's cavalry thundered forwards, with the king himself at the centre restoring order and taking command of the battle. Arsuf was a tremendous moral victory for the Franks and a public humiliation of Saladin, a small repayment for the Templars he slaughtered after the battle of Hattin. The victory also partly resurrected the Kingdom of Jerusalem.

Jerusalem Again

After the death of Saladin his empire fell apart; rival factions of his dynasty, the Ayyubids (Ayyub being Saladin's father's name), ruled in Cairo and Damascus but all the rest was lost. Occasional skirmishes followed between Outremer and the Muslim powers but more often relations were regulated by repeated truces, while in the West enthusiasm for crusading against the Muslim East momentarily declined. The Fourth Crusade, launched against Egypt with the aim of ultimately recovering Jerusalem, was diverted by the Venetians, who supplied the ships, to Constantinople, which in 1204 was sacked, with Latin Christians replacing the rule of the Orthodox Christian Emperors until the Byzantines reconquered their city in 1261. As discussed earlier, France and the Papacy looked to the enemy within when the Albigensian Crusade against the Cathars was launched in 1209. Neither of these crusades improved the position of Outremer.

Returning to the object of regaining Jerusalem, in 1217 the Papacy launched the Fifth Crusade, though the means of doing so was to attack Egypt. The Templars were involved in this new crusade from the start, with the Templar treasurer at Paris overseeing the donations that were to fund the expedition. Forces under King Andrew of Hungary and Leopold, Duke of Austria, were joined by men under John of Brienne, the King of Jerusalem, which included Templars, Hospitallers and Teutonic Knights – the last being a new military order founded along Templar lines by Germans who had been on the Third Crusade.

With no single outstanding leader among this mixed force, the Fifth Crusade was placed under the authority of the Papal legate Pelagius, a man of no military experience. Nevertheless, early in 1219 the Crusaders captured the port of Damietta in the Nile Delta, thanks largely to the Templars, who not only fought admirably on horseback but demonstrated a remarkable talent for innovation, adapting their engineering and tactical skills from the arid conditions of Outremer to the watery landscape of the Delta where they commanded ships and built floating pontoons to win the victory.

The loss of Damietta so unnerved the Sultan of Egypt, Saladin's nephew al-Kamil, that he offered to trade it for Jerusalem. But the Templar Grand Master argued that Jerusalem could not be held without controlling the lands beyond the Jordan, and so the Crusaders rejected the offer and continued their campaign in Egypt. Meanwhile they were awaiting the arrival at Damietta of another army led by the Holy Roman Emperor Frederick II. Despite its failure to appear, the Papal legate Pelagius impatiently urged the Crusaders to advance up the Nile towards Cairo. United under the command of an experienced leader, the Fifth Crusade might have been a success. But at Mansurah, al-Kamil cut off the Crusaders' rear, opened the sluice gates of the irrigation canals and flooded the army into submission. In 1221 Pelagius agreed to give up Damietta, not in exchange for Jerusalem, but to save the lives of the Crusaders, who immediately evacuated Egypt and returned to Acre.

Frederick II did eventually appear in the East, but only eight years later, by when he was openly at loggerheads with the Church. Crowned Holy Roman Emperor in 1212 at Frankfurt, Frederick was also king of both Germany and Sicily. He preferred to rule from Palermo, where he had been raised amid the Norman, Byzantine, Jewish and Arab influences at the Sicilian court. He learnt German, Italian, French, Latin, Greek and Arabic, and was a student of mathematics, philosophy, natural history, medicine and architecture, as well as being a talented poet. These accomplishments contributed to his broadness of outlook, his exceptionally cultivated mind and his rather idiosyncratic character, which earned him the title of *Stupor Mundi*, Wonder of the World. But they also engendered suspicion. It was rumoured that Frederick did not believe in God, and it was put about that he scoffed at the virgin birth of Jesus and described Mohammed, Jesus and Moses as 'the three impostors or deceivers of the world'.

This might have been the black propaganda of the Papacy at Rome, which was worried at being encircled by his domains and was also agitated by Frederick's claim to supreme authority and his boast that he would revive the Roman Empire, to which the Papacy countered by saying the Church had a higher authority in God.

Frederick had been twenty-one when he was crowned Holy Roman Emperor and vowed to take the cross, but he failed to appear in Egypt during the Fifth Crusade and time and again put off his departure for the East. But in 1225, when John of Brienne, the aged King of Jerusalem, came West seeking a husband for his fourteen-year-old daughter Yolanda, whom he had crowned queen at Acre, Frederick saw his opportunity. Marrying her at Brindisi, Frederick broke his promise that John of Brienne could continue as regent; instead Frederick claimed the right as Yolanda's husband to become king, a move that would confirm him, he imagined, as the supreme sovereign in the Christian world.

Now in 1228 at the age of thirty-six Frederick finally set out for the Holy Land, but he fell ill en route and rested in Italy for a while before continuing his journey. Pope Gregory IX, who distrusted Frederick's imperial intentions in Italy, excommunicated him at once, using the excuse that this was yet one more instance of the Emperor's failure to fulfil his crusading vow. Then when Frederick eventually arrived at Acre in September, the Pope again asserted his authority, excommunicating him again, this time for attempting to go crusading without having first obtained Papal absolution for his earlier excommunication. Frederick was not impressed, but the barons and clergy in Outremer were, as were the Templars and the Hospitallers who owed their allegiance to the Pope, only the Teutonic Knights braving Papal wrath to support their fellow German.

However, even before Frederick had left Sicily, he and al-Kamil had been in secret negotiations over the objects of this Sixth Crusade. Frederick wanted Jerusalem if only because it would be useful in promoting himself as the supreme power in the West. Al-Kamil was prepared to oblige provided Frederick helped him capture Damascus. But by the time Frederick arrived in Outremer, al-Kamil had changed his mind. Determined to gain Jerusalem, Frederick now made a feint towards Egypt, in November leading his army from Acre towards Jaffa. The Templars and Hospitallers followed a day behind, not wanting to seem part of a crusade led by an excommunicant, but when Frederick placed the expedition under the nominal authority of his generals, the orders abandoned their scruples altogether and joined up with the main force. The show of unity did not last long.

Frederick's advance was enough to make al-Kamil fear that he would have to abandon his siege of Damascus, and he quickly agreed a deal with Frederick: a ten-year truce and the surrender of Jerusalem to the Christians. It was a sudden and sensational result and gave Frederick what he wanted, but it outraged the Patriarch and the military orders. The walls of Jerusalem had been torn down during the Fifth Crusade; if it was going to be given to them then, the intention was that it should not be defensible, and that remained the idea now, for part of the agreement was that the city should remain unfortified, and its only connection to the coast should be a narrow corridor of land. Moreover the orders were forbidden to make any improvements to their great castles of Marqab and Krak des Chevaliers of the Hospitallers and Tortosa and Chastel Blanc of the Templars. And then there was the galling provision – a necessary face-saver for al-Kamil – that the Temple Mount should remain under Muslim control and that the Templars were absolutely forbidden to return to their former headquarters at the al-Aqsa mosque.

On 29 March 1229 Frederick was crowned King of Jerusalem at the Church of the Holy Sepulchre. The Patriarch had placed an interdict on the city, forbidding church ceremonies while Frederick was in Jerusalem, and so with no priests to crown him, and with the Templars and the Hospitallers keeping away, it was left to Frederick to place the crown of Jerusalem on his own head. Calling himself God's Vicar on Earth, the title usually reserved for the Pope, Frederick swore in the presence of the Teutonic Knights to defend the kingdom, the Church and his empire. He afterwards toured the city, and going to the Temple Mount he entered the Dome of the Rock through a wooden lattice door, put there he was told to keep the sparrows out. Venting his feelings about his Papal enemies to whom he had restored the holy city, Frederick pronounced, 'Now God has sent you pigs.'

Frederick stayed in Jerusalem for only two days. He had achieved what he wanted and was eager to get back to Europe and the serious business of expanding his powers there. But he also feared that the Templars might make an attempt upon his life while he was in the city. Chroniclers as far apart as Sicily, Damascus and England reported this story, which if nothing else reflected the intensity of ill-feeling and suspicion between the Emperor and the Pope, an enmity in which the Templars had become involved. When Frederick returned to Sicily he seized the property of the military orders there, released their Muslim slaves without paying compensation and imprisoned the Templar brothers. Yet again the Pope excommunicated him, and again Frederick ignored the Pope. It was a foreboding of what could happen when the Templars stood in the way of the needs and ambitions of a secular prince.

The Rise of the Mamelukes

In 1239 the ten-year truce had run out, but there was no immediate threat to Outremer. Al-Kamil had died the year before and Egypt was riven by factions, while the bitterness between the Cairo and Damascus branches of the Ayyubid family had increased. Nevertheless the Templars remained opposed to the rapprochement between Outremer and Egypt brought about by Frederick II, and with good reason: Templar emissaries sent to Cairo in 1243 were held as virtual prisoners for six months, and the Egyptians would still not return Gaza, Hebron and Nablus in accordance with the truce.

The Templars saw this as a delaying tactic by the new Egyptian Sultan al-Salih Ayyub, giving him time to overcome Damascus and other Muslim rulers, and then to overwhelm Outremer. Templar policy was to favour Damascus, and this showed some results: the Christian kingdom gained by negotiation all the land west of the Jordan except Hebron and Nablus, and the Franks were given a free hand to celebrate Christian services in every former church throughout Jerusalem, and to expel the Muslims from the Temple Mount and to reconvert to Christian use the al-Aqsa mosque and the Dome of the Rock.

When war broke out again between Cairo and Damascus in spring 1244 the Templars persuaded the barons of Outremer to

Four Mamelukes, brandishing shields and sabres, illustrate a medieval manual of horsemanship and military practise produced in Syria and Egypt

intervene on the side of the Damascene ruler Ismail. The alliance was sealed by the visit to Acre of al-Mansur Ibrahim, a Muslim prince of Homs, who on behalf of Ismail offered the Franks a share of Egypt when al-Salih Ayyub was defeated. The continuing factionalism in Cairo meant that al-Salih could not rely on the regular army, but he had taken steps to counter that by purchasing Mamelukes in large numbers.

These military slaves were mostly Kipchak Turks from the steppes of southern Russia; bought, trained and converted to Islam, they became al-Salih's powerful private army. Also al-Salih had bought the help of the Khorezmian Turks, ferocious mercenaries then based in Edessa, who had been displaced from Transoxiana and parts of Iran and Afghanistan by the expansion of the Mongols. In June the Khorezmian horsemen, twelve thousand strong, swept southwards into Syria, but deterred by the formidable walls of Damascus they rode on into Galilee, captured Tiberias, and on 11 July broke through the feeble defences of Jerusalem and brutally massacred everyone who could not retreat into the citadel. Six weeks later the defenders emerged, having been promised safe passage to the coast. The garrison together with the entire Christian population, six thousand men, women and children, left the city but were cut down by Khorezmian swords, only three hundred making it to Jaffa. For good measure the Khorezmians ransacked the Church of the Holy Sepulchre, tore up the bones of the Kings of Jerusalem from their tombs, set the place alight and burnt all the other churches of the city, pillaged its homes and shops, then left the smoking wreckage of Jerusalem to join al-Salih's Mameluke army at Gaza.

The Mamelukes

The Mamelukes as seen through the eyes of Ibn Khaldun, fourteenth-century North African historian:

It was God's benevolence that he rescued the faith by reviving its dying breath and restoring the unity of the Muslims in the Egyptian realms, preserving the order and defending the walls of Islam. He did this by sending to the Muslims, from this Turkish nation and from among its great and numerous tribes, rulers to defend them and utterly loyal helpers, who were brought from the House of War to the House of Islam under the rule of slavery, which hides in itself a divine blessing. By means of slavery they learn glory and blessing and are exposed to divine providence; cured by slavery, they enter the Muslim religion with the firm resolve of true believers and yet with nomadic virtues unsullied by debased nature, unadulterated with the filth of pleasure, undefiled by the ways of civilised living, and with their ardour unbroken by the profusion of luxury. The slave merchants bring them to Egypt in batches, like sandgrouse to the watering places, and government buyers have them displayed for inspection and bid for them ... Thus, one intake comes after another and generation follows generation, and Islam rejoices in the benefit which it gains through them, and the branches of the kingdom flourish with the freshness of youth.

From Bernard Lewis, *Islam from the Prophet Muhammed to the Capture of Constantinople*, Oxford University Press, 1987

Catastrophe at La Forbie and the Seventh Crusade

The Frankish forces which had been scattered throughout the castles of Outremer gathered at Acre. Not since Hattin had such a considerable Christian army been put into the field, its numbers including over 300 knights from the Templars, at least another 300 from the Hospitallers, also some Teutonic Knights, and a further 600 secular knights, as well as a proportionate number of sergeants and foot soldiers. To these were added the yet more numerous if lighter-armed forces of their Damascene ally under the command of al-Mansur Ibrahim and a contingent of Bedouin cavalry.

On 17 October 1244 this Christian-Muslim army drew up before the smaller Egyptian army with its elite core of Mamelukes and the Khorezmians outside Gaza on a sandy plain at a place called La Forbie. The Franks and their allies attacked, but the Egyptians stood firm under the command of the Mameluke general Baybars, and while the Franks were pinned in place, the Khorezmians tore into the flank of al-Mansur Ibrahim's forces. The Damascene forces turned and fled; the

Franks fought on bravely but after a few hours their entire army was destroyed. At least 5000 Franks died in the battle, among them 260 to 300 Templars, while over 800 Christians were captured and sold into slavery in Egypt, including the Templar Grand Master, who was never seen again. The catastrophe was comparable to Hattin, and when Damascus fell to al-Salih the following year it looked as though time had run out for Outremer.

Relief to Outremer came in the form of the Seventh Crusade, led by King Louis IX of France, Saint Louis as he afterwards became thanks to his incessant warfare against enemies of the true faith, be they Muslims or Cathars – it was during Louis' reign that the Cathars were finally beaten and incinerated at the stake. Now in the summer of 1249 he landed with his French army at the Delta port of Damietta with the familiar idea of overturning the Ayyubid regime in Cairo. Al-Salih Ayyub was suffering from cancer and when he died in November his wife, Shagarat al-Durr, hid his corpse and kept morale alive by pretending to transmit the Sultan's orders to his army of Mameluke slave troops led by Baybars.

In February 1250 the French advanced through the Delta towards Cairo but owing to the impetuosity of the king's brother, the Count of Artois, suffered heavy losses at Mansurah. He had urged the Crusader knights to charge into the town, where they were trapped within the narrow streets, the Templars alone losing 280 mounted knights, a massive blow so soon after La Forbie. A stalemate followed and the Crusaders were weakened by scurvy and plague. In April they retreated but were captured by the Mamelukes, along with King Louis himself, who was released only after a huge ransom was paid to which the Templars, who as bankers to members of the crusade had a treasure ship offshore, refused to contribute.

That same year Shagarat al-Durr openly declared herself sultan, basing her claim to the succession on having borne al-Salih a son, though the child had predeceased the father. The Abbasid caliph refused to recognise her, so she married Aybek, one of her Mameluke slave warriors, and ruled through him instead, then murdered him in 1257 when she suspected him of turning his attentions to another woman. Purchased

Fifteenth-century painting of Louis IX's invasion of Egypt, which met with disaster in 1250 at Mansurah, the Templars alone losing 280 knights

as a slave by al-Salih, then made one of his concubines, Shagarat al-Durr had eventually become his wife, and then became the first and last female ruler of Egypt since Cleopatra. Owing to her courage and resourcefulness she had saved Egypt from the Seventh Crusade, but she proved to be the last of the Ayyubid line. Aybek's supporters killed her and threw her naked body over the wall of the Citadel at Cairo to be devoured by the dogs. The Mamelukes then made themselves the masters of Egypt in the person of their first sultan, Qutuz.

But it was the shock of the Mongol invasion of the Middle East that established the Mamelukes as the legitimate defenders of Islam against the infidels of East and West. In February 1258 the Mongols, led by Hulagu, a grandson of Genghis Khan, captured Baghdad, put the Abbasid caliph to death, then plundered and destroyed the city. In January 1260 they took Aleppo, and in March Damascus fell. The Mongols appeared to be unstoppable. The Franks sent urgent letters westwards pleading for help; 'a horrible annihilation will swiftly be visited upon the world,' went a message carried by a Templar to London. But it was the Mamelukes who responded to the threat. That summer when Mongol ambassadors arrived in Cairo demanding Egypt's submission, they encountered an adversary more ferocious than themselves; Qutuz had them killed on the spot. And in September, after being allowed free passage through Christian lands, a Mameluke army under Qutuz inflicted a stunning defeat upon the Mongols in the battle of Ain Jalut southeast of Nazareth.

But among the jealous Mamelukes victory was no guarantee of success, and a month later Qutuz was murdered by a group of fellow Mamelukes, among them Baybars, al-Salih's general at La Forbie, who then became sultan. With Syria and Egypt under Baybars' control, Outremer was encircled, and the Franks were confronted by one of the most formidable fighting machines in the world.

Abandoned by God

Medieval Christians believed that God's judgement was revealed through history, and that he often declared his will by determining the outcome of a battle. As Saint Bernard had written in his panegyric *In Praise of the New Knighthood*, a Templar was a knight of Christ and 'the instrument of God for the punishment of malefactors and for the defence of the just'. A defeat in battle could mean that the Christians were paying the price for some sin. Confession, prayers and penance would cleanse their souls and lead to ultimate victory. But what were Christians now to make of the repeated defeats in the Holy Land? After Baybars captured Caesarea and Haifa in 1265, a Provençal troubadour called Bonomel, who may have been a Templar, sang that given this, 'Then it is really foolish to fight the Turks, now that Jesus Christ no longer opposes them ... Daily they impose new defeats on us: for God, who used to watch on our behalf, is now asleep, and Bafometz [Mohammed] puts forth his power to support the sultan.' Another Provençal poet wrote that because God and Our Lady wanted Christian troops to be killed, he would become a Muslim. As defeats continued it became impossible to attribute Muslim victories to the sins of the generality of Christians, and increasingly the military orders and especially the Templars attracted the suspicion and resentment of a disillusioned Christian world.

Templar Plans for Defending the Holy Land

In a series of devastating campaigns Baybars captured Caesarea and Haifa in 1265, the Templar castle of Saphet in 1266, Jaffa and the Templar castle of Beaufort both in 1268, and then struck at Antioch in the north, which he captured that same year, treating its inhabitants with a murderous brutality that shocked even Muslim chroniclers. The Templar castle at Baghras in the Amanus mountains was now utterly isolated. Baghras had been their first castle, but now the Templars had no choice but to abandon it. Chastel Blanc of the Templars was surrendered in 1271 together with the Hospitallers' great castle of Krak des Chevaliers. Baybars then marched on Montfort between Acre and the Sea of Galilee and that too was soon handed over to the Muslims by its garrison of Teutonic Knights.

With all their great inland fortresses taken, the Franks were pinned to their remaining coastal defences, crucially Acre and Tripoli, both powerfully fortified cities, and the Templars' stronghold of Tortosa, which had held out against Saladin, and their castle of Athlit, south of Haifa. But meanwhile the Franks gained some relief when Prince Edward, the future Edward I of England, led a fresh crusade to the East and in 1272 persuaded Baybars to agree to a ten-year truce.

Acre, capital of the Kingdom of Jerusalem and headquarters of the military orders, was the most powerfully defended city in Outremer. And according to the Templar of Tyre, who knew it well, 'The Temple was the strongest place of the city, largely situated along the seashore, like a castle. At its entrance it had a high and strong tower, the wall of which was twenty-eight feet thick. On each side of the tower was a smaller tower, and on each of these was a gilded lion *passant*, as large as an ox ... On the other side, near the street of the Pisans, there was another tower, and near this tower on the Street of St Anne, was a large and noble palace, which was the Master's ... There was another ancient tower on the seashore, which Saladin had built one hundred years before, in which the Temple kept its treasure, and it was so close to the sea that the waves washed against it. Within the Temple area there were other beautiful and noble houses, which I will not describe here.'

In 1273 the Templars elected a new Grand Master, William of Beaujeu, a man with considerable experience of fighting in the East

Aerial view of Acre and the walls surrounding the town

and administering the order. One of his first missions was to attend the Church Council of Lyons, which was convened by the Pope in 1274 for the principal purpose of launching a new crusade. At the council William spoke against a proposal to send 500 knights and 2000 infantry to the Holy Land as the vanguard of a mass levy like that of the First Crusade, arguing that unruly hordes of enthusiasts would not serve the needs of Outremer. Instead a permanent garrison was required which would be reinforced from time to time by small contingents of professional soldiers. And he also argued for an economic blockade of Egypt, the Mamelukes' power base.

Such a blockade would not be possible, however, as long as Outremer depended on the ships of the Italian maritime republics, for these were the very same merchant marines who traded so profitably with Egypt. The Venetians, for example, supplied Baybars with the metal and timber that he needed for his arms and siege engines, and the Genoese even provided him with Mameluke slaves. Instead the Christians needed to gain the naval ascendancy in the Eastern Mediterranean. William's advice was accepted and the council ordered the Templars and the Hospitallers to build their own fleets of warships.

William of Beaujeu had arrived at this plan not least because he recognised the contribution that was already being made by the French monarchy to sustaining the existence of Outremer. William's own uncle had fought with Louis IX in Egypt, and through his paternal grandmother he was related to the Capets, the French royal family. The kings of France were already paying for a permanent force of knights and crossbowmen at Acre, and the ambitious Charles of Anjou, who was king of Sicily and the younger brother of Louis IX, was helping to extend French power throughout the Mediterranean. But William's plans were overthrown by a popular uprising in 1282 known as the Sicilian Vespers, which sent Charles fleeing from the island to Naples.

Pope Martin IV, who was himself French, now declared a crusade against the Sicilian rebels and their supporters, the house of Aragon in Spain. Worse, he ordered funds held at the Paris Temple and intended for Outremer to be diverted to the house of Anjou in support of their war against fellow Christians to regain control over Sicily. Christians throughout Europe and in particular the Templars were outraged, and a few years later, after the fall of Tripoli, one Templar told Martin's successor Pope Nicholas IV, 'You could have relieved the Holy Land with the power of kings and the strength of the other faithful of Christ ... but you preferred to attack a Christian king and the Christian Sicilians, arming kings against a king to recover the island of Sicily' – another example of the growing trend to put secular interests over religious ideals.

Charles of Anjou's ambitions to build a Mediterranean empire and to combine his Kingdom of Sicily with the Kingdom of Jerusalem had kept Baybar's own ambitions somewhat in check. But in 1277 Baybars had died, and after a brief power struggle the most capable among the Mamelukes was elevated to the sultanate, Baybar's brilliant commander Qalaun. The Sicilian Vespers, followed by Charles' death in 1285, removed any Mameluke hesitation in pursuing the destruction of the Christian states in the East.

Lonely Outposts

The fall of the Crusader castles to the Mamelukes needs some explanation. How could such magnificent structures, built at such vast cost and effort, incorporating the latest military design of the age, and defended by men of undoubted courage, have so rapidly capitulated or been captured? There is no single answer. Several factors worked in combination.

The Templar castle of Beaufort, overlooking the southern end of the Bekaa valley in Lebanon, fell to Baybars in 1268 with the help of first-class military engineers. They assembled something like twenty-six siege engines, that is battering rams and siege towers as well as catapults, the wooden frames and metal parts bought from Venetian merchants sailing into Egyptian ports. In this case the Templars were overwhelmed by technology. But two years earlier when the Templar castle of Saphet (Safad) fell to Baybars it had been down to treason.

Saphet was the castle in northern Galilee which the Templars had spent a fortune rebuilding less than thirty years before, a worthwhile expense as it guarded against raids of Bedouins and Turks who would formerly

Beaufort castle, a Templar outpost, still commands a strategic position overlooking southern Lebanon and northern Israel. It has been occupied by the PLO, Hezbollah and the Israeli Defence Forces.

cross over the Jordan with impunity. Traders could safely conduct their pack animals and wagons between Acre and Galilee, farmers could cultivate their fields in security, and pilgrims could freely visit many sites associated with the ministry of Jesus. Muslim sources acknowledged its efficacy by describing Saphet as 'an obstruction in the throat of Syria and a blockage in the chest of Islam' – that is until Baybars brought about its downfall in 1266. He did so not by attack – he tried three times that year and failed – but by sowing dissent between the small garrison of Templars and the much larger numbers of Syrian Christian servants and native troops inside. He promised the latter free passage and so many wanted to defect that the defence of the castle was called into question. The Templars agreed to negotiate and a safe conduct was arranged, for Templar knights and locals alike. But when the gates were opened, Baybars grabbed all the women and children and sold them into slavery and decapitated all the knights and other men.

The willingness of the Templars garrison at Saphet to negotiate points to another factor at work: a sense of isolation and feeling overwhelmed, which seems to have played an important part in the fall of the Templar castle of Chastel Blanc (Safita) and the Hospitallers' Krak des Chevaliers to Baybars within two months of one another in 1271. Both castles stood in the Jebel al-Sariya, that mountain range separating the interior from the sea; but both became increasingly isolated amidst the Muslim advance. Perhaps also the Templar master at Tortosa thought it wiser to concentrate his forces on the coast, but whatever the reason he ordered the evacuation of Chastel Blanc.

Likewise Krak des Chevaliers was not taken but given away. The Hospitallers could no longer raise sufficient manpower to garrison the castle and for its diminished complement of Hospitaller knights the waiting became a terrible immurement. After a month's siege, Baybars delivered a forged note purportedly from their master at Tripoli, urging them to surrender. Their defences and supplies might have allowed them to hold out for years, but it must have seemed to them that Krak was drifting anchorless and rudderless upon an irresistible Muslim tide. Weary, dejected and demoralised, on 8 April 1271 the Hospitallers accepted Baybars' offer of safe conduct to the sea.

Within twenty years the few Crusader possessions along the coast would also fall and the 200-year adventure in the Holy Land would end.

The Fall of Acre

The truce with the Franks had allowed the Mamelukes to direct their energy towards renewed Mongol threats, but once that had been accomplished, and even before the truce had ended, Sultan Qalaun renewed Mameluke aggression against the Franks. Now the coastal cities and castles began to go the way of the inland defences; in 1285 Qalaun took the Hospitaller castle of Margat, perched on a salient of the Jebel al-Sariya overlooking the sea, and in 1287 he easily took the port city of Latakia after its walls were damaged in an earthquake.

Yet in 1286, in the midst of these campaigns and with extraordinary insouciance, the Franks celebrated the visit of King Henry II of Cyprus, who had come to assume the crown of Jerusalem. The Templar of Tyre recorded the festivities at Acre, when the king 'held a feast lasting fifteen days at the Auberge of the Hospital of Saint John. And it was the most splendid feast they had seen for a hundred years ... They enacted the tales of the Round Table and the Queen of Femenie, which consisted of knights dressed as women jousting together. Then those who should have been dressed as monks dressed up as nuns, and they jousted together.'

Beyond the walls of Acre, however, the outlook was grim. In 1289 Qalaun overwhelmed Tripoli: 'The population fell back to the port where some escaped on ships', recorded the historian Abu al-Feda. 'Of the rest, the men were all put to death and the women and children taken as slaves, and the Muslims amassed an immense booty. Just off the headland there was a small island with a church, and when the city was taken many Franks took refuge there with their families. But the Muslim troops swam across to the island, massacring the men and carrying off the women and children. I myself went out to the island on a boat after the carnage, but I was unable to stay, so strong was the stench

A nineteenth century depiction of the Mamelukes breaking through the defences of Acre in 1291

of corpses.' When the killing and looting were finished, Qalaun razed the city to the ground.

Vowing not to leave a single Christian alive in the city, Qalaun set out from Cairo for Acre in November 1290, but he fell ill and died along the way. His son al-Ashraf Khalil pledged to continue the war against the Franks, and in early spring 1291 his armies from Syria and Egypt converged on Acre, together with over a hundred siege engines, including various kinds of catapults. On 5 April Sultan al-Ashraf Khalil himself arrived and the siege began. At most the Franks were able to muster about 1000 knights and 14,000 foot soldiers; the population of Acre was 40,000, and every able-bodied man took his place on the ramparts. On 15 April William of Beaujeu, the Templar Grand Master, led a night attack on a section of the Muslim lines. At first, surprise won them the advantage, but the Christians got caught up in the enemy's tent ropes and were eventually beaten back. Under a hail of arrows and a bombardment of stones by the catapults, Mameluke engineers were able

The Templars' fortress of Château de la Mer at Sidon on the coast of southern Lebanon. The order's treasure was brought here before the fall of Acre, and then taken away to Cyprus

to advance close against the walls and mine the defences, bringing down tower after tower over the following weeks.

On 15 May, after six weeks of constant battering, the Accursed Tower commanding the vital northeast salient of the city's walls was taken by the Mamelukes. William of Beaujeu was fatally wounded trying to force the enemy back. He was placed on a shield and carried to the Temple enclave where he was buried before the high altar while the desperate fighting continued outside. By now townspeople were pressing onto the quays to board whatever ships they could to escape from the doomed city. Merchant captains made fortunes extorting money from the rich desperate to escape, as did also, it is thought, Roger of Flor, captain of a Templar galley called *The Falcon*, who used his profits to found his later career as a pirate. As the Mamelukes stormed through the streets they killed everyone in sight, including women and children; those who hid indoors were taken captive and sold on the slave market of Damascus, where the glut of women and girls reduced their price to a single drachma.

By the evening of 18 May all Acre was in the hands of the Mamelukes except for the Templar fortress at the seaward extremity of the city. There they held out, commanded by their marshal, together with civilians who had sought protection within their walls, and were kept supplied by sea from Cyprus. On 25 May the Templar marshal agreed to surrender provided those inside were granted safe passage out of Acre, but as the Muslims entered they began to molest the women and boys, provoking the Templars to fight back. That night the Templar commander Theobald Gaudin was sent out of the fortress with the order's treasure and sailed up the coast to Château de Mer, the Templars' sea-castle just off the coast at Sidon. The Templar fortress in Acre fell three days later and at Sultan al-Ashraf Khalil's command all those left alive were led outside the walls where their heads were cut off, and the city was smashed to pieces until almost nothing was left standing. Forty years later a German traveller came upon the spot and found only a few peasants living amidst the desolation of what had once been the splendid capital of Outremer.

The Last Templars in the East

From Sidon, Theobald Gaudin sailed to Cyprus with the Templar treasure. His intention was to bring back reinforcements. But Gaudin never returned. Instead a message came from the Templars in Cyprus urging their brethren in Sidon to abandon their castle there, and on the night of 14 July they put to sea. Cyprus had long been a Frankish kingdom. A century earlier Richard the Lionheart had seized it from the Byzantines, and after a brief period in Templar hands, Richard sold it on again to Guy of Lusignan, the former King of Jerusalem, whose dynasty would continue to rule Cyprus for nearly three hundred years. Meanwhile the Templars and the Hospitallers had built castles on Cyprus, and now as the Franks were being driven from the coast of Outremer the island became a refuge for both military orders.

In the Holy Land, after the fall of Acre and Sidon, only Tortosa and Athlit remained in Christian hands. Both were Templar strongholds, but as the Mamelukes gathered for the kill, the knights slipped away to Cyprus from Tortosa on 3 August 1291 and eleven days later from Athlit. 'This time', wrote the Templar of Tyre, 'everything was lost, so that the Christians no longer held a palm of land in Syria.' As the Templars looked back along the receding mainland, the devastation was already beginning. For some months after the fall of Tortosa in 1291, Mameluke troops laid waste to the coastal plain. Orchards were cut down and irrigation systems wrecked, while native Christians fled into the Jebel al-Sariya. The only castles left standing were those far back from the sea, and Margat, high upon its mountain. Anything that might be of value to the Crusaders should they ever attempt another landing was destroyed.

Even four centuries after the Franks were driven from this coast, the devastation wrought by the Mamelukes was still apparent, in 1697 the English traveller Henry Maundrell recording the 'many ruins of castles and houses, which testify that this country, however it be neglected at present, was once in the hands of a people that knew how to value it, and thought it worth the defending'.

Part 4

The Fall

1291–1314

A variety of siege engines was employed by the Crusaders. The tables were turned when the Mamelukes built their own machines, using metal and timber supplied by Venetian merchants.

Exile from the Holy Land

Lost Souls

Though not unexpected, the fall of Acre came as a shock in the West. The sins of the inhabitants of Outremer were blamed, as was the failure of the leaders of European Christendom to provide ample and timely aid, and the Italian merchant states which had traded with Mameluke Egypt, and the military orders, Templars and Hospitallers alike. No one was exempt.

But it was the Templars who felt the loss most intensely. The defence of the Holy Land and the protection of pilgrims was their *raison d'être*. For the Hospitallers the ethos of their charitable work took precedence; they had never abandoned their original function of caring for the sick. But the Templars were founded as a knighthood, their role to fight against the infidel, and in that cause to service crusades and direct the finances of Popes and kings. Now cast out from the Holy Land, the Templars found themselves in limbo.

Dreams and New Realities

Of course, the dream of recovering the Holy Land was not yet over, certainly not in the mind of James of Molay who in 1293 became the Templars' new Grand Master. He had spent thirty years in the order, much of it in Outremer, and his vision for the Templars was that they should take the lead in a new crusade. The fall of Acre did not seem like the decisive end of things, more an interlude, and there were expectations that the mainland would be regained. The Templars had established their new headquarters on Cyprus, and they still held the tiny island of Ruad (Arwad) just two miles off the coast of Syria opposite Tortosa, and from these places James of Molay envisioned that the counterattack against the Mamelukes would begin.

The inauguration of James of Molay as Grand Master of the Templars, by the nineteenth-century painter François-Marius Granet

Meanwhile on the mainland there were numerous local insurrections against Mameluke rule, which was brutal and repressive. Already in 1291, while Sultan al-Ashraf Khalil was busy fighting the Crusaders at Acre and elsewhere along the coast, Shia Muslims living in the northern part of the Bekaa valley and in the mountains northeast of Beirut had joined with Druze in an uprising against the Sunni Mamelukes which was finally crushed only in 1308.

Across Palestine, Syria and Lebanon, the Christian denominations survived but were greatly diminished. Muslims taunted the native Christians, saying that the failure of Christ to save them against the Mameluke onslaught proved that he was just a man; so demoralised were many Christians in the East that they converted to Islam. Things were particularly difficult for the Maronites. They had been condemned by the Church as heretics in the seventh century for their belief not in the single nature of Christ, Monophysitism, but in the single will of Christ, Monothelitism, but in 1182 the Crusaders helped bring them into communion with the Catholic Church at Rome. Over fifty thousand Maronites were said to have died fighting alongside the Crusaders during the twelfth and thirteenth centuries to defend Outremer against the Muslims. When the Crusaders left, some Maronites went with them to Cyprus, but those who remained never surrendered their connection with Rome, despite persecution by the Mameluke jihad. Instead they escaped into the mountains of northern Lebanon where surnames such as Franjieh, meaning Frank, and Salibi, meaning Crusader, are current to this day.

Nor had the Mongols gone away. Since their defeat at the hands of the Mamelukes in 1260 they had shown an interest in forming an alliance with the Christians in the West, and indeed the conversion of two Mongol emissaries at the Council of Lyons in 1274 had raised hopes that the Mongols might convert wholesale to Christianity. Twice, in 1281 and 1299, the Mongols advanced into northern Syria, and when news came from the West in 1300 of a new crusade, the Mongols offered the Christians the Holy Land if they would help them beat the Mamelukes.

Waiting for the Mongols

Eager to take the initiative in recovering the Holy Land, in 1294 James of Molay travelled from Cyprus to the West to promote the Templars as the vanguard of a new crusade. He received encouragement from Pope Boniface VIII in Rome and King Edward I in London and practical assistance too, with both Pope and king making it easier for the Templars to raise new funds in Europe in order to rebuild their forces after their terrible recent losses at Acre and elsewhere in Outremer. Foodstuffs and treasure were shipped from European ports to the Templars in Cyprus and galleys were bought from Venice, part of the war fleet that the Templars would need to lead the attacks against the Syrian and Egyptian coasts.

The Mongols, led by Hulagu, a grandson of Genghis Khan, captured and destroyed Baghdad in 1258 and put to death the Abbasid caliph. For a time the West looked upon the Mongols as possible allies against Islam.

A wave of excited anticipation swept across Europe in 1300 at the prospect of this new expedition to the East. The mood was reminiscent of those days when Pope Urban II had preached the First Crusade. The Mongols had invaded deep into Syria the year before and the Mamelukes had withdrawn, and there were rumours that Jerusalem had fallen into Mongol hands. Being the 1300th anniversary of the birth of Christ, the Pope declared this to be a jubilee year, promising full remission of sins to those who visited the Basilica of Saint Peter in Rome. Two hundred thousand pilgrims answered his call and were welcomed by a triumphant Pope Boniface sitting on the throne of Constantine the Great and holding the symbols of temporal dominion, the sword, the sceptre and the crown, and bellowing to the crowd, 'I am Caesar!' In the familiar battle between the Church and the secular claims of kings, no one could be left in doubt that the Pope was proclaiming the universal jurisdiction of the Church over the monarchs of the West and celebrating the victory yet to come over the infidels in the East.

In the summer of 1300 the Templars, together with the Hospitallers and the king of Cyprus, launched a series of probing attacks against Alexandria and Rosetta, and at Acre, Tortosa and Maraclea. These were preliminaries to a planned joint operation with the Mongols, and they were followed up in November by a combined Templar, Hospitaller and Lusignan force from Cyprus, about 600 knights in all, which was landed on the island of Ruad opposite Tortosa; this, together with Athlit, had been the last stronghold abandoned by the Templars in 1291. From there they made further raids against Tortosa, waiting for the Mongols to appear; instead in the face of a Mameluke threat the Crusaders withdrew to Cyprus, and when the Mongols finally did appear in February 1301 it was too late.

Nevertheless, later in that year the Templars returned to Ruad, this time establishing a considerable force on the island and rebuilding its defences. In preparation for a serious assault on the Syrian mainland, they garrisoned Ruad with 120 knights, 500 archers and 400 servants, almost half the number of Templar knights and auxiliaries as would normally have defended the entire Kingdom of Jerusalem in the twelfth century. Possibly they were waiting for the Mongols to return; instead

The island of Ruad off the Syrian coast was the last redoubt of the Templars in Outremer. Their castle can be seen to the left of centre

they found themselves isolated on their tiny island against which the Mamelukes sent a fleet of sixteen ships in 1302. A prolonged siege and repeated attacks finally wore down the starving Templars, who surrendered on condition of safe conduct, a promise that was betrayed, the Templars being slaughtered or sold into slavery.

Philip IV, the Most Christian King

Despite this setback in the East, Pope Boniface VIII was no less adamant about his claims of Papal supremacy in the West, which he reinforced with a bull in 1303 called *Unam Sanctam*. This asserted that there was only one holy (*unam sanctam*) Catholic Church, and that to attain salvation it was necessary to submit to the Pope in all matters both spiritual and material. The bull was in response to various trespasses against the authority of the Church that had been committed by King Philip IV of France, often known as Philip the Fair for his golden locks if nothing else, who was forever in need of money to finance the expansion of his kingdom and make war against Flanders and England, and so imposed taxes against the clergy. To Philip this was no different to raising taxes for a crusade, for he ruled with a divine mission; in 1297 he had obtained a sainthood for his grandfather, the crusading Louis IX, and was convinced that France was the chosen kingdom of God. In effect the conflict was between the universalist claims of the Church and the new phenomenon of nationalism as asserted by the king of France, both claiming to have God on their side. The Pope might be the Vicar of God, but Philip, according to his admirers, was 'more than a man, wholly divine', and 'the most Christian king of France'.

When Philip still showed no sign of repentance nor of bowing to the Pope's will, Boniface prepared a bull of excommunication against the king and his minister William of Nogaret. But before it could be published a force of French soldiers led by William of Nogaret himself burst into the Pope's summer palace at Agnani in the hills southeast of Rome with the aim of taking Boniface as prisoner back to France to stand trial on charges of heresy, sodomy and the murder of the previous Pope. Boniface, who was guarded by only a handful of Templars and Hospitallers, challenged his enemies to kill him, saying, 'Here is my neck, here is my head.' But Boniface had been born at Agnani and the townsfolk rallied to him; and before his captors could do more than slap him around and beat him up, they rushed to his defence and drove the French out. He was a broken man, however, and a month later when he died in Rome any serious pretension of the Catholic Church to universal dominion over spiritual and material affairs died with him. The age had truly begun of European nation states led, whatever their religious claims, by secular leaders with secular aims.

Pope Clement's New Crusade, King Philip's New Order

After the death of Boniface, the College of Cardinals elected a new Pope, but he died within a year. After long deliberation and pressure from Philip IV, the College produced a Frenchman who came to the Papal throne in 1305 as Clement V. Never throughout his Papacy did Clement set foot in Rome nor indeed Italy; instead he moved between Lyons and Poitiers until March 1309 when he set up court at Avignon in Provence, which at that time technically lay outside the jurisdiction of the kings of France. Clement then went on to pack the College of Cardinals with Frenchmen; not surprisingly the next six Popes all resided at Avignon, and all were French.

This did not mean that Clement V was a puppet of Philip IV, rather the new Pope understood that if he was to achieve his Papal ambitions it would not be, as Boniface had insisted in *Unam Sanctam*, by trying to make Philip submit to his authority but by cultivating their relationship and securing Philip's cooperation. Clement's great ambition was a new crusade, but it would need the collaboration and leadership of the French king. The proposed venture had its difficulties, however, not least because since the fall of Ruad the Mongols had converted en masse to Islam, not to Christianity as had been hoped.

Another difficulty was presented by Philip himself. Clement succeeded in persuading the king to take the cross at the end of December 1305; he freed Philip from the distraction of local conflict by negotiating a peace between the French king and King Edward I of England; and he diverted 10 per cent of the Church's income in France to Philip's coffers to finance the new crusade. But in Philip's view a prerequisite for a successful crusade was the merging of the two military orders, the Templars and the Hospitallers. Moreover, Philip would command the new order; it would become an instrument of France, for Philip's propagandists also insisted that eventually his command should pass to one of his sons who likewise should succeed him as king of Jerusalem.

Then again, there was a large element of hypocrisy in these French plans; recovering the Holy Land was not really Philip's priority, rather his ambition was to conquer the Christian Byzantine Empire and to establish himself on the ancient imperial throne at Constantinople.

The Last Days

In May 1307 Pope Clement met with the Templar and Hospitaller Grand Masters at his court in France where they submitted their own views on the proposed crusade and the unification of the orders. The comments made by the Grand Master of the Hospitallers, Fulk of

Villaret, about the merging of the orders do not survive, but it seems that he was opposed as his proposal for the crusade assumed that the Hospitallers and the Templars would operate independently. Fulk favoured a small initial expedition to the East, a policy the Hospitallers in fact pursued in June of that very same year when they seized the island of Rhodes, which had been a Byzantine possession, an enterprise that gave them a well-fortified and independent state of their own. A large crusade, went Fulk's argument, should follow only after forward bases had been secured.

But after the Templars' experience of the failure at Ruad, James of Molay opposed a small-scale

Clement V depicted in Andrea Buonaiuti's fresco, The Triumph of Thomas Aquinas, in Santa Maria Novella, Florence

expedition and wanted an all-out crusade. This meant calling on the kings of England, Germany, Sicily, Spain and France to raise an army of between 12,000 and 15,000 knights and 5000 soldiers on foot. This enormous force was to be raised secretly and transported on Venetian, Genoese and other Italian ships to Cyprus, from where it was to be launched against the coast of Palestine. James of Molay's plan was based on a serious and realistic assessment of the military problems facing a crusade aimed at the recovery of the Holy Land, though he knew that this was not in line with popular opinion, which wanted the rhetoric of crusade without the effort or commitment, and moreover it flew in the face of Philip's hypocritical intentions.

On the matter of uniting the two orders, James of Molay was also unaccommodating. He admitted that there could be some advantages in the merger, principally that a united order would be stronger. But he also pointed out that the question had been raised before, only to be rejected. Competition between the Templars and the Hospitallers made the orders more effective, he said, as it provided the stimulus for each to outdo the other; nor did one duplicate the functions of the other, rather they were complementaries, placing different emphases on providing alms, transporting men and supplies across the sea, protecting pilgrims and Crusaders, and making war against the infidel.

Unfortunately, for the Templars there was no hope of the sort of mass crusade envisioned by James of Molay. The Hospitallers had shown a keener awareness of current realities by going for the lesser option, one which all but guaranteed their survival by creating a state of their own on Rhodes. The Templars once again were left in limbo and were now increasingly the victims of attacks on their seeming idleness.

The Templars, wrote Rostan Berenguier, a poet of Marseilles at around this time, 'waste this money which is intended for the recovery of the Holy Sepulchre on cutting a fine figure in the world; they deceive people with their idle trumpery, and offend God; since they and the Hospital have for so long allowed the false Turks to remain in possession of Jerusalem and Acre; since they flee faster than the holy hawk; it is a pity, in my view, that we do not rid ourselves of them for good.'

After his meeting with the Pope, James of Molay travelled to Paris where on 12 October 1307 his apparent intimacy with the royal family was evident for all to see when he walked in procession holding one of the pall cords at the funeral of Philip IV's sister, Catherine of Courtenay. Other Templar leaders, usually based in Cyprus, were also in Paris at this time. However, at dawn on the following day, Friday 13 October, James of Molay was arrested by the king's men, led by William of Nogaret.

Philip's order for the arrest of the Templar leadership in Paris and of every Templar throughout France had been circulated secretly the month before: 'A bitter thing, a lamentable thing,' went the opening lines of the order, dated 14 September, 'a thing which is horrible to contemplate, terrible to hear of, a detestable crime, an execrable evil, an abominable work, a detestable disgrace, a thing almost inhuman, indeed set apart from all humanity.'

The Trial

A Highly Efficient Affair

The Templars were taken quite by surprise when Philip IV's officers came for them in the early hours of the morning of Friday 13 October 1307. They were arrested simultaneously throughout France – about 2000 men in all, from knights down to the most humble agricultural workers and household servants. There was no resistance. Most of the Templars were unarmed and many were middle aged or even elderly, and except for the Paris Temple their houses were unfortified. The arrests were made in the name of the Inquisition and the Templars were all brought to Paris where they were imprisoned in their own headquarters.

The efficiency of the operation probably benefited from previous raids when King Philip struck against Italian bankers resident in France in 1291 and against Jews in 1306, in each case arresting them, throwing them out of the country and seizing their property and their money. A few Templars did escape, about twenty-four it seems, though only one of any importance, Gerard of Villiers, the master of France. Several were apprehended later, despite disguising themselves by a change of dress and shaving off their beards; some had gone to ground in the countryside, one was picked up off the streets of Paris where he was living as a beggar, and another fled to England where he was arrested later. The medieval world was very hard on fugitives, and it is unlikely that many could have survived for long.

Accusations and Defamation

The charge against the Templars was heresy. When being inducted into the order, initiates were required to deny Christ, spit on the cross and place obscene kisses about the body of their receptor. They were also obliged to indulge in sexual relations with other members of the order if requested, and they wore a small belt which had been consecrated by touching a strange idol which looked like a human head with a long beard called Baphomet (possibly an Old French distortion of Mohammed).

At their trial, the Templars were accused of defiling the image of Christ on the Cross

The arrest and charging of the Templars was unusual in that though authorised by the Papal Inquisitor in France, the action was effected not by the Church but by the king. The normal procedure in heresy cases at this time was for the Church to make the arrests and try the accused heretics under Church law, only releasing them to the secular authorities for punishment if this was the verdict of the court. Yet here was a military order which for nearly two hundred years had owed its loyalty directly and solely to the Papacy, from which it had enjoyed complete protection, and suddenly its brothers were arraigned by a secular power. This alone must have come as a shock to the arrested Templars.

That Philip was able to arrest and charge the Templars was owed to a loophole in the law going back to the time of the Cathars and their trials nearly eighty years before. So serious was the spread of the Cathar heresy that in 1230 Pope Honorius III had bestowed extraordinary powers on the Inquisitor in France, extending his reach even to the exempt orders, the Templars, the Hospitallers and Saint Bernard's Cistercians, whenever there was a suspicion of heresy. After the Cathar heresy was eradicated this grant of powers was forgotten by the Papacy, but it was never revoked. This meant that the Templars, though otherwise untouchable, were vulnerable to the charge of heresy – a discovery made by Philip IV's assiduous lawyers, who now used it to devastating effect.

Heresy was the one possible charge that the king could successfully level against the Templars, and so heresy it had to be. The royal lawyers gathered information about the inner life of the Templar order with the aim of selecting and extrapolating from their proper context those elements which could be presented as crimes against religion. These were then put together in such a form that they created the impression of a coherent heretic creed. The royal lawyers then presented this evidence to the French Inquisitor, a Franciscan called William of Paris who was in connivance with the king, who denounced the Templars as heretics.

The accusations against the Templars were also calculated to exploit a degree of residual hostility towards the order after the fall of Acre and the loss of the Holy Land in 1291, while the mere charge of heresy had the immediate effect of blackening the order's reputation. No time was wasted in mounting the propaganda campaign against the Templars: the king's minister William of Nogaret announced the heresy before a large crowd in Paris, and the Franciscans spread the news in their sermons under instructions from the Inquisitor, Brother William of Paris.

The Charges Against the Templars

The charges made against the Templars at the time of their arrest on 13 October 1307 can be summarised as follows:

✠ The Templars held their reception ceremonies and chapter meetings in secret and at night.

✠ During the reception ceremony initiates were required to deny Christ;

✠ to spit, piss or trample on the cross or images of Christ;

✠ to exchange kisses with the receiving official on the mouth, navel, base of the spine, and sometimes on the buttocks or the penis; and

✠ to agree to submit to homosexual practises as required within the order, which practised institutionalised sodomy.

✠ The brothers did not believe in the sacraments and the Templar priests did not consecrate the host.

✠ The brothers worshipped an idol in the form of a head or a cat called Baphomet.

✠ Though not ordained by the Church, high Templar officials, including the Grand Master, absolved brothers of their sins.

✠ The Templars failed to make charitable gifts as they were meant to do, nor did they practise hospitality.

The King's Motives

It is quite possible that Philip and his government really did believe the accusations of heresy that they made against the Templars, and as will be seen there were some grounds for suspicion. This was an age when people believed that the devil was constantly trying to spread corruption throughout Christian society. By attacking the weak points of the social structure the devil aimed to cause the collapse of society altogether. Therefore the task of the faithful was to be vigilant, to expose evil, and to cut out corruption at an early stage before the whole of society succumbed. Philip had given himself the role of a sacred king ruling over a holy country; if there was anything about the Templars that smacked of heresy, the king and his supporters could easily have taken this as a danger that needed to be immediately eradicated. As for the Templars posing a physical threat to the king, there is no evidence for this and it seems unlikely: they were involved with no faction, and they were largely unarmed. Nevertheless, their protection under the Pope and their immunity from the secular law would likely have seemed an offence to Philip's notions of absolute sovereignty, and there had already been a clash of sovereign claims between Philip and Pope Boniface VIII.

But Philip's most powerful immediate motive was the desire, indeed the need, to get his hands on the wealth of the Templars. He had already stolen from the Italian bankers and the Jews, he had debased the currency, and it was his exactions from the clergy that provoked his first confrontation with Boniface VIII. His wars against England and in Flanders had cost him a great deal of money, and he had inherited a huge debt from his father's wars. The Templars were a tempting target, for unlike the Hospitallers, whose wealth was entirely in land, the Templars from their banking activities also had liquid wealth which the king could quickly and easily grab. By accusing them of heresy Philip could turn the Templars into reprehensible religious outsiders like the Jews, against whom persecution was readily rationalised.

Many foreign observers, especially those in northern Italy where there was a more complete understanding of the power of money than anywhere else in fourteenth-century Europe, were convinced that getting his hands on the Templars' cash and precious metals was the primary motive for Philip's attack. Dante famously attacked the king's actions in *Purgatorio*, the second book of *Divine Comedy*, written in the immediate aftermath of the Templars' arrest:

> *I see the second Pilate's cruel mood*
> *Grow so insatiate that without decree*
> *His greedy sails upon the Temple intrude.*

from *The Portable Dante*, ed. Paolo Milano, Penguin, 1977

Spies, Tortures and Confessions

The order went out on 14 September 1307 to make the arrests that took place at dawn a month later, on 13 October, but the case had been prepared years before. French government spies had joined the Templars to discover its inner workings and to gather anything with which they could be slandered. The sinister force behind this was William of Nogaret, who in 1303 had taken part in the attempt to overthrow Pope Boniface VIII, since when he had remained excommunicated. William's family had suffered persecution because his grandfather had been a Cathar, but by his cleverness and cynicism he had risen in Philip's court and was ennobled in 1299, becoming the king's Keeper of the Seals and his right-hand man. These facts may have contributed to William of

Anything was permitted in torture provided blood was not drawn and bones were not broken. One of the tortured Templars said he would have been willing 'to kill God' to end his torment

Nogaret's contempt for the Papacy and his unscrupulous ambition to make France the greatest power in the world.

Many of those arrested were simple men, not battle-hardened Templar knights, but ploughmen, artisans and servants who helped keep the order running, and these would have succumbed to torture or even the threat of torture fairly quickly. The knights themselves, however, had been long prepared for the worst in Outremer, for that day when they might be captured and thrown into a Muslim dungeon, be tortured or face execution unless they abjured their faith. And yet these too rapidly and all but unanimously confessed. The tortures could be savage: scores died undergoing what was called 'ecclesiastical procedure', which was meant not to break limbs or draw blood but routinely included being kept chained in isolation and fed on bread and water; being drawn on the rack until the joints were dislocated; being raised over a beam by a rope tied to the wrists that had been bound behind the victim's back; and having fat rubbed into the soles of the feet, which were then placed before a fire – one tortured Templar priest being so badly burnt that the bones fell out of his feet. Another of the accused said that he would have agreed 'to kill God' to stop his torment.

Yet physical torture was far from the only element in the confessions. Instead, one of the worst problems for the Templars was the overturn of their spiritual and social universe. They had spent their lives in the enclosed world of a military elite group to which they owed absolute loyalty and were constantly reminded of the support they in turn received from the rest of society. But now they were reviled, told that they were heretics, and no support seemed to be forthcoming from any quarter. The walls, ceiling and floor of their enclosed world had fallen away leaving them exposed, bewildered and lost. Under these conditions it is not surprising that James of Molay, the Grand Master, and Hugh of Pairaud, whose rank of Visitor made him the most elevated Templar in Western Christendom after James of Molay, were both among the near unanimity of Templars who rapidly confessed – and indeed there is some uncertainty whether the Grand Master was ever tortured.

The further truth of the confessions was that they were gained quickly because the Templars were accused of something that actually

James of Molay appears before the Inquisition in Paris

existed and to which they could admit, though it had been distorted in the hands of the Inquisitor. This was the fruit of the information gathered by the government spies.

On 19 October 1307 the Inquisitorial hearings began at the Paris Temple. On 25 and 26 October James of Molay was called to testify. His confession was recorded and sent to the Pope as proof of heresy. In less than two weeks since their arrest, the Templars' honour had been stained forever, and the news of their guilt reverberated throughout the whole of Christendom.

The Pope Acts

Pope Clement V was stunned when, on 14 October, a messenger brought the news to his court at Poitiers that the Templars had been arrested the previous day. Though the action had been taken on the nominal authority of the French Inquisitor, there was no doubt that the arrests represented an attack on the Papacy and the Catholic Church by the secular monarchy of France. The matter concerned not the Templars only; the survival of the Papacy was at stake, and Clement immediately summoned all his cardinals for an emergency meeting of the Curia which began on 16 October and lasted three days.

Another Pope at another time might have excommunicated Philip. But Clement was doubly vulnerable – after Philip's coup against Boniface in Italy, and as a resident on French soil. Instead Clement issued a bull, *Ad Preclarus Sapientie*, which gave Philip a way out: it said that the king had acted unlawfully and had tarnished the reputation of his grandfather Saint Louis, but he could make up for his rashness by handing the Templars and their possessions over to the Church. To achieve this, in November the Pope sent two cardinals to Paris to take into custody the men and property of the Temple. But the king had made himself absent and his counsellors refused access to the Templars, let alone handing them over to the Church, arguing that a Papal inter-vention was superfluous as they were self-confessed heretics.

When the cardinals went back to Poitiers with the news that the French monarchy was flatly refusing to obey an express command of the Pope, the Curia was plunged into crisis. According to one report, ten cardinals threatened to resign if the Pope showed himself to be a puppet of the French king. Clement was faced with replacing the cardinals at the cost of causing a schism in the Church, or he could excommunicate Philip and fall victim to a royal coup.

But the Pope found another way and, acting with some dexterity within the difficult constraints of his situation, he did what he could to put himself in charge of events. First on 22 November 1307 he issued a bull, *Pastoralis Praeeminentiae*, asking all the kings and princes of Christendom to arrest the Templars in their lands and to hold their property in safekeeping for the Church. In this way proceedings were initiated against the Templars in England, Iberia, Germany, Italy and Cyprus – but in the name of the Church. By doing this the Pope was delivering an implied ultimatum to King Philip, that what was true in the rest of Europe must also be so in France. He praised the French king for his good faith and religious zeal, but Clement was making it clear that the case against the Templars was being removed from the king's authority and was now being taken into the hands of the Papacy.

As for the crisis that had arisen when the king's officials rebuffed the two cardinals, the Pope simply pretended that the incident had never happened. Instead in December he sent the two cardinals back to Paris as if for the first time. But now they brought with them the power, granted by the Pope, to excommunicate Philip on the spot and to place the whole of France under an interdict if the king persisted in his refusal to hand over the Templars. The move was effective: on 24 December 1307 Philip wrote to the Pope that he would hand over the Templars.

On about 27 December 1307 the cardinals met James of Molay and other leading Templars, who denied everything to which they had formerly confessed. According to one source the Grand Master said that he had confessed only under heavy torture, and he showed the wounds on his body, though it is not clear if this source can be trusted. Nevertheless, retracting the confessions was a risky move because under the rules of the Inquisition relapsed heretics were handed over to the secular authorities to be burnt. That the Grand Master and others took that risk shows that they were confident that a great injustice was about to be overturned. Certainly James of Molay's retraction marked a turning point in the trial.

Deadlock Between Pope and King

Although the Church was granted this brief access to the leading Templars, Philip had still not transferred any Templars to Church control. In February 1308 Pope Clement suspended the Inquisitor William of Paris and the whole French Inquisition. In reply the king's officials tried to force the Pope to reopen the trial by marshalling public and theological opinion in France. The chief agent in this was William of Nogaret, who instigated a campaign of libel, slander and physical intimidation against the Pope; Clement was threatened with deposition and menaces were directed against his family. But Clement stood his ground against the king, and to settle their differences they met in May and June at Poitiers. There they agreed that the Pope would set up two kinds of inquiry, one by a Papal commission to look into the Templars as an institution, the other consisting of a series of provincial councils, each supervised by the bishop of a diocese, to investigate the guilt or innocence of individual Templars. For his part Philip finally consented to release a number of Templars into the physical custody of the Church so that they could be interviewed directly by the Pope.

Philip chose seventy-two Templars from among his prisoners in Paris and sent them, chained to one another and under a military escort, by wagon to Poitiers. Most of these were renegades or at best sergeants selected to make a poor impression on the Pope, and with them he sent the Grand Master and four other high officers of the Templar order. But suddenly when the convoy reached the royal castle of Chinon the seventy-two were sent on to Poitiers but the leaders were detained, the king claiming they were too ill to undertake the journey. This was an obvious lie as Chinon lay not far from Poitiers. The king probably feared that if the Pope interviewed the Templar leaders he would find them free of heresy and grant them absolution.

The Pope Hears the Strange Testimony of the Templars

The Pope ignored Philip's deceit over the Templar leaders held at Chinon. Instead of walking into a destructive confrontation with the king, Clement got on with examining those Templars who had been sent to him. From 28 June to 1 July 1308 the seventy-two Templars were heard at Poitiers by a special commission of cardinals and by the Pope himself. On 2 July Clement granted absolution to the Templars, who had confessed and had asked for the forgiveness of the Church. Had the Templars been found guilty, the Pope would never have forgiven them; but on the other hand had they been innocent he would have acquitted them without requiring any show of repentance.

The Templars were not heretics, Clement had decided. An account of the examination was kept in the form of marginal notes made at the time. Damaged and mislaid in the Vatican archives, these notes have only recently been discovered, deciphered and published. Together with the Chinon Parchment, they show how the Pope came to understand the true nature of the Templars' strange practises.

The Templars attended mass, they went to Holy Communion and confession, and they complied with their liturgical duties. But they also confessed to the Pope that at their entrance ceremony they denied Christ and spat on the cross, though they insisted that they had never consented to this in their souls and as soon as possible had confessed to a priest and asked for absolution. The Pope found these induction rituals too confused to be taken seriously; at one moment the novice spat on the cross, but then kissed it in adoration; and the novice denied the divinity of Christ saying, 'You, who are God, I deny', which was no denial at all. If the Templars were heretics, they were the most inconsistent and unconvincing adherents any heresy could have. The Templars had fallen into peculiar ways and needed reform, but that, decided the Pope, was all.

In fact Clement had already heard something of these bizarre practises from James of Molay himself when the two met at Poitiers in May 1307, five months before the arrests. In the Pope's words, the Grand Master had told him of 'many strange and unheard-of things' which had caused Clement 'great sorrow, anxiety and upset of heart'. The Grand Master feared that these initiation ceremonies, which had been going on for a century or more, were getting out of hand, and the Pope agreed to instigate an inquiry to root out these practises before they erupted into scandal. In August 1307 Clement had also written to King Philip on this count, telling him that 'we could scarcely bring our mind to believe what was said at that time'. But Philip's spies within the Templars had informed the king of these practises long before that, providing Philip with the material that he cynically manipulated with such devastating effect.

Clement's understanding of these strange Templar practises was that they were simply an entrance ritual, a custom which was common, with variations, in every military elite since early antiquity. This was a secret rite of passage after the formal ceremony, a compulsory test to which all new Temple brothers had to submit, a peculiar tradition (*modus ordinis nostri*) which demonstrated to the initiate the violence that the Templars were likely to suffer at the hands of their Muslim captors, and how they would be compelled to deny Christ and to spit on the cross. The aim of the test was to strengthen the souls of recruits, and it took the form of a very realistic performance. To this first part was added another test, that of kissing the master who had received him on the lower spine, on the navel and finally on the mouth; its purpose was to teach the novice that in all circumstances whatsoever he owed absolute obedience to his superiors. This seems to have been the original and true form of the ritual, but the local masters made changes, and in time this secret ritual became quite coarse and sometimes even violent.

The Templars were not heretics but they were not innocent either for they had actually denied the divinity of Christ even if it was all a pretence. Apostasy could be forgiven but sinners had to repent and submit to harsh penance. That was how Clement dealt with the seventy-two Templars he interviewed at Poitiers. But he could not do the same for the leaders without seeing them, and though he issued a formal summons for the appearance of James of Molay and the other leading Templars, this was refused by the king with the repeated claim that they were ill.

The Mystery of Chinon

In the summer of 1308 the Pope absolved James of Molay and the other Templar leaders held prisoner at Chinon. Seemingly no proper report of this hearing had survived, and until recently it was doubted that any such event had taken place – that is until the discovery of the Chinon Parchment in the Vatican archives in 2001 and its publication by the Vatican in 2007. This showed unequivocally that despite the chief Templars being held prisoner by the king, a hearing had somehow been arranged within the royal castle at Chinon.

This was set in motion on 14 August 1308 when three cardinals left the Papal court at Poitiers for an unknown destination. They were Etienne of Suisy, Landolfo Brancacci and Bérenger Frédol, the last being one of the outstanding canon lawyers of his time and a nephew of the Pope; secretly they formed a special apostolic commission of inquiry with Clement's full authority. Two or three days later the cardinals arrived at Chinon where, in addition to the royal jailer, there were two important royal officials, identified in French records only by their initials, but who are thought to have been William of Nogaret and a lawyer who acted on his behalf called William of Plaisians.

If there were any hidden negotiations between the parties at Chinon, the fact is unknown. Instead what followed seems to have taken place under the noses of the king's officials but without their knowledge. According to the Chinon Parchment, no royal officials attended the hearings that took place at Chinon from 17 to 20 August; they were held quickly and presumably in all secrecy to avoid the intervention of the royal officers. Apart from the three cardinals and the Templars they examined, the others at the hearing were a handful of witnesses, all clerks and humble people, none of them closely linked to King Philip. This at last was the Papal trial of the Templar leaders; it was entirely a Church affair.

During the first three days of the trial the three cardinals examined Raimbald of Caron, the master of Cyprus; Geoffrey of Charney, master of Normandy; Geoffrey of Gonneville, master of Poitou and Aquitaine; and Hugh of Pairaud, the Visitor. On the final day, 20 August, they heard the testimony of the Grand Master, James of Molay. The details varied between the testimonies, but taken all together they amounted to a restatement of the practises previously mentioned in testimony by the seventy-two Templars at Poitiers.

When the cardinals reported back to the Pope, Clement accepted the explanation of James of Molay and the other Templar leaders that the charges against them of sodomy and blasphemy were due to a misunderstanding of the knighthood's arcane rituals, which had their origins in their struggle against the Muslims in Outremer. Denying Christ and spitting on the cross, as well as kissing other men's behinds, were understood to simulate the kind of humiliation and torture that a knight might be subjected to by the enemy if captured. They were taught to abuse their own religion 'in words only, not in spirit'.

Noting that the Templars had asked his pardon, the Pope wrote, 'We hereby decree that they are absolved by the Church and may again receive Christian sacraments.' Of James of Molay in particular the Pope recorded that after hearing what he had to say, 'We concluded to extend the mercy of absolution for these acts to Brother James of Molay, the Grand Master of the order, who denounced in our presence the described heresy and any other heresy, and swore in person on the Lord's Holy Gospel, and humbly asked for the mercy of absolution, restoring him to unity with the Church and reinstating him to communion of the faithful and sacraments of the Church.'

At this point Clement was still trying to save the Templars as an order; his object was reform, and then probably to combine the Templars with the Hospitallers. But the Pope failed to make the details of his absolution public because the scandal of the Templars had aroused extreme passions; Clement was still trying to avoid either a confrontation with Philip or a schism within the Church.

The Chinon Parchment

Everything written about the trial – and beliefs – of the Knights Templar has become redundant since the discovery of the Chinon Parchment. Uncertain and unexplained circumstances surrounding the fall of the order had led to a variety of theories about their activities and the motives of others involved in their trial. The accepted view of historians, over the centuries, had tended to be that the Templars were not heretics but that they were guilty of something – but of what? Historians also saw Pope Clement V as the pliant and weak creature of Philip IV of France, with whom he was thought to have colluded to destroy the Templars and seize their fortune.

The Chinon Parchment records the Pope's verdict that the Templars were not guilty of heresy. But it was mislaid in the Secret Vatican Archives and went undiscovered until 2001.

The discovery of the Chinon Parchment has thrown a new and clarifying light on these mysteries and misconceptions. The parchment is a contemporary account of the testimony of James of Molay and other Templar leaders at a secret Papal hearing held at the royal castle of Chinon from 17 to 20 August 1308. The document reveals that the Pope found no heresy among the Templars and granted absolution to its leaders. Indeed, he fought with some determination to protect the Templars against the French king. Fatally, however, the Pope delayed making his absolution public owing to the extreme passions of the time. And so Phillip IV was able to have James of Molay and the other Templar leaders put to death before the Pope's verdict could be published.

Subsequently the Chinon Parchment was mislabelled and misplaced amid the labyrinthine files of the Secret Archive until Barbara Frale, an Italian researcher at the Vatican School of Paleontology, found it and recognised its significance. She deciphered its tangled and coded writing and published her findings in the *Journal of Medieval History* in 2004. This was followed in 2007 by a facsimile publication of the parchment by the Vatican itself – no doubt eager to avoid the appearance of yet more conspiracy amid the fallout from their fictional machinations in Dan Brown's bestselling novel *The Da Vinci Code*.

The Papal Examination

The Papal Examination of James of Molay at Chinon castle 20 August 1308 as translated from the Chinon Parchment:

Then on the twentieth day of the month, in our presence, and in the presence of notaries and the same witnesses, brother-knight James of Molay, Grand Master of the Order of Knights Templar, appeared personally and having sworn in the form and manner indicated above, and having been diligently questioned, said it has been forty-two years or thereabouts since he was received as a brother of the said Order by brother-knight Hubert de Pérraud, at the time Visitor of France and Poitou, in Beune, diocese of Autun, in the chapel of the local Templar commandery of that place.

Concerning the way of his initiation into the order, he said that having given him the cloak the receptor showed to him the cross and told him that he should denounce the God whose image was depicted on that cross, and that he should spit on the cross. Which he did, although he did not spit on the cross, but near it, according to his words. He also said that he performed this denunciation in words, not in spirit. Regarding the sin of sodomy, the worshipped head and the practise of illicit kisses, he, diligently questioned, said that he knew nothing of that.

When he was asked whether he had confessed to these things due to a request, reward, gratitude, favour, fear, hatred or persuasion by someone else, or the use of force, or fear of impending torture, he replied that he did not. When he was asked whether he, after being apprehended, was submitted to any questioning or torture, he replied that he was not.

After this, we decided to extend the mercy of absolution for these acts to brother James of Molay, the Grand Master of the said order, who in the form and manner described above had denounced in our presence the described and any other heresy, and swore in person on the Lord's Holy Gospel, and humbly asked for the mercy of absolution, restoring him to unity with the Church and reinstating him to communion of the faithful and the sacraments of the Church.

The Templars Rally

In March 1309 the Papal court established itself at Avignon, which in those days was not within the kingdom of France and had the added benefit of offering the Pope a quick escape over the Italian border. In November 1309 the Papal commission into the order of the Templars began its sittings; this was the inquiry that Clement had agreed to establish after his meeting with Philip at Poitiers the previous year.

Slowly the accused Templars rallied, and instead of confessing they began mounting a defence. By early May 1310 nearly six hundred Templars were defending their order, and they denied their previous confessions. In contrast to the Cathars, who truly were heretics and went to their deaths for what they believed, not one Templar was prepared to be martyred for the heresies which members of the order were supposed to have guarded so fiercely for so long, quite simply because there was no heresy, only the malignant interpretation put on their practises by a malignant king.

Deeply worried by this growing confidence among the Templars, Philip took drastic action and had the Archbishop of Sens, a royal nominee, reopen his episcopal inquiry against individual Templars in his diocese. Obedient to his king, the archbishop found fifty-four Templars guilty as relapsed heretics – in other words guilty of having revoked their earlier confessions – and handed them over to the secular authorities. On 12 May 1310 in a field outside Paris the fifty-four Templars were burnt at the stake. Yet even after these burnings not all the remaining Templars were cowed nor was their morale completely crushed, though this intimidation by burning did have its effect, and many Templars fell silent or returned to their confessions.

The Suppression of the Templars

Since 1308 Pope Clement had been intending to hold an ecumenical council at Vienne in the Rhone-Alps region of France to consider three great matters: the Templars, the Holy Land and the reform of the Church. Originally scheduled for October 1310, it had to be postponed a year because the Pope's contest with the king of France over the Templars was dragging on. Now in the summer of 1311 Clement had gathered information about the Templars from investigations all round France and abroad to present at the council. What he found was that only in France and in regions under French domination or influence were there substantial confessions from Templars – that is areas where the French authorities and their collaborators had applied ferocious tortures to their victims, or where their testimony was deliberately distorted to turn admitted irregularities into heresy. Clement was becoming eager to wind up the Templar matter before its controversies caused wider and deeper troubles for the Church.

Clement had senior advisors who argued that no time should be wasted on discussion or defence, and that the Pope should use his executive powers to abolish the Templars forthwith. One said that the Templars had 'already caused the Christian name to smell among unbelievers and infidels and have shaken some of the faithful in the stability of their faith'. He added that suppression of the order should take place without delay in case 'the capricious spark of this error ignites in flames, which could burn the whole world'. But then in late October a dramatic event occurred which did much to counter the arguments of those in favour of swift abolition – seven Templars appeared at the council to argue for the defence of the order. The Pope reacted swiftly and had them locked up.

But this was not a matter that the overwhelming majority of the clergy attending the council was prepared to overlook. As Henry Ffykeis, an Englishman attending the council, wrote home to the bishop of Norwich on 27 December 1311: 'Concerning the matter of the Templars there is great debate as to whether they ought in law to be admitted to the defence. The larger part of the prelates, indeed all of them, excepting five or six from the council of the King of France, stand on their behalf. On account of this the Pope is strongly moved against the prelates. The King of France more so; and he is coming in a rage with a great following'. Indeed Philip was soon demonstrating his usual technique of intimidation by appearing at various places upriver from Vienne, creating the powerful sensation in the Pope that the king was about to descend upon him. On 2 March 1312 the king sent a thinly veiled ultimatum to the Pope, reminding him of the crimes and heresies of the Templars, 'Which is why, burning with zeal for the orthodox faith and in case so great an injury done to Christ should remain unpunished, we affectionately, devotedly and humbly ask Your Holiness that you should suppress the aforesaid order'. Just in case Clement did not get the message, on 20 March the king with his brothers, sons and a considerable armed force arrived at Vienne.

On 3 April, having silenced the members of the council on pain of excommunication, and with the King of France sitting at his side, the Pope made public his decision, already committed to writing twelve days earlier in the form of a bull, *Vox in Excelso*, dated 22 March 1312, that the Templars, though not condemned, were suppressed on the grounds that the order was too defamed to carry on. Under the circumstances it was probably the best that Clement could do. Another bull, *Ad Providam*, dated 2 May, granted the Templars' property to the Knights Hospitaller. Soon after, Philip extracted a huge sum of money from the Hospitallers in compensation for his costs in bringing the Templars to trial.

The Burning of James of Molay

The Church had now washed its hands of the Templars. In accordance with Church practise, once it had decided on a defendant's fate he was handed over to the secular authorities for punishment. In this case almost all the Templars in France had been in royal hands all along, and the dispensal of their fates did not require the transfer of their persons. The treatment meted out by the royal authorities to individual Templars varied. Those who had confessed were subjected to penances, and these were sometimes heavy, including lengthy imprisonment. Others who had confessed to nothing or were otherwise of little account were sent to monasteries for the rest of their lives.

The leading Templars, including the Grand Master, had to wait until 18 March 1314 before their cases were disposed of. They might well have expected that their cases had been disposed of long before at Chinon when they received Papal absolution, and almost certainly they would now have been expecting to be treated accordingly. But the hearings at Chinon still remained secret, and instead Hugh of Pairaud, Geoffrey of Gonneville, Geoffrey of Charney and James of Molay were brought for final judgement before a small commission of French cardinals and ecclesiastics at Paris, among them that same archbishop of Sens who had so happily for the king burned fifty-four Templars in May 1310.

The sentence was handed down. On the basis of their earlier confessions, as twisted by the crown, all four men were condemned to harsh and perpetual punishment – in effect to starve and rot in prison until they were released by a lingering death. Hugh of Pairaud and Geoffrey of Gonneville accepted their fate in silence. 'But lo', wrote a chronicler of the time, 'when the cardinals believed that they had imposed an end to the affair, immediately and unexpectedly two of them, namely the Grand Master and the master of Normandy, defending themselves obstinately against the cardinal who had preached the sermon and against the archbishop of Sens, returned to the denial both of the confession as well as everything which they had confessed.'

James of Molay was in his seventies; he and Geoffrey of Charney, the master of Normandy, had been in the king's dungeons for the last seven

*The end of the Templars came on 18 March 1314 when the last Grand Master,
James of Molay, was taken to the Isle de Javiaux in the Seine, just east of
Notre Dame cathedral, and was bound to the stake and burnt to death*

years. For six of those years they had lived under the expectation that
their absolution by the Pope would free them from their nightmare, that
they would live again in sunlight among those loved by the Church and
Christ. But now in the midst of betrayal and despair they refused to give
themselves into perpetual incarceration in a living hell. Loudly protest-
ing their innocence and asserting that the order of the Templars was
pure and holy, James of Molay and Geoffrey of Charney put themselves
into the hands of God.

At once the king ordered that they be condemned as relapsed heretics,
and on that same evening, at Vespers, they were taken to the Ile des
Javiaux, a small island in the Seine east of Notre Dame, and bound to
the stake. The chronicler described their last moments: 'They were seen
to be so prepared to sustain the fire with easy mind and will that they
brought from all those who saw them much admiration and surprise for
the constance of their death and final denial.' The last of the Templars
went to their deaths with courage, in the tradition of their order.

Vatican Backs Templar Link with the Turin Shroud

The Turin Shroud is claimed to be the linen cloth that covered the body of Jesus after the Crucifixion. A relic answering to its description was among the treasures that were taken from Constantinople when the city was sacked by the Fourth Crusade in 1204. In a letter sent the following year to Pope Innocent III, a Byzantine aristocrat complained that 'the Venetians partitioned the treasures of gold, silver and ivory while the French did the same with the relics of the saints and the most sacred of all, the linen in which our Lord Jesus Christ was wrapped after his death and before the resurrection'. But the certain provenance of the Shroud can only be traced back to 1357 when it was displayed in the church at Lirey in the diocese of Troyes by the widow of a French knight called Geoffrey of Charney who, it is said, was the nephew of that same Geoffrey of Charney burnt at the stake with James of Molay. This has led some historians to believe that after the sack of Constantinople the linen relic passed into the hands of the Templars who took it to France, where it formed part of their famous treasure. But is this true?

Remarkably, in April 2009 support came from the Vatican itself, where Barbara Frale, the scholar who discovered the Chinon Parchment, found a further document, this one the testimony of Arnaut Sabbatier, a young Frenchman who entered the order in 1287. As part of his initiation, he said, he was taken to 'a secret place to which only the brothers of the Temple had access', where he was shown 'a long linen cloth on which was impressed the figure of a man' and was told to venerate the image by kissing its feet three times. The Templars had rescued the Shroud to ensure that it did not fall into the hands of heretics such as the Cathars, who claimed that Jesus did not have a true human body but only the appearance of a man and neither died on the Cross nor was resurrected. For their pains they were burnt at the stake.

Not that this discovery has any bearing on the authenticity of the Shroud. The Vatican leaves the question of whether or not the Shroud is a medieval forgery to the faith of believers. But it does suggest that the cloth today known as the Turin Shroud, fake or not, was in the possession of the Templars, that they believed it to be real, and that for a century it played a central part in their initiation ceremonies.

Part 5

The Aftermath

Some have argued, not least masons themselves, that the Freemasons are the descendants of the Templars. George Washington, first president of the United States, was a Freemason, and he wore his Freemason's apron when he laid the foundation stone of the Capitol building in Washington DC.

Survivals

The New Orders

A German pilgrim visiting the Holy Land in 1340 came upon two elderly men in the mountains overlooking the shores of the Dead Sea. They told him they had been Templars, and they recalled for him their last memories of their order, of their fellow knights being slaughtered during the desperate fighting at the fall of Acre in 1291. The two men had been taken captive, and for nearly fifty years they had eked out their lives as woodcutters, entirely cut off from news of Western Christendom. Now, with the help of the pilgrim, they were repatriated to France where they learnt that the order of the Templars was no more, and that the last Grand Master had been burnt at the stake as a heretic. Despite this the two old men were respectfully received at the Papal court at Avignon and were given the means to live out their days in peace.

Few Templars could still have been alive by that time. Some might have been grimly hanging on to life in the royal dungeons of France, others left to live quietly in monasteries on pensions, while some are known to have turned mercenary and to have taken wives. The lifespan of the Order of the Knights Templar coincided almost exactly with the claim of the Papacy to universal spiritual and temporal dominion, but Europe was now entering into a new world of rising nation states. By the time the two old Templars returned to France from the shores of the Dead Sea, their order and the world it had bestrode for two hundred years had become old news.

The Survival of the Hospitallers

It seems unlikely that the Knights Hospitaller were entirely free of strange rituals similar to those practised by the Templars, yet the Hospitallers survived the destruction of the Templars and indeed benefited from their demise by acquiring the greater part of their properties. Possibly they survived Philip IV's avarice and ambition because their headquarters was on Rhodes, though this can hardly be the whole explanation as most of their property was in France. Certainly in 1312 Philip was already making menacing noises about 'reforming' the Hospitallers, and in that same year, as if to put the initiative back into Papal hands, Clement V announced his own inquiry and programme of reforms. But both Philip IV and Clement V died within a year of James of Molay, and it is this that may have saved the Knights Hospitaller.

But though no accusations of heresy, blasphemy or sodomy were made against the Hospitallers, their reputation was in some measure tarnished by the atmosphere of charges made against the Templars. Even Pope Clement VI, the namesake of that earlier Clement who had struggled to save the Templars, was writing sadly in 1343 that it was 'the virtually unanimous and popular opinion of the clergy and laity' that the Hospitallers were doing nothing to advance the interests of Christendom or to promote its faith.

Nevertheless, the Hospitallers held on to Rhodes until it fell to the Ottoman Turks in 1522. They then retreated to Malta, where they withstood a five-month Ottoman siege in 1565, and six years later Hospitaller ships were part of that great Western armada which defeated the Ottoman fleet at Lepanto off the coast of western Greece, the battle that

The Hospitallers captured Rhodes in 1309 and turned it into a formidable fortress that withstood the Muslim onslaught for another two hundred years

finally put into permanent reverse the Muslim aggression that had begun when the Arabs first conquered the Holy Land nine hundred years before. But marooned on Malta, the order of the Knights Hospitaller became enfeebled; in 1792 the French National Assembly confiscated its estates, and in 1798 the Hospitallers offered no resistance when Napoleon came to Malta and after a one-day siege expelled them from the island.

The Hospitallers were dispersed throughout Europe, though they reformed, with the Tsar as Grand Master, in Russia, while in the 1820s the Most Venerable Order of the Hospital of Saint John of Jerusalem was founded in the 1820s with the intention of forming a mercenary army to liberate Greece from Ottoman rule. But this order soon took on an entirely pacific nature devoted to charitable works, as did offshoots and revivals in Britain (where Henry VIII had confiscated the property of the original order), Germany and Italy. The latter, the Sovereign Order of Malta, has its headquarters in Rome and has observer status

The present-day Order of the Hospital of St John in Jerusalem has its headquarters at St John's Gate in London

(as a quasi-sovereign state) at the UN. It has recently returned to Malta, whose government granted it a lease on the Fort Sant Angelo.

In Britain, the modern-day Hospitallers – the (largely Protestant) Order of the Hospital of Saint John of Jerusalem – are best known for their service organisation, the Saint John's Ambulance Brigade. This was established in 1887, though already in 1882 the order had established its Saint John's Eye Hospital in Jerusalem. The order remains active in Britain, the Commonwealth and the USA, and maintains its headquarters at St John's Gate in Clerkenwell, London – in what had been the gatehouse to the medieval English Grand Priory of the Knights Hospitaller.

The Templars in Britain

In 1307, when Philip IV of France ordered the suppression of the Templars, Edward II of England dismissed the charges laid against them as implausible. Despite considerable pressure by the French king and the Pope, Edward resisted the Inquisition, which had no standing in English common law. Eventually each Templar was permitted to make a public statement saying 'I am gravely defamed' by the accusations, and for that reason, not because of any proven guilt, each asked for and was granted reconciliation with the Church and was sent to live peaceably at some monastic foundation. Nor was the king keen to hand over Templar properties to the Church, arguing that they had originally been donated by the English nobility, which was entitled to have them back. Though the Hospitallers did receive some Templar possessions, the king felt free to redistribute much of it as he liked. This reintegration of Templar property into the fabric of English life helps explain why so much of the Templar past survives today.

Scotland was caught up in a series of wars as the days of the Templars came to an end. Robert the Bruce had killed his rival John Comyn, Lord of Badenoch, in 1306, an act which set Scot against Scot even as the Bruce was fighting to keep Scotland free from the English armies under Edward II. Finally the battle of Bannockburn in 1314 – the very year that James of Molay was burnt at the stake – won Scottish independence for centuries to come. In recent years the writers of 'alternative history' have given the Templars a considerable role in these events and have argued for their continued survival 'underground' or disguised as, for example, the Freemasons. These speculations are examined in the following chapter on 'Conspiracies'.

As for the more prosaic world of reality, the fate of the Templars in Scotland was that, as in England, they went unpunished, but their order was dissolved and their land was for the most part handed over to the Hospitallers. The original ownership of the land has not been forgotten, however, for even today such properties are designated in transactions as 'Templarland'.

Spain – the Order of Montesa

The Templars had always been enthusiastically welcomed in Spain for the invaluable assistance they gave in the long struggle to free the Iberian peninsula from Arab occupation. Though the order was found guilty of heresy and other crimes in France, those Templars who were put on trial in Aragon were pronounced innocent.

Despite the protests of King Jaime II of Aragon, Pope Clement's bull suppressing the order could not be averted. But Jaime had no intention of allowing Templar properties in Aragon and Valencia to pass to the

Hospitallers. Instead in 1317, with the permission of the Papacy, he formed the new Order of Montesa – a body not essentially different from that of the Templars – which acquired the old Templar assets and was charged with the defence of the frontier. And so the Templars continued in Spain under another name. Another 175 years would pass before Ferdinand of Aragon and Isabella of Castile drove out the last Muslim invaders when Granada fell to them in 1492, years in which the descendants of the Templars continued to play a vital role. The order declined thereafter and in 1587 Philip II joined the office of Grand Master with that of the crown.

The Order of Christ in Portugal

In Portugal the contribution that the Templars had made to the emergence and independence of the kingdom during its wars against the occupying Muslims was not forgotten. In 1319, with Papal permission, the Portuguese King Diniz reconstituted the Templars as the Order of Christ (*Ordem dos Cavaleiros de Nosso Senhor Jesus Cristo*), and – after four years of negotiation – he was authorised by Pope John XXII to endow the order with the Templars' possessions. Moreover, in 1357 the Order of Christ, which initially had been based in the Algarve, was transferred to the Templars' former headquarters northeast of Lisbon at Tomar, with its magnificent rotunda patterned after Constantine's domed Church of the Holy Sepulchre in Jerusalem. In essence the Order of Christ was the Templars under another name, the main difference being that, in addition to their vows of poverty and chastity, the knights pledged obedience to the king; they had been nationalised and now existed to serve the interests of the Portuguese crown.

Successive kings of Portugal were able to install royal princes or other favourites as Grand Master of the new order. The greatest of these was Prince Henry the Navigator, appointed in 1418, who used the wealth of the order to establish the navigators' school at Sagres from where the first great wave of exploratory voyages, likewise financed by the order, were launched down the coast of Africa, around the Cape of Good Hope and eventually to Asia. Vasco da Gama, who discovered

Prince Henry the Navigator and other figures from Portugal's Age of Discovery are commemorated by this monument in Lisbon. The Templars, reconstituted in Portugal as the Order of Christ, played an all-important role in financing the explorations that led to the discovery of the New World.

the sea route round Africa to India in 1497, was himself a member of the order, and soon the Templar cross, adopted by the Order of Christ, was emblazoned on the sails of Portuguese ships sailing to Brazil, India and Japan. By the end of the fifteenth century the order possessed 454 commanderies in Portugal, Africa and the Indies. It is no exaggeration to say that Templar wealth, given a new purpose in the vision of Prince Henry the Navigator, inaugurated the new Age of Discovery that would transform the world – and open up the New World – over the next four centuries.

The Order of Christ was secularised in 1789 and in 1834 lost all of its possessions, under an anti-Church government. However, it was re-established – and survives – as an order of merit awarded for outstanding service to the Portuguese republic.

Prince Henry the Navigator, Grand Master of the Reconstituted Templars

Prince Henry was a younger son of King John I of Portugal and a grandson of John of Gaunt of England. In 1415, at the age of twenty-one, he commanded the expedition which achieved Portugal's first overseas conquest when it captured Ceuta in North Africa from the Muslims. The crusading legacy in Portugal exerted tremendous influence during Prince Henry's time. The expulsion of the Arabs and Berbers from the Algarve was still a part of the living memory of most Portuguese, and bodies of knights, including the Order of Christ, continued to man castles throughout the kingdom.

Fulfilling the mission of the Templars, reconstituted as the Order of Christ, of which he was the Grand Master, Prince Henry's ships carried on a constant war against the infidel. But though still pursuing his crusading ideal, Henry increasingly mounted his explorations for the sake of knowledge, leading to a series of discoveries down the coast of Africa and out in the Atlantic, including the Madeira islands in 1418 and the Azores and the Cape Verde islands in 1456.

Though Henry did not himself sail with these expeditions, he was their intellectual inspiration and through the Order of Christ he provided the financial wherewithal. He based himself at Sagres on a wild and windswept Atlantic headland of the Algarve, from where the first long caravels were launched, revolutionising shipping with their wide hulls and small adaptable sails, and their ability to sail close to the wind. Here at Sagres Henry attracted astronomers, geographers, cartographers and sailors, a community of scholars and adventurers who joined together under his direction to conquer the unknown.

Prince Henry died and was buried at Sagres in 1460, but the impetus of his work continued. The achievements of Vasco da Gama, who found the first sea route round Africa to India in 1498, of Ferdinand Magellan, who in 1519 initiated the first voyage round the world, and of Christopher Columbus, who discovered America in 1492, were all the fruits of Prince Henry the Navigator's lifelong endeavour as Grand Master of what had been the Templars.

The Templar Archives

Monastic orders were scrupulous in preserving documents, both their own and those left with them for safekeeping such as deeds and wills, and the Templars were no different. Indeed their entire banking system with its record keeping, credit notes and statements was an elaboration of the archival activities of monasteries. The Templars were also land-lords, traders and shipowners, activities that required documents to be filed and maintained over long periods of time. And then there was the Templars' military, religious and diplomatic activity, all of it requiring continuous correspondence and archiving. Yet today the only surviving documents which point to the existence of the Templar archives are copied transcripts from the originals which were held in Outremer and are to do with the granting of property in the East.

The Templars kept their archive at their headquarters on the Temple Mount in Jerusalem – that is in the al-Aqsa mosque, which the Crusaders

Kolossi was a Hospitaller castle in Cyprus but briefly, after the fall of Acre in 1291, it was the headquarters of the Knights Templar, who may well have kept their archives and their treasure here

assumed stood on the site of Solomon's Temple. At the fall of Jerusalem to Saladin in 1187 the archives would have been removed to Acre where most likely they would have been held in the tower by the sea where the Templars stored their treasure; or perhaps they used their castle of Athlit, south of Haifa, which was a secure alternative. The archives were at least as valuable as any portable wealth that the Templars possessed, for they contained the evidence for the Templars' mortgages, loans, possessions and even their right to exist which was granted in the form of Papal charters. As Acre fell in 1291 the Hospitallers managed to get their archives out to Provence, and so there is no reason why the Templars should not also have succeeded, probably taking them to Cyprus, which became the new Templar headquarters.

James of Molay had no reason to bring the Templar archives with him to the West just before his arrest; indeed the Grand Master was looking forward to the day when a new crusade would return the Templars, with their archives, to the Holy Land. Nor have searches of the French royal archives and the Papal archives turned up a hint of the Templar archives. The most likely explanation is that they remained on Cyprus where they were taken over by the Hospitallers along with the Templars' possessions on the island in 1312. The Hospitallers moved their headquarters to Malta in 1530, but the Templar archives and those archives of the Hospitallers that specifically related to Cyprus were not taken with them, and both archives were probably destroyed when the Ottomans overran the island in 1571. The Hospitaller's documents relating to Cyprus have never been found either.

That explains why almost everything we know about the Templars, apart from their Rule itself, comes from sources other than themselves – from bodies like the canons of the Holy Sepulchre, the Italian trading communities, the Hospitallers, and the various chroniclers and pilgrims in the Holy Land, from the Papal archives and the prosecution documents of Philip IV's lawyers.

The loss of the Templar archives is a blow for serious historians of the order, but it has been a boon for those who prefer their speculations to be uninhibited by facts. For more on which, read on.

Conspiracies

Something to Do with Everything

For many people at the time and since, the destruction of the Templars was inexplicable. How could such an important and powerful organisation seemingly devoted to the defence of Christendom and enjoying the protection of the Papacy have fallen to charges of blasphemy, heresy and sodomy – charges pressed by the king of France, aided by Church inquisitors, and apparently condoned by the Pope himself?

But since the recent discovery of the Chinon Parchment and its publication in 2004 the mystery has been solved. The reality is that the Templars were the victims of a titanic power struggle between France and the Papacy, between emerging European nationalism on the one hand and the universalist claims of the Church on the other. The Templars did indeed practise various strange rituals, not uncommon among military organisations, but their admission of these was deliberately twisted by the French state to appear as heresy and so forth. The Pope himself understood that these rituals were fundamentally innocent and personally cleared the Templars of the charges – but he kept his absolution secret for the time being for fear of a French assault on the institution of the Papacy itself and then died before he could publicly set the record straight. In the commotion of returning the Papacy from Avignon to Rome the Chinon Parchment got lost among the jumble and went unrecognised until 2001.

For nearly seven hundred years, therefore, the public and historians and experts of every kind were confronted with an incomplete account, one with many gaps and seeming contradictions but so dramatic that it demanded explanation – and became an open invitation to speculation and conspiracy theories. These have long taken on a life of their own – 'The Templars have something to do with everything', as Umberto Eco wrote in *Foucault's Pendulum* – and not even the discovery of the Chinon Parchment is likely to put them to rest.

The Immediate Reaction

Some of the most sensible reactions to the charges against the Templars and the destruction of the order came at the time. Dante, as we have seen, who wrote his *Purgatorio* during the trial of the Templars, had nothing to say about the supposed avarice of the order. But he was in no doubt about the greed, power-seeking and dishonesty of King Philip IV of France and the malign influence of his entire Capetian dynasty. Dante's Italian compatriots generally thought the same: Italian bankers in France, like the Jews, had already been made to suffer Philip's rapaciousness, while in the following generation the writer and poet Boccaccio, author of the *Decameron*, supported the Templars' innocence and ridiculed the Inquisition.

In Portugal, the French assault on the Templars was also seen for what it was, and with royal support, and the permission of the Papacy, the Templars continued to flourish in Portugal under another name. The Germans and the English, too, tended to be sceptical about Templar guilt. In fact it was really only in France and among people under French sway that the story of Templar heresy was swallowed. Ramon Lull is an example. He was a Catalan philosopher and mystic who eagerly expected that Philip IV would lead a new crusade to the East.

At first he believed in the honour and good faith of the Templars, but in 1308, during the trial and the full force of the French monarchy's propaganda campaign against the order, he fell into line with the French court and changed his mind; but if he thought that the condemnation of the Templars would purify Christians and lead to a new crusade, he was disappointed.

Meanwhile, as the flame of the Crusader ideal flickered and died, the Templars were taking on a mythic life of their own.

The Romance of the Templars

Well before the end of the Order, the Knights Templar were entering into the realm of myth. The first mention of the Templars in literature came in about 1220 in *Parzival* by the German knight and poet Wolfram von Eschenbach. He based his work on Chrétien des Troyes' romance *Perceval, The Story of the Grail*, begun in 1181 and left unfinished at his death in 1190. Chrétien's association with Troyes may be significant: it was the capital of the counts of Champagne who played an important role in the founding of the Templars and also in promoting their great champion Bernard of Clairvaux. Certainly Troyes represented a link with the East through Chrétien's patroness, the countess Marie of Champagne, who was the daughter of Eleanor of Aquitaine. Eleanor was the lively young wife of Louis VII, the incompetent leader of the Second Crusade; she accompanied him on the venture, and upon her arrival in the East lost no time in embarking on a flagrant affair with her uncle Raymond of Antioch. She later married Henry II, king of England. Bernard of Clairvaux did not much approve of the free-spirited Eleanor of Aquitaine, whom he found flighty and indecorous. But for a poet she made good copy, and it is not hard to imagine her inspiring Chrétien when he invented the character of Guinevere in his earlier work *Lancelot, the Knight of the Cart*, which he wrote specifically at Marie's request.

The hint of a Templar link in Chrétien's romance was made manifest in Wolfram von Eschenbach's *Parzival*, in which he makes the Knights Templar the guardians of the Grail. Eschenbach had visited Outremer in about 1200 and he set sections of his poem in the East. His Templars are pure warriors, defenders of the sacred territories which contain the Grail, just as the real Templars defended the Holy Land:

> [They] are continually riding out on sorties in quest of adventure. Whether these same Templars reap trouble or renown they bear it for their sins. I will tell you how they are nourished. They live from a stone whose essence is most pure. If you have never heard of it I shall name it for you here. It is called "Lapsit exillis". By virtue of the stone the Phoenix is burned to ashes, in which he is reborn.

Eschenbach explains that *Lapsit exillis*, the name given to the Grail, is a stone that was once set in Lucifer's crown but which fell with him from heaven, and which serves the Templars as an elixir of life – a notion that would not be entirely out of place in a dualist cosmology.

'Grail' originally meant a serving dish. In this French illustration dating from c1316, Perceval, Galahad and Bohors carry the great silver grail to the mystical island of Sarras

The Grail Quest

The Grail was invented in the late twelfth century by Chrétien de Troyes: no mention of a Grail had ever been made before. Curiously, there was nothing explicitly religious about Chrétien's Grail; he did not write about it as the cup or chalice at the Last Supper. For that matter he did not describe it as a cup or chalice at all, but rather as a serving dish, which is the usual and original meaning of the Old French word *graal*. But there is something wonderful about the Grail's first appearance in the pages of Chrétien's story at the beginning of a rich man's feast, and all the more wonderful and strange because Chrétien never finished his story. This is how it makes its first appearance on the page:

Then two other squires entered holding in their hands candelabra of pure gold, crafted with enamel inlays. The young men carrying the candelabra were extremely handsome. In each of the candelabra there were at least ten candles burning. A maiden accompanying the two young men was carrying a grail with her two hands; she was beautiful, noble, and richly attired. After she had entered the hall carrying the grail the room was so brightly illumined that the candles lost their brilliance like stars and the moon when the sun rises. (*Arthurian Romances*, Penguin, 1991)

What is tantalising about this appearance of the Grail is that Perceval, the hero of the romance, knows exactly what it is, but he fails to tell us before the story breaks off (when Chrétien dies). Is the story allegorical? People have argued over that point for more than eight hundred years. And if allegorical, is the allegory religious? That too has never been resolved. But this haunting image was soon inspiring writers to complete the tale – among them Wolfram von Eschenbach, who in *Parzival*, his thirteenth-century German adaptation, introduced the Knights Templar to literature by making them guardians of the Grail.

Chrétien de Troyes was writing when medieval Western society, so attached to its tradition, was opening onto a wider world, the world of the Mediterranean, the world of the East, to worlds of ideas and beliefs that it was discovering or rediscovering, not least on account of the Crusades. Writing about the Grail meant writing about this cultural and spiritual quest, and yet strangely it has always been a genre, regardless of its religious overtones, that has belonged to secular writers, never to the Church. And so, free from doctrine and canon, the Grail has been endlessly reinvented down to the present time.

Templars and Witchcraft

It is curious that it was precisely as Europe was moving out of the Middle Ages and into the ages of awakening and reason that the first sinister mystifications about the Templars were developed in both the popular and learned imaginations. The story begins in 1487 with the publication of the *Malleus Maleficarum*, ironically one of the earliest books to be printed – the invention of the printing press is usually taken to mark the end of the Middle Ages.

There had always been a belief in evil spirits, but there had also been a confidence that the Church could shield believers from their influence; exorcism was routinely practised by the clergy to banish unclean spirits, while external threats, such as the Muslim conquests, would be countered by the Crusades and the knightly class, including the military orders. But the failure of the Crusades and the loss of confidence in the Church helped set off a pathological fear that demons were taking possession of Christian people.

The Malleus Maleficarum, published by the Papal Inquisition in 1487, was a handbook for identifying and punishing witches. As supposed heretics, the Templars were incorporated into this paranoid world of the esoteric.

By the end of the fifteenth century the fear of witchcraft had grown into an epidemic which forced the Church to intervene. In 1484 a Papal bull, *Summis Desiderantes Affectibus*, legitimised the belief in witches and granted permission to bishops and secular authorities to prosecute them if there were no representatives from the Inquisition. The *Malleus Maleficarum* was published three years later; written by two experienced and enthusiastic Dominican witch-hunters, it established the procedural rules for witchcraft trials and quickly became notorious. The title, which translates as 'The Hammer of the Witches', in effect means the persecution of witches – a term which was applied to anyone from heretics, devil-worshippers and practitioners of magic to prostitutes and superstitious old women. By a chance remark made in a book published a generation later, the Templars became associated with this murky and paranoid world of the esoteric.

The book was *De Occulta Philosophia*; it was by a German, Henry Cornelius Agrippa, and after its publication in 1531 it became the most widely read and influential of the Renaissance magical texts. Agrippa was a serious humanist scholar whose interests spilled over into folklore and the occult. The purpose of his book, he said, was 'to distinguish between the good and holy science of magic and the scandalous and impious practises of black magic, and to restore the former's good name'. In the process he examined the various ways in which the powers emanating from spirits and demons could be harnessed and controlled. And then he wrote these fateful lines: 'It is well known that evil demons can be attracted by bad and profane arts, in the manner in which Psellus relates that the Gnostic magicians used to practise, who used to carry out disgusting and foul abominations, like those formerly used in the rites of Priapus and in the service of the idol called Panor, to whom people used to sacrifice with their private parts bared. Nor were they much different, if what we read is truth and not fantasy, from the detestable heresy of the Templars; and similar things are known about the witches and their senile craziness in wandering into offences of this sort.'

By placing the Templars alongside witches as his two examples of perverted Christian magicians Agrippa thrust the order into the phantasmagoria of occult forces which were the subject of the persecuting craze for which the *Malleus Maleficarum* was a handbook. Suddenly the Templars were raised from the depths of half-forgotten failures and became the focus of the darkest disturbing forces in the European mind – its victims or its masters. In this way the Templars entered the Renaissance and were to advance into the Age of Enlightenment.

Solomon's Temple and the Freemasons

At a time when most workers were tied to the land, masons were freelancers who sought work where they could, and in Scotland and England during the Middle Ages they began to form themselves into mutual help associations. There were two kinds of masons, the 'rough masons' who worked in hard stone, laying foundations and raising walls, and the more mobile masons who carved the fine facades on cathedrals from softer stone, freestone as it was called, and these elite masons were called freestone masons, or freemasons for short. As the freemasons travelled round Britain they would stay at lodges, and after the Reformation in the sixteenth century one of their activities at their lodges was to read the Bible. The Catholic Church had discouraged the translation of the Bible into the vernacular, fearing that the Bible would replace the Papacy as the font of authority. This was precisely what Protestants in Scotland and England were eager to do, for the Bible was discovered to have revolutionary implications; for example it spoke of prophets who had overthrown wicked kings, and at the same time it failed to support the notion that the bishop of Rome, that is the Pope, should be the supreme leader of a universal Church.

On the other hand the Protestants decided that the Bible was itself the word of God, and those who were freemasons paid close attention to the Second Book of Chronicles with its description of how Solomon asked Hiram to build the Temple, and to the detailed measurements of the Temple, which God would only have troubled to mention, in their view, because they contained some profound theological truths. The freemasons were particularly impressed by that other Hiram, not Hiram the king of Tyre, but Hiram the widow's son, the one they called Hiram Abiff. The most remarkable work at Solomon's Temple had been done by Hiram Abiff, the casting of the enormous basin known as the Sea of Bronze and of the huge bronze pillars known as Jachin and Boaz. As the Bible said, this Hiram was a man 'filled with wisdom and understanding'.

The efficacy of these freemasons' mutual assistance associations depended on their exclusivity, that they should be clubs open to free-masons only, and the point was made by developing a system of signs and rituals supposedly passed down from ancient times and by means of which adherents gained access to the private meetings. One such ritual concerned Hiram Abiff, to whom the masons gave a history that went far beyond his brief mention in the Bible. Hiram Abiff, they said, knew the secret of the Temple. Three villains kidnapped Hiram and threatened to kill him if he did not reveal the secret 'Master's word' – a term used by the masons in their trade to differentiate the pay and assignments of workers, but also, as the ritual now implied, bearing deeper and mystical significance. But Hiram refused to reveal the secret, and his assailants murdered him.

When Solomon heard about this, he wondered what was Hiram's secret, and he sent three masons to look for his body, also telling them that if they could not find the secret, then the first thing they saw when they found Hiram's body should itself become the secret of the Temple. The masons found Hiram Abiff's coffin, and when they opened it the first thing they saw was his hand – and from this the masons made the handshake and other signs of recognition the new secret. On the basis of this story, the masons developed the ritual by which a Freemason advances through degrees, the first being apprentice mason, the second being entered apprentice, and so to the third degree when he becomes a master mason. Advancing to the third degree requires that the initiate must agree to undergo the sufferings of Hiram Abiff should he ever reveal the Freemasons' secrets, and that if he ever broke his oath it would be right for his fellow Freemasons to cut out his heart, his liver and his entrails, in the same way as a traitor was disembowelled as part of the process of being hanged, drawn and quartered.

But already these associations of artisan freemasons were undergoing a transition that would alter their fundamental nature. To enhance the standing of their associations, freemasons invited influential people to serve as patrons. This gave the freemasons a social appeal which together with their study of the Bible began to attract an inquiring elite comprising gentlemen and scholars, professionals and merchants, so that by about 1700 these 'admitted' or 'speculative masons' outnumbered 'operative masons', as the artisans were called. In fact the modern institution that we recognise as Freemasonry was born when a group of four London lodges made up of both operative and admitted masons merged in 1717 to create a Grand Lodge. They placed at their head not a practising mason but a gentleman, and never again would a true stonemason ever serve as a Grand Master.

Enlightenment and Mystery

The meaning of the Hiram story is unclear as perhaps it was meant to be, for its true purpose may have been to link the Freemasons with antiquity. For all that educated people of the Enlightenment looked towards the future, they also looked back towards the past for they believed that antiquity had possessed much learning and wisdom that had since been lost, and that it was their duty to recover what they could from biblical and classical times. For example, Sir Isaac Newton made such recovery a major part of his work and attempted for years to decipher the wisdom hidden in biblical prophecy and alchemy. His *Principia Mathematica*, published in 1687, which described gravitation and the laws of motion, was central to the scientific revolution and the acceptance that rational investigation can reveal the inner workings of nature – and yet Newton was convinced that it was merely a rediscovery of ancient knowledge.

Isaac Newton by William Blake, engraving with pen and ink and watercolour, 1795

Though Newton, who died in 1727, was never himself a mason, Freemasonry did attract eminent intellectuals, including several members of the Royal Society, in effect the British academy of sciences, men who stood for rationalism and deism, but who also found it entirely appropriate that the Freemasons should identify themselves with the Temple of Solomon, built by Solomon and Hiram Abiff, those mysterious exemplars of ancient wisdom.

Sir Isaac Newton and the Temple of Solomon

One of the greatest figures of the Enlightenment, the scientist and mathematician Sir Isaac Newton, wrote something like four hundred and seventy books – many of them on theological subjects and several about the Temple of Solomon. Newton was convinced that Solomon was the greatest philosopher of all time, and he also believed that he owed his own breakthrough formulation of the law of gravity to his close reading of those portions of the Bible, 1 Kings and 2 Chronicles, which give in great detail the measurements of Solomon's Temple. Moreover Newton saw in those same figures all manner of prophecies of great and terrible events that would take place over the coming four hundred years, including the Second Coming of Christ in 1948.

Freemasons and Templars

News of the formation of London's Grand Lodge and the activities of British Freemasons soon spread across Europe. By the 1730s masonic lodges had been founded in the Netherlands, France, Germany and elsewhere, often by representatives of the London Grand Lodge who travelled abroad for the purpose, but sometimes by local residents who were inspired by the Grand Lodge but were not under its direction. But if Freemasonry proved popular in Europe, it was also alien and troubling for some. It did not grow out of the old artisan organisations of France, Germany and elsewhere on the continent, which had long since ceased to exist. Instead it was imported from Britain, home of the

Glorious Revolution of 1688 that had definitively curtailed the powers of the king and divided authority between the monarchy, Parliament and the judiciary, and that had instituted a degree of religious toleration. Britain was widely admired by the people of Europe as a progressive and tolerant nation, but its institutions and inventions, not least Freemasonry, were deeply distrusted by Europe's autocratic rulers and the Catholic Church.

Though the Freemasons in Britain were an innocuous and largely middle-class fraternal organisation, whose lodges fulfiled a similar social function as the London coffee house, they acquired a cult of secrecy and linked this to a mysterious knowledge associated with Solomon's Temple. Earlier, Agrippa had linked the Templars to witchcraft and occult powers. It remained for these elements to be drawn together into one powerful occultic myth, and this is what happened when the Freemasons were directly linked to the Templars – which happened not in Britain but in continental Europe.

The first step was taken in 1736 or 1737 by a Scotsman called Andrew Michael Ramsay, a Jacobite exile living in France who, as chancellor of the French Grand Lodge, introduced a fictitious Crusader background to the Freemasons and notions of aristocratic class. British Freemasonry was democratic in nature; its members included artisans and aristocrats, professional men, learned men and middle-class traders, all content to rub shoulders with one another. But neither rubbing shoulders nor belonging to an institution that had grown from working-men's beginnings appealed to the upper strata of French society. The gentry and nobility of France wanted recognition of social distinctions, and they wanted it reinforced by style, nostalgia and romance. Ramsay gave it to them by the bucketful, suggesting that the stonemasons had also been knightly warriors in the Holy Land, and soon he had turned the French Freemasons into an ancient chivalrous international secret society. 'Our ancestors, the Crusaders, who had come from all parts of Christendom to the Holy Land, wanted to group persons from every nation in a single spiritual confraternity', Ramsay announced in his Oration to Saint John's Lodge in Paris, variously dated 27 December 1736 or 21 March 1737.

A Freemasons' lodge in England in about 1730

In Ramsay's version of the past, the Crusaders had attempted to restore the Temple of Solomon in a hostile environment and had devised a system of secret signs and rituals to protect themselves against their Muslim enemy, who otherwise would infiltrate their positions and cut their throats. Ramsay also said that at the collapse of Outremer the Crusaders returned to their homelands in Europe and established Freemason lodges there. But their lodges and their rites were neglected over time and it was only among Scotsmen that the Freemasons preserved their former splendour:

> *Since that time Great Britain became the seat of our Order, the conservator of our laws and the depository of our secrets. ... From the British Isles the Royal Art is now repassing into France. ... In this happy age when love of peace has become the virtue of heroes,*

this nation, one of the most spiritual in Europe, will become the centre of the Order. She will clothe our work, our statutes, our customs with grace, delicacy and good taste, essential qualities of the Order, of which the basis is wisdom, strength and beauty of genius. It is in future in our Lodges, as it were in public schools, that Frenchmen shall learn, without travelling, the characters of all nations and that strangers shall experience that France is the home of all nations.

At the time Ramsay said nothing about the Templars, perhaps because he might have offended the still powerful French monarchy and Church. In 1749, however, six years after his death, Ramsay's monumental work *The Philosophical Principles of Natural and Revealed Religion* was published in Glasgow, and in it Ramsay said, 'every Mason is a Knight Templar', a remark that was not forgotten.

The Crusader link was further developed in Germany in about 1760, when a Frenchman who pretended to be a Scottish nobleman and called himself George Frederick Johnson claimed to have direct access to Templar secrets. This too served local tastes, as Germany was an old-fashioned society dominated by notions of rank which resisted the egalitarian and rationalist ideas inherent in British Freemasonry. A spurious connection with Templars provided the German Freemasons with Gothic atmosphere and a strong flavour of the occult.

According to Johnson's concoction of history, the Templar Grand Masters had spent their time in the East learning the secrets and acquiring the treasure of the Jewish Essenes, later famous for the Dead Sea Scrolls, and the people with whom John the Baptist probably had some association. This learning and this treasure was handed down from one Grand Master to another, and so came into the possession of James of Molay – who according to the story also bears the name of Hiram. On the night before his execution, James of Molay was said to have ordered a group of Templars who were somehow still at large to enter into the crypt of the Paris Temple and make off with the treasure, which consisted of the seven-branched candelabra stolen from the Temple by the Roman Emperor Titus, the crown of the Kingdom of Jerusalem and a shroud. These were taken to the Atlantic port of La Rochelle from where eighteen Templar galleys made their escape to the Isle of Mull where they called themselves Freemasons. The Scottish Freemasons, said Johnson the fake Scotsman, were the Templars' direct heirs.

Then came the French Revolution in 1789, which shook the European public to the core. In an effort to understand those dramatic events, many accepted the fiction that secret organisations were manipulating public affairs.

The Revenge of James of Molay

James of Molay was burnt to death in Paris on the evening of 18 March 1314. The one eyewitness account of the burning of Molay, written by an anonymous monk, says that he went to his death 'with easy mind and will'. There is no contemporary reference to him uttering a curse, yet it has since been said that as the flames engulfed the Templars' last Grand Master he cried out for vengeance and called on the king and Pope to appear with him before the tribunal of God within a year and a day. Less than five weeks later, on 20 April, Pope Clement V died of the long and painful illness that had afflicted him throughout his pontificate. And still within that same year King Philip IV died, on 29 November, after falling from a horse while hunting.

The supposed secret survival of the Templars through the centuries opened the way for agents of the order to take their revenge for the burning of James of Molay. With a sense of prophecy owing everything to hindsight, James of Molay was now remembered to have brought his curse down on the heads of the king and Pope. The downfall of the French royal house of Capet, and the humbling of the Catholic Church in France, would come with the French Revolution – brought about by a secret conspiracy controlled by the Templars working through the Freemasons. That anyway was the belief of some extreme conservative elements in France, among them Charles de Gassicour, the author of *Le Tombeau de Jacques Molay*, published in 1796. Describing the death by guillotine of Louis XVI, Gassicour has someone rise up and shout, 'James of Molay, you are avenged!' – a hated Freemason, or a Templar, whose subversive organisation had overturned the established order.

A story was invented during the French Revolution that as James of Molay went to the stake he cursed the Pope and the king of France. Both died within the year, but the curse lived on, claiming the life of Philip IV's descendant Louis XVI, who went to the guillotine.

Gassicour also claimed that James of Molay had founded four lodges, one in Edinburgh; that the Templars/Freemasons were associated with the Assassins and the Old Man of the Mountain; that they supported Oliver Cromwell; and that they had stormed the Bastille.

Others added their voices to the story. For example in 1797 Abbé Augustin Barruel published *Memoirs*, his account of the French Revolution, which he helped explain by saying that Freemasonry had derived from the Templars after their suppression, when:

> *a certain number of guilty knights, having escaped the proscription, united for the preservation of their horrid mysteries. To their impious code they added the vow of vengeance against the kings and priests who destroyed their Order, and against all religion which anathematised their dogmas. They made adepts, who should transmit from generation to generation the same hatred of the God of the Christians, and of Kings, and of Priests.*

Addressing the Freemasons directly, he continued:

> *These mysteries have descended to you, and you continue to perpetuate their impiety, their vows, and their oaths. Such is your origin. The lapse of time and the change of manners have varied a part of your symbols and your frightful systems; but the essence of them remains, the vows, the oaths, the hatred, and the conspiracies are the same.*

A few years later Barruel added Jews to the conspiracy, seeing them as the real power behind the Templars and the Freemasons and the ultimate manipulators of European events – a conspiracy theory that culminated in the gas ovens of the Third Reich.

Barruel was in exile from revolutionary France and published his *Memoirs* in London, where he was politic enough to thank the British government for granting him asylum and wrote that his claims of dangerous Freemason activities did not apply to the respectable Freemasons of Britain. The British government agreed. Worried about the virus of revolution from France, in 1799 it passed the Unlawful Societies Act, although this specifically excluded the Freemasons.

A Scottish History for the Knights Templar

The eighteenth and early nineteenth centuries saw an explosion of orders, degrees and societies, among them benevolent societies that survive to this day such as the Oddfellows and the Royal Antediluvian Order of Buffaloes, or spiritual groups such as the Druids, given to pantheistic nature worship in imitation of Bronze Age Celtic Druids. By 1800 there were hundreds, maybe over a thousand, of these organisations in Britain, and like the Freemasons they gave themselves antique histories; the Oddfellows, for example, traced their spiritual origins back to the Jews at the time of their Babylonian exile in 586 BC. In addition to these organisations, there were other orders or degrees, about thirty in all, which claimed to be masonic, indeed were often operating unofficially within local lodges, among them the Knights Templar. Chivalry and mysticism were very much in fashion, and though at first both the

The 'traditional history' that Templars helped Robert the Bruce win the battle of Bannockburn in 1314 was invented by Freemasons in 1843

English and Scottish Grand Lodges rejected the Knights Templar, saying they were a foreign corruption, in the age of Romanticism the fashion proved irresistible and eventually the Templars were accepted within British Freemasonry.

In 1843 the Order of the Knights Templar in Scotland published a *Historical Notice of the Order*, which was written by the Scottish masonic Templars themselves and gave an account of their origins:

> *It is agreed by all hands, even the French, that the Templars joined the standard of Robert the Bruce and fought in his cause until the issue of the Battle of Bannockburn in 1314 securely placed him on the throne. That Monarch was not ungrateful.*

The account explains that after the suppression of the Knights Templar in France, local Scottish Templars gave their support to Robert the Bruce during his war of independence against the English, and that at the battle of Bannockburn on 24 June 1314, three months after the burning of James of Molay, a troop of Templars charged against the English at the decisive moment and gave the victory to the Scots. In gratitude, Robert the Bruce protected the Templars by assimilating them into a new order, the Freemasons.

None of this had been recorded by any Scottish chronicler at the time. It was entirely made up in the nineteenth century. The masonic Scottish Templars had done what masons always do: they invented a tradition, a connection with the past, and a very flattering one for Scots Freemasons. These inventions were never meant as factual history. This is explained by Robert Cooper, Freemason and curator at the Grand Lodge of Scotland in Edinburgh in his book *The Rosslyn Hoax?*:

> There are a number of branches within Freemasonry. Each has its own 'story', its own traditional history, which underpins that particular part of the Masonic system... The Royal Arch Chapter is concerned with the building of a new or second Temple, often referred to as Zerubbabel's Temple. Another branch of Freemasonry has for its traditional history the story of Helena, wife of Constantine, and her search for the place of Christ's crucifixion... All branches of Freemasonry, therefore, have a 'traditional history' on which their ceremonies are based. As well as having considerable colour (the Temple at Jerusalem must have seemed very exotic to the stonemasons of Scotland), King Solomon's Temple added a great deal of prestige to a group of honest working men ... None of the traditional histories of any of the branches of Freemasonry are, or were, intended to be taken literally. Our forebears in all the Masonic Orders manufactured suitable 'pasts' for allegorical purposes. They did so with romantic notions at heart but understood that these histories manufactured by, and for, themselves were not literal truths.

But many people, both masons and non-masons, failed to separate fantasy from fact. For example, in his *History of Free Masonry* published in Edinburgh in 1859, Alexander Laurie, who was himself a Freemason, wrote, 'It will be necessary to give some account of the Knight Templars, the fraternity of Freemasons, whose affluence and virtues aroused the envy of contemporaries, and whose unmerited and unhappy end must have frequently excited the compassion of posterity. To prove that the order of the Knight Templars was a branch of Free Masonry would be a useless Labour, as the fact has been invariably acknowledged by Free Masons themselves, and none have been more zealous to establish it than the enemies of their order.'

Evidence and proof were irrelevant to Laurie. He asserted that it was not necessary to prove that the medieval Order of the Knights Templar was an outgrowth of the Freemasons because Freemasons already knew it, as did the enemies of Freemasonry, people like the Abbé Barruel.

The myth of the Knights Templar was taking its modern shape. The medieval order had survived but in another form. The battle of Bannockburn was established as a central event in the myth. What was needed was a central place, and its invention began in 1982 with the publication of *The Holy Blood and the Holy Grail* and has continued with other 'alternative histories' such as *The Hiram Key* (written by two Freemasons) and *The Templar Revelation*, not to mention *The Da Vinci Code*, Dan Brown's novelised synthesis of these pseudo-histories, which all worked to bring Rosslyn Chapel, south of Edinburgh, and its founding family the St Clairs into the myth.

The Sinclairs (as the St Clairs are known in English) were themselves Templars, and Rosslyn Chapel became a repository for the Templars' treasure or their secrets, or for some powerful iconic object such as the embalmed head of Jesus Christ or the Ark of the Covenant or the Holy Grail. Or so the story goes.

The Templars Discover America

The Templars discovered America. The evidence is found at Rosslyn Chapel, richly decorated with carvings. Among these are carvings that have been identified as maize, a plant native to North America, and also carvings identified as 'aloe cactus' and described as a New World plant. Rosslyn Chapel was built in 1456; whoever carved the maize and aloe at Rosslyn must have known about America nearly fifty years before it was discovered by Christopher Columbus in 1492.

This realisation makes sense of an old stone tower at Newport, Rhode Island. The Newport Tower is round and stands on round arches; there are those who say it was a round church built by Templar colonists who came to America. The Templars would have come in about 1308 after the suppression of their order in France, escaping with their fleet from La Rochelle, some sailing for Scotland, others for the New World; or they came in the person of Henry Sinclair, Earl of Orkney and the son and heir of William Sinclair, Lord of Rosslyn. Henry Sinclair was a Templar, and he took charge of a voyage by the Venetian brothers Nicolo and Antonio Zeno, who in maps and letters later claimed to have reached Nova Scotia via Greenland in 1389 and explored some of the North American coastline more than a hundred years before the voyage of Columbus.

But there are difficulties with this account, which was first proposed by Christopher Knight and Robert Lomas, the authors of *The Hiram Key* published in 1996, and elaborated by others since. The carvings identified as maize do not really look like maize at all except in the authors' minds. The 'aloe cactus' at Rosslyn could in fact be almost any kind of plant; once again its identification is owed merely to the assertion of the authors. Nor is aloe a cactus; it is a succulent; and it is native to Africa, not America, and it certainly could not have grown in New England, which has severe winters. And though Rosslyn Chapel was built in 1456, the carvings were added only after its completion. They are not carved from the stone of the structure, rather the carvings throughout the chapel were carved separately and subsequently attached, 'glued on' as it were, and therefore give no reliable dates.

As for the Newport Tower, it was built as a windmill for grinding grain in the seventeenth century and is mentioned in 1677 as 'my stone build Wind Mill' in its owner's will. Two archaeological excavations at the tower, one in 1951, another in 2006, both concluded that the tower was built between 1650 and 1670. The Zeno brothers are known through the publication of their purported letters and a map in 1558, over a hundred and fifty years after their supposed voyage, but the documents are widely regarded as a hoax. Nor do the letters mention Henry Sinclair; they mention someone called Zichmni, the commander of the expedition, and only with some effort and imagination has he been turned into Sinclair. The matter is summed up by an article in the *New Orkney Antiquarian Journal* in 2002:

> *Henry Sinclair, an earl of Orkney of the late fourteenth century, didn't go to America. It wasn't until 500 years after Henry's death that anybody suggested that he did. The sixteenth-century text that eventually gave rise to all the claims about Henry and America certainly doesn't say so. What it says, in so many words, is that someone called Zichmni, with friends, made a trip to Greenland. None of Henry Sinclair's contemporaries or near-contemporaries ever claimed that he went to America; and none of the antiquaries who wrote about him in the seventeenth century said so either, although they made other absurd claims about him. The story is a modern myth, based on careless reading, wishful thinking and sometimes distortion, and during the past five years or so it has taken new outrageous forms.*

In one version of this 'alternative history', the Templars' voyage to America is undertaken in ships of their fleet, part of the same fleet that sailed for Scotland from La Rochelle in northern France. But this much-vaunted fleet is itself a myth. The Templars did have a fleet of ships to carry pilgrims and supplies and personnel across the Mediterranean between Marseilles and Acre, but these were not suitable for ocean voyages, nor could they carry enough water for more than a few days. As for warships, the Templar 'fleet' is unlikely to have numbered more than four galleys. And given that Templar activities were in the Mediterranean and that their chief European port was Marseilles, it is most unlikely that more than a very few Templar ships of any kind, if any ships at all, would have been based at La Rochelle.

Nevertheless this 'Templar fleet', wherever it was based, has given rise to another invented history. When the order was suppressed and the fleet made its escape, the Templars altered their red cross to a skull and crossbones and continued their resistance to the Papacy and the crowned heads of Europe, all except the Scottish, by living the lives of pirates on the high seas.

The New World Order

In the United States there has been a well-established legend that the Freemasons were behind the American Revolution. They are said to have instigated violent resistance to the British and to have defied British attempts to impose taxation without representation by holding the Boston Tea Party in 1773; they drew up the Declaration of Independence in 1776, provided the leadership during the Revolutionary War, and drafted the Constitution in 1787.

But the role of the Freemasons has been exaggerated. A few Freemasons may have participated in the Boston Tea Party, but it was planned and executed by a group of radical artisans called the Sons of Liberty. Of the Committee of Five who drew up the Declaration of Independence, only one, Benjamin Franklin, was a Freemason; the Declaration was almost entirely written by Thomas Jefferson, who was not a Freemason. Of the fifty-five Americans to sign the Declaration of Independence, only nine were certainly Freemasons; and of the thirty-nine who approved the Constitution, only thirteen were or later became Freemasons. George Washington had become a Freemason at the age of twenty but did not take it seriously, regarding his lodge as a social club and showing up for only two meetings in the next forty-one years. The higher ranks of Freemasonry in the American colonies were pro-British and remained loyal to the Crown, as did at least a third of the American population. Benedict Arnold, who won the first great battle of the revolutionary war for the Americans at Saratoga, and who then defected to the British (so that in America his name is synonymous with treason) was a Freemason.

Yet in 1793, at the dedication of the Capitol building, George Washington, in his capacity as first president of the United States, but wearing his masonic apron, placed a silver plate upon the foundation stone and covered it with masonic symbols of maize, oil and wine. An inscription on the silver plate made the identification of the new republic with masonry absolutely clear: the stone had been laid, it stated, 'in the thirteenth year of American independence, and in the year of Masonry, 5793' – that being the generally accepted number of years

George Washington wearing his Freemason's apron while laying the foundation stone of the Capitol building in Washington DC

since God's creation of the world. After the successful conclusion of the War of Independence, and for a generation after, Freemasonry was widely considered to be the foundation stone of the republic. The explanation lies in the creation of the revolutionary army with Washington at its head. His officers had been thrown together from a diversity of regional origins, religions and social rank, and had great responsibilities thrust upon them. Freemasonry had been popular among officers in the British army in North America, and the revolutionary army continued the practise of having military lodges, which it turned to good account. Freemasonry's ideals of honour and fraternity offered American officers the bonds on which to build the camaraderie necessary for the survival of the army, and therefore of the American republic.

But for mythomanes there is more to it than that. The monumental building constructed to house the Senate and the House of Representatives on Capitol Hill was part of the grand plan for the entire city designed in 1791 by Pierre Charles L'Enfant, a Frenchman who served in General George Washington's staff as a military engineer throughout the revolutionary war. Though Washington appointed L'Enfant to lay out the new city, L'Enfant was not a Freemason, but the conspiracy theorists insist he was; and they say that his rectangular street grid overlaid by diagonal avenues creates a series of masonic patterns that also reflect the pattern of the stars. The harmony between the heavens and the earth would work its powers on those who inhabited the city, the capital of the new republic. As once the god Shalem had manifested himself on the Ophel Hill as the evening star, confirming Jerusalem as a sacred place, so Washington would become the new Jerusalem, its activities sanctified by its relationship with the spiritual world as symbolised by the stars.

Powerful masonic symbols have also been discerned in the Great Seal of the United States, which is reproduced on the reverse of the dollar bill. The seal was commissioned by Congress on 4 July 1776, immediately after it had voted its approval of the Declaration of Independence, but it would pass through three committees and take six years before a final design was approved. Benjamin Franklin, who was on the first committee, was the only Freemason involved, and his non-masonic suggestion that the seal should depict the Jews escaping from the tyranny of pharaoh was rejected. The obverse of the seal shows an eagle clutching thirteen arrows, an olive branch with thirteen leaves and thirteen fruits, the eagle defended by a shield with thirteen stripes, and above his head thirteen stars arranged in the form of the Seal of Solomon, also known as the Star of David. Thirteen represents the original thirteen American colonies that rebelled against Britain and came together to form the United States. The motto reads 'E Pluribus Unum', meaning 'Out of Many, One'. The arrangement of the stars has aroused speculation, but biblical and Hebrew symbolism were as common in the eighteenth and nineteenth centuries as classical symbolism. Charles Thomson, a Latinist who was Secretary of Congress and the person who set the various ideas for a seal into their final form, explained simply that 'the constellation of stars denotes a new State taking its place and rank among other sovereign powers'.

The reverse of the seal shows a pyramid surmounted by an eye. The pyramid has thirteen courses and is inscribed at its base with MDCCLXXVI. There are two mottoes, one above the eye, the other below the pyramid. Again Charles Thomson gave his explanation: 'The pyramid signifies strength and duration: The eye over it and the motto, *Annuit Coeptus* [He [God] Has Favoured Our Undertakings], allude to the many interventions of Providence in favour of the American cause. The date underneath is that of the Declaration of Independence, and the words under it, *Novus Ordo Seclorum* [A New Order of the Ages], signify the beginning of the new American era in 1776.'

But 'alternative histories' and conspiracy theorists see things differently. They say that the pyramid and the eye on the reverse of the Great Seal are masonic and amount to a code. Expert Freemasons deny this, saying that the seal is not a masonic emblem, nor does it contain hidden masonic symbols. Certainly the pyramid is not masonic. But the eye does figure in masonic imagery, and it even appears on the Freemason's apron worn by George Washington.

The point, however, is that there is nothing specifically masonic about the all-seeing eye, which was part of the cultural iconography of the seventeenth and eighteenth centuries. For example in 1614 the frontispiece of Sir Walter Raleigh's *History of the World* showed an eye in a cloud labelled 'Providentia' overlooking a globe. Nevertheless, for those given to conspiracy theories the meaning lies elsewhere. For Robert Langdon, the hero in Dan Brown's *Angels and Demons*, *novus ordo seclorum* translates as 'new secular order', and for others it prefigures the 'new world order' announced by George H.W. Bush before a joint session of Congress after Saddam Hussein had invaded Kuwait and the United States was mustering a coalition to drive the Iraqi forces back. 'Out of these troubled times', Bush told Congress, 'our fifth objective – a New World Order – can emerge: a new era.' The speech was delivered on 11 September 1990, exactly eleven years before that other '9/11'.

Mormons, Freemasons and the Key to Solomon's Temple

In 1844 when Joseph Smith, the founder of the Mormons, was being attacked by a mob in Illinois, he barely managed to cry out, 'Oh Lord, my God' before he was shot and killed. These were the first words of a recognised distress call among Freemasons – 'Oh Lord, my God, is there no help for the widow's son?' The phrase arises from the ritual enacted by Freemasons who are being admitted to the third degree, that of Master Mason, which allows them to participate fully in all aspects of their brotherhood. The drama at the centre of this initiation ritual is the murder of Hiram, 'the widow's son' of the Bible, whom the Freemasons call Hiram Abiff. The initiate acts out the sufferings of Hiram Abiff, who while vowing to protect the Freemasons' secrets with his life, calls out, 'Oh Lord, my God, is there no help for the widow's son?'

Joseph Smith was himself a Freemason, as were his brother and his father and many of their friends and co-religionists; Brigham Young, who was Smith's successor as leader of the Mormons and led them into Utah where they founded Salt Lake City, was likewise a Freemason. In America Mormonism and Freemasonry grew out of the same soil. Indeed there are many parallels between Mormonism and Freemasonry, including degrees of elevation, sacred treasures hidden in the earth, an interest in ancient Israel and Egypt, symbolic clothing, secret means of recognition and a belief in the creative role of a supreme being.

Also both organisations have made extensive use of such motifs as the beehive, the square and compass, the all-seeing eye, the two right hands clasped to one another, and the sun, the moon and the stars. In particular, Masonic legends of a lost sacred word, once engraved upon a triangular plate of pure gold, profoundly affected the Smith family, which became well known for its treasure-hunting activities; and it was on such plates of gold, unearthed by Joseph Smith in upstate New York, that he found what he said were the words of the Angel Moroni and which he translated and published as the *Book of Mormon*, the gospel of the new faith of which Smith himself was its prophet. The mission of the Mormons is to restore the true revelation which became corrupted after the death of Jesus. And according to the Mormons their rituals and symbolism have come to them by divine revelation and originate in Solomon's Temple.

'Oh Lord, my God, Is there no help for the widow's son?' is the Freemasons' distress call and refers to the murder of Hiram Abiff. Joseph Smith, founder of the Mormons, began this cry for help just before he was shot and killed by a mob in 1844.

Skull and Bones

For some a New World Order (*Novus Ordo Mundi*) means a constructive ordering of world affairs through institutions like the United Nations. For others it is a conspiracy conducted by a small and secretive but powerful group to eliminate or neutralise sovereign states, to restrict individual freedom, and to establish a world government answerable to no one but themselves. This latter idea has much in common with the beliefs of Charles de Gassicour and the Abbé Barruel, who saw the French Revolution as the culmination of an ancient historical plot by the Templars and Freemasons who were in league with everyone from the Assassins to the Jews.

According to the conspiracy theorists, the infrastructure of this New World Order is already largely in place in the form of such organisations as the International Monetary Fund, the World Bank, the Council on Foreign Relations, the Trilateral Commission, the Bilderberg Group, NATO, the European Union – and indeed the United Nations. They point to the statement given by David Rockefeller to the United Nations Business Council in September 1994: 'We are on the verge of a global transformation. All we need is the right major crisis and the nations will accept the New World Order.' But this remark is almost always quoted without context, with the suggestion that it refers to an event like 9/11, when in fact Rockefeller was referring to the need to take united action against global warming and over-population.

The 11th of September 2001 is itself seen as a conspiracy, a not uncommon version being that the attacks were a joint operation between elements in the United States government and Mossad, Israel's secret service. The Freemasons are also blamed, as in this quotation from a website run by a former United States Air Force officer and professor of aerospace systems:

> 'What happened on September 11, 2001, was nothing less than an elaborate, carefully crafted and dynamically staged satanic ritual. I believe the tumbling down of the twin towers of the World Trade Center was a blood sacrifice ... A satanically energized variation of the third degree ritual of Freemasonry was staged – the Master Mason degree – in which the candidate (playing the role of Hiram Abiff, the antichrist) lying in a coffin, is raised by the strong grip of the Lion's Paw. In the ritual it is noted that the two pillars (towers), Jachin and Boaz, have fallen and are in need of restoration. What transpired on September 11th was a black magic ceremony intended to bring about the restoration of the Temple of Solomon in Jerusalem and the raising of its twin pillars which had fallen ...'

For a small and secretive but powerful group promoting the New World Order, one does not have to go farther than the campus of Yale University in New Haven, Connecticut. On High Street a windowless Graeco-Egyptian building, familiarly known as the Tomb, houses the

Order of Skull and Bones. Though known as Bonesmen to the outside world, they call each other knights, and their symbol, the skull and crossbones, is the very sign that the Knights Templar are said to have adopted in exchange for their red cross. At any rate if you were Dan Brown that is something you might work in to your next novel.

Skull and Bones was founded in 1832 in rivalry to the Phi Beta Kappa fraternity. But in fact they are very different organisations. Even in the 1830s Phi Beta Kappa already had chapters at seven universities (and now extends to nearly three hundred), while Skull and Bones has remained exclusive to Yale. Phi Beta Kappa recruits members in their freshman year and has half a million living members at any one time, while Skull and Bones never has more than eight hundred and does not accept members until their senior year, by when it can have some confidence that its members will rise to positions of exceptional eminence in the future.

Originally, Skull and Bones is said to have been the American chapter of a German student organisation that called itself the Eulogian Club, after Eulogia, the goddess of eloquence. The story, however, might have been a cover. A few years earlier, in 1826, a Freemason called William Morgan was murdered in New York for revealing masonic secrets, and there was such a popular outrage and backlash that Freemasonry was all but destroyed in the United States. If the real intention had been to found a Freemason's lodge, it would have been wise to disguise it as something else. Why the skull and bones was ever chosen as the name and symbol is unexplained. The '322' on the order's stationery is said to mark the date of death of the great orator Demosthenes, but '32' might refer to the year of the order's inception, with '2' signifying that it was the second chapter after the German original.

The invitation to join the Skull and Bones comes in a student's junior year with a tap on the shoulder as the tower clock strikes eight and a Bonesman demands, 'Skull and Bones, accept or reject?' President William Howard Taft and various Chief Justices of the Supreme Court and other important figures in the highest ranks of American government have been members. But not a great deal is known about the workings of the order, for everyone is sworn to secrecy, and this is closely observed. President George W. Bush was asked about his time there but would only say, 'In my senior year I joined Skull and Bones, a secret society, so secret I can't say anything more.' And when Senator John Kerry, Bush's rival in the 2004 presidential election, was asked what it meant that both he and Bush were Bonesmen, he replied, 'Not much because it's a secret.' George W. Bush's father, George H. W. Bush, was also a Bonesman; he was president from 1988 to 1992, and had earlier been head of the CIA. While it is not true that the OSS, the predecessor to the CIA, was founded by Bonesmen, it is true that the Skull and Bones can boast of a disproportionately large number of its alumni, called Patriarchs, in the intelligence services and high places in government and business.

Bonesmen including future president George H. W. Bush (left of clock)

Conspiracy theorists see the Skull and Bones as the proponent of a New World Order motivated by Hegelian philosophy and believing that the state is supreme and change is generated only by conflict, which has infiltrated all the elite control groups in the United States. One journalist who tried to get inside information warned, 'They don't like people tampering and prying. The power of Bones is incredible. They've got their hands on every lever of power in the country. It's like trying to look into the Mafia.' But George W. Bush dismisses such talk as 'the kind of connect-the-random-dots charges that are virtually impossible to refute'.

The Templars Forever

The history of the Templars begins with their formation in Jerusalem in 1119 and ends with their destruction two centuries later in France. But in another sense it goes back three thousand years to the Ophel Hill and continues into the future. The secrecy of the Templars, their hybrid nature as monks with swords, the exotic worlds that they encompassed, their romance and sudden fall, and the mysteries left unanswered by the disappearance of their archives, have enlarged them in the popular imagination where they survive and flourish. Powerful associations with such places as the Church of the Holy Sepulchre and the Temple Mount have extended the spiritual dimensions of the order and added layers of history, legend and myth. Romantics and Freemasons, charlatans and lunatics, radicals and reactionaries, Christians, Jews and Muslims, have all contributed to the story.

Just as the search for holy relics in the Middle Ages turned up the most unlikely objects in the most convenient places, so each new pseudo-history or fanciful novel follows the money and adds new places, events and notions to the myth – so that Scotland and the French Revolution are already well established as playing a part, and America is being developed. An imminent leap from Rosslyn to Washington DC via Rhode Island, Salt Lake City and New Haven would not be surprising.

In Umberto Eco's *Foucault's Pendulum* some publisher's editors are thinking up a new series of books to appeal to academics, cultists and conspiracy theorists, something 'in these dark times to offer someone a faith, a glimpse into the beyond', and make a little money. One suggests that they take a few dozen notions and feed them into a computer, 'for example, the Templars fled to Scotland, or the Corpus Hermeticum arrived in Florence in 1460', and add 'a few connective phrases like "It's obvious that" and "This proves that"'. And so they begin at random: 'Joseph of Arimathea carries the Grail into France'; 'According to Templar Tradition, Godefroy de Bouillon founded the Grand Priory of Zion in Jerusalem'; 'Debussy was a Rosicrucian'; 'Minnie Mouse is Mickey's fiancée'. No! They must not overdo it, an editor warns, but the first replies, 'We must overdo it. If we admit that in the whole universe there is even a single fact that does not reveal a mystery, then we violate hermetic thought.' 'That's true', says another. 'Minnie's in. And, if you'll allow me, I'll add a fundamental axiom: The Templars have something to do with everything.'

Part 6
Locations

palais du grand maitre

eglise S.t Jean

An old drawing of Acre shows the palace of the Hospitaller Grand Master and the church of Saint John. Still less survived of the Templar quarter, which was to the left.

Outremer

The Templars in the East

Outremer – French for 'the land across the sea' – was the general name for the Crusader states which ran along the eastern seaboard of the Mediterranean from Asia Minor to Egypt. These were the Kingdom of Jerusalem, the County of Tripoli, the Principality of Antioch and the County of Edessa. Today the region encompasses Israel, the Palestinian Territories, Jordan, Lebanon, Syria and parts of Turkey. But the principal sites associated with the Templars that visitors can see today are in Israel and Syria, and most notably in the Old City of Jerusalem.

Outremer would have fallen much sooner than it did had it not been for the Templars. They defended the Holy Land on the battlefield, and also in numerous castles and fortified cities, remains of which survive across the region. In addition to Jerusalem and Acre, the Templars were based at Tortosa on the Syrian coast, on the island of Arwad, and inland at Safita, which, along with the Hospitaller castle of Krak des Chevalier, guarded the strategically important Homs Gap. All of these places are worth visiting today.

Israel

Jerusalem is central to the story of the Templars. Here in the Church of the Holy Sepulchre on Christmas Day 1119 the founding knights took their vows before patriarch and king, and in the al-Aqsa mosque atop the Temple Mount they established their headquarters. When Saladin captured Jerusalem in 1187, the Templars removed themselves to Acre, the port city which now became the principal metropolis of Outremer, and here too the story of the Templars can be traced among the stones of its walls and towers, and through the secret Templar tunnel to the harbour from where they spirited away their treasure at the final fall of Outremer.

JERUSALEM: THE OLD CITY

Jerusalem has been the centre of the Jewish faith for three thousand years, since Solomon built his Temple here in the tenth century BC. As the site of the crucifixion and resurrection of Jesus in the first century

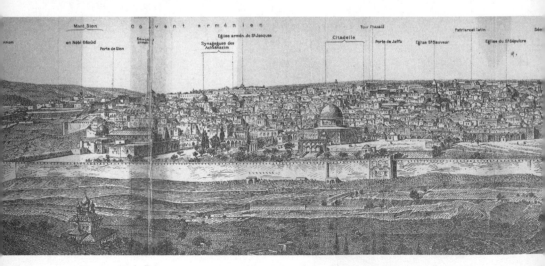

AD, Jerusalem also stands at the fulcrum of the Christian world. For Muslims the Prophet Mohammed's Night Journey in the seventh century AD made Jerusalem Islam's third holiest city after Mecca and Medina. The key Jewish, Christian and Muslim sites are all within the Old City, enclosed within its medieval walls.

The Walls

The walls that enclose the Old City of Jerusalem today were rebuilt by the Ottoman Sultan Suleiman the Magnificent in 1537–41, though they have been restored many times since. They closely follow the line of the walls as they were at the time of the First Crusade in 1099. Today visitors can gain excellent views of the city and its surroundings by walking the circuit of its walls, partly atop its ramparts and partly along the outer footing, a distance of four kilometres in all.

The ramparts can be walked from the Jaffa Gate in the west to Saint Stephen's Gate in the east via the Damascus Gate and Herod's Gate along the northern wall. Just to the east of Herod's Gate is the spot where,

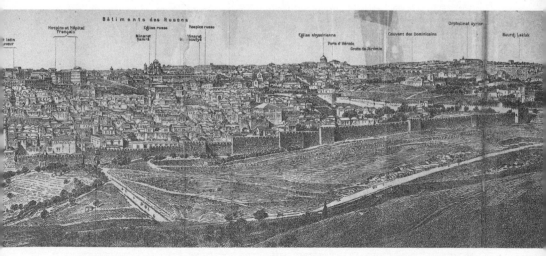

A panorama of Jerusalem from Baedeker's guide to Syria and Palestine, 1912. The al-Aqsa mosque is on the left. To the right of it is the Dome of the Rock.

during the successful First Crusade, at around noon on 15 July 1099, Godfrey of Bouillon fought his way onto the northern battlements and was quickly followed by Tancred and his men, who pushed into the city towards the Temple Mount. Eighty-eight years later, Saladin directed his attack against this same stretch of the northern wall when he laid siege to the city in 1187, leading to its surrender on 2 October. To walk the southern half of the circuit, from Saint Stephen's Gate back to the Jaffa Gate, you must come down from the ramparts and follow the outside of the city wall. The route takes you round the massive retaining walls of the Temple Mount at the southeast corner of the Old City.

Since medieval times the Old City enclosed within these walls has been home to four distinct religious communities, which have gathered into neighbourhoods: the Muslim quarter in the northeast, the Christian quarter in the northwest (but excluding the Armenians, who have their own quarter in the southwest) and the Jewish quarter in the south-central part of the city.

The Church of the Holy Sepulchre

The Church of the Holy Sepulchre is in the Christian quarter in the northwest corner of Jerusalem and stands on the traditional sites of the crucifixion, burial and resurrection of Jesus, which in the first century AD were outside the city walls.

The discovery of the True Cross and also the site where Jesus was entombed and rose on the third day was made by Helena, mother of the Roman emperor Constantine the Great, during her visit to the Holy Land in 326–8. First Constantine ordered that a basilica called the Martyrium (meaning place of witness) be built to encompass the site of Golgotha, that is Calvary, the place of crucifixion, and this was dedicated on 17 September 335. The interior of Constantine's Basilica was faced with multi-coloured marble and its coffered ceiling was covered with gold which was said to ripple and swell like an ocean in the changing light. But the great domed Rotunda, also called the Anastasis (meaning resurrection), erected over the tomb of Jesus took longer to build and was not completed until 340.

The Martyrium and the Rotunda were linked by a court and surrounded by lesser buildings, to which a tumultuous history has lent a hand, so that the church you see today has often been restored. In 614 the Persians attacked Jerusalem, stole the True Cross and set the church alight, destroying its roof and many of its decorations. The church was again put to the torch by rioting Muslims in 938 who also devastated the Golgotha Chapel within Constantine's Basilica and the tomb chapel within the Rotunda. Yet again, and this time on the orders of the Fatimid caliph al-Hakim, in 1009, the church and the tomb were destroyed. A few decades later, and with permission from Cairo, Byzantine emperors rebuilt the church on the old foundations using salvaged material.

The Templars had their origins here in this rebuilt church when on Christmas Day 1119 Hugh of Payns and his eight companions took

The Rotunda of the Church of the Holy Sepulchre during Easter mass. The church encompasses the traditional sites of the crucifixion, burial and resurrection of Jesus.

their vows of poverty, chastity and obedience before the Patriarch of Jerusalem. Calling themselves the Poor Fellow-Soldiers of Christ, they dedicated themselves to defending pilgrims against attack along the roads to the holy places. The Templar Church in London, consecrated by the Patriarch of Jerusalem in 1185, takes its circular design from the Church of the Holy Sepulchre, the holiest place in the Crusaders' world.

Large parts of the Church of the Holy Sepulchre were altered and rebuilt between 1150 and 1180 by the Crusaders. The entrance facade is mostly Crusader work and incorporates Romanesque and Gothic styles, the five-storey bell tower was added in 1153 and Constantine's Basilica, the Martyrium, was rebuilt in Romanesque style, but the Rotunda was left essentially intact. This is the church you see today. During the Kingdom of Jerusalem, the church was the royal burial place, but the tombs were pillaged in 1244 when the Khorezmian Turks sacked the church and massacred the Christians huddled for safety inside.

The Temple Mount

The Hebrew for Temple Mount is Har ha-Bayit, but the mount is better known by its Arabic name, al-Haram ash-Sharif, the Noble Sanctuary. In the days of Kings David and Solomon in the tenth century BC a limestone ridge rose from the Ophel Hill in the south where David built his city (now the City of David Archaeological Garden outside the city walls) and climbed northwards as Mount Zion, reaching its peak where the Dome of the Rock stands today. Thereabouts was the threshing floor of Araunah, the last Jebusite king, where David built an altar and where perhaps Solomon sited the Holy of Holies, the shrine of the Ark of the Covenant, when he built his Temple.

Solomon carved the ridge into a platform for the Temple; the same platform was reused for the Second Temple in the sixth century BC; and then Herod constructed a vaster masonry platform atop the ancient bedrock when he built his immense renovated and extended Temple in the first century BC. Though the Temple was destroyed by the Romans in AD 70, much of the masonry platform and its retaining walls remained.

Over the centuries Jews from all over the world have come to pray at the Western Wall, famously known as the Wailing Wall for the laments heard here, an exposed section of the retaining wall which has come to symbolise not only the lost Temple of Herod but the Temple of Solomon built on this spot three thousand years ago. After the Arab conquest the Muslims built the Dome of the Rock and the al-Aqsa mosque atop the mount. In Crusader times the Temple Mount became an integral part of the city, and the entire southern half of the mount was a Templar complex; indeed their very name is taken from their close association with the Temple Mount.

The Temple Mount is administered by the Muslim authorities, and the Western Wall, at its base, by the rabbinic authorities. Access to the Mount is allowed to all religions, although Orthodox Jews will not visit the Temple Mount at all. Only the Jewish high priest was permitted to enter the Temple's Holy of Holies, and as its exact position remains uncertain, the Orthodox fear walking upon that most sacred of spots.

The Dome of the Rock

The sacred nature of Jerusalem is confirmed for Muslims by the Night Journey in which the angel Gabriel brought Mohammed to the Temple Mount, the site of Solomon's Temple, from where they ascended to Paradise (*Koran 17:1*). Octagonal in plan and topped with a golden dome, and standing over the oblong rock from where the ascent was made, the Dome of the Rock is more a shrine than a mosque, a place where the faithful come on pilgrimage and circle round the ambulatories in prayer. It is the second most important place of pilgrimage after Mecca.

Begun in 687 by order of the Umayyad caliph Marwan and completed in its essentials in 691, the Dome of the Rock was built by Syrian craftsmen in the Byzantine tradition and was covered inside and out with mosaics of gold and coloured tesserae. The interior mosaics round the outer ambulatory are original and date to 691; they bear designs of palm trees, sprays of foliage, garlands of flowers and fruits, and bunches of grapes. Elsewhere the interior mosaics have been renewed several

In this aerial view of the Temple Mount, the Dome of the Rock, which stands on the site of the Temple of Solomon, is at the centre and the al-Aqsa mosque, which the Templars made their headquarters, is on the right.

times, for example by Saladin though also as recently as the late 1950s, but they faithfully follow the designs of the originals. The exterior mosaics were replaced with Turkish tiles in the sixteenth century and these were renewed in the late 1950s. The present dome was put in place in 1961 but like the original it is made of wood and is covered with gilded lead.

The structure is also decorated both inside and out with calligraphic inscriptions which are composed of all the Koranic references to Jesus, including the warning to Christians (Koran 4:171) that their faith, based on the divinity of Jesus, is false: 'People of the Book, do not transgress the bounds of your religion. Speak nothing but the truth about God. The Messiah, Jesus the son of Mary, was no more than God's apostle and His Word which He cast to Mary: a spirit from Him. So believe in God and His apostles and do not say: "Three". Forebear, and it shall be better for you. God is but one God. God forbid that He should have a son! His is all that the heavens and the earth contain. God is the all-sufficient protector.'

But traditions about the rock directly beneath the dome long antedate the Muslim conquest of Jerusalem. The rock is the peak of the mount now covered over by the man-made platform, and so it is the highest point in the Old City. An early Christian source, known only as the Bordeaux Pilgrim, who visited the Holy Land in AD 333, noted the Jewish attachment to the rock, writing that it is a 'perforated stone to which the Jews come every year and anoint it, bewail themselves with groans, rend their garments, and so depart'. To Jews it is known as the Foundation Stone, for they believe that this is where David offered up his sacrifice after purchasing the threshing floor from Araunah the Jebusite.

Though secular scholars may debate the exact position of Solomon's Temple and its plan, many Jews have no doubt that the rock formed the base of the Holy of Holies and was the spot where the Ark of the Covenant stood. They also believe that during the Second Temple, when the Ark had vanished or was hidden, the stone was where the high priest sprinkled the blood of sacrifices and offered up the incense during the Yom Kippur service.

There is a chamber beneath the rock, reached by a flight of marble stairs; the chamber is about six feet high and nearly square with each side measuring about fifteen feet. The first mention of an opening in the rock was made by the Bordeaux Pilgrim, but the first documented reference to the cave beneath the rock was made by an Arab visitor called Ibn al-Faqih in 903: 'Under the rock is a cavern in which the people pray. This cavern is capable of containing 62 persons.' The Crusaders installed the marble entrance to the stairway and recut the chamber, which they used for confession.

After the Crusader capture of Jerusalem in 1099 the Dome of the Rock was turned into a church, the *Templum Domini* or Temple of the Lord, and also served as the residence of the Latin Patriarch of Jerusalem. The canons of the Church of the Holy Sepulchre established a convent in the northeast corner of the outer court and the Templars also built some living quarters here and planted gardens.

The Mystery of the Rock and Its Subterranean Chamber

There is no mention of the rock nor the chamber beneath it during the Jewish period. This is not surprising as the man-made platform on which the Temples of Solomon and Herod stood entirely covered the rock. There is evidence to suggest that the Roman emperor Hadrian reduced the summit of the Temple Mount by several feet with the purpose of erasing the Jewish nature of Jerusalem. Only then, as the upper level of Herod's platform was cleared away, did the rock become exposed. Originally the rock had marked the summit of the mount, but once it was covered by the platform it bore no particular relationship to the siting of the altar nor to the Holy of Holies in the Temples of Solomon and Herod. As for the chamber beneath the rock, it is thought to have been a tomb cut four thousand years ago and forgotten long before Araunah had his threshing floor here. After lowering the platform, Hadrian had intended to build a shrine to Jupiter on this spot, but he never did. The rock and subterranean chamber were left exposed, leaving Jewish and Muslim traditions to lend religious significance to the site.

The Temple Mount is riddled with tunnels and caverns, but this nineteenth-century cross-section, by Italian engineer Ermete Pierotti, is entirely fanciful in showing a tunnel running between the cave beneath the Dome of the Rock (right) and the al-Aqsa mosque (left)

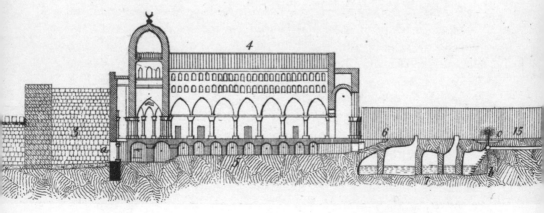

Al-Aqsa Mosque

After the Arab conquest of Jerusalem in 638 the Muslim commander, Umar, had a temporary mosque built at the southern end of the Temple Mount. Umar's mosque was replaced sixty years later when work began on the mosque of al-Aqsa, which was completed in 715. Al-Aqsa means 'the farthest' and was originally applied to the entire Temple Mount, being that farthest place where Mohammed ascended into Paradise according to an interpretation of *Sura 17:1* in the Koran. Al-Aqsa, a basilica with a lead dome that shines silvery in the sun, became the great congregational mosque of Jerusalem, the place of Friday prayers and the midday sermon.

Fatimids, Ayyubids, Mamelukes, Ottomans and, since the 1920s, the Supreme Muslim Council have altered, extended or rebuilt the mosque, so that it is a palimpsest of thirteen centuries of architectural history. The Crusaders also played an important role. In 1099 it became the headquarters of the Crusader leader Godfrey of Bouillon, and for several years it served as a palace for Baldwin I, the first king of Jerusalem. The Crusaders called it the mosque of the *Templum Solomonis* because they believed that it stood on the site of Solomon's Temple, so that when Baldwin gave the building to the new knighthood of the Poor

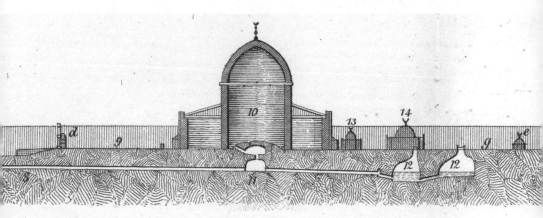

Fellow-Soldiers of Christ in 1119 it was not long before they were calling themselves the Poor Fellow-Soldiers of Christ and of the Temple of Solomon – or, simply, the Templars.

Al-Aqsa was the Templars' administrative, military and religious headquarters for over sixty years. They made various structural alterations and extensions to provide chambers for the Grand Master and other officers of the order and their staff, living quarters for the knights, and storage rooms for food, clothing and arms, but they took care not to damage the fine Arab decorations. Some Templar work survives, most notably the annexe they built to the east of the mosque which is now incorporated in the Women's Mosque and the Islamic Museum, and they also left their mark on Solomon's Stables.

Solomon's Stables

Solomon's Stables were in fact vaulted cellars built by Herod the Great to support his immense platform of the Temple Mount when he extended and refurbished the Second Temple in the first century BC. The vast masonry underpinning raised the ground level at the southeast corner of the Temple Mount by 150 feet. There are thought to be four levels of vaulting, but only the topmost level is accessible, and at present this is closed to tourists. The Umayyads reused Herodian masonry to restore this topmost level in the late seventh and early eighth centuries, and later the Templars rebuilt the arches. In addition to offering structural support for the Temple Mount platform and later the al-Aqsa mosque built above this spot, the cellars may have served Herod's Temple as storerooms. The Templars were probably the first to use them as stables, and there are still rings attached to many of the pillars which were used to tether their horses.

A tunnel runs from the southern retaining wall of the Temple Mount underneath Solomon's Stables. At a distance of 100 feet the tunnel is blocked by pieces of stone and debris, and archaeologists have not been able to examine it further because of objections from the Muslim authorities. But from the way the tunnel was constructed, often using large blocks from the period of Herod's Temple, archaeologists have concluded that it was built as a postern by the Templars. The entrance would have been somewhere on the surface of the Temple Mount, and its exit in the southern wall would have allowed the Templars to emerge and make sudden surprise attacks against their enemies.

The Islamic Museum

Architectural fragments and other objects removed from the various structures on the Temple Mount during renovations have been put on display at the Islamic Museum. Among these are some items of Crusader workmanship. But the finest thing about the museum is the Templar vaulted hall, which serves as the chief exhibition space. The hall was built in the 1160s and was part of that magnificent complex described by Theoderich, a pilgrim who visited the Holy Land in 1172.

> On another side of the [al-Aqsa] palace, that is to say, on the western side, the Templars have erected a new building. I could give the measurements of its height, length and breadth of its cellars, refectories, staircases and roof, rising with a high pitch, unlike the flat roofs of that country; but even if I did so, my hearers would hardly be able to believe me.

In fact what you are seeing is only the western half of the hall, which after Saladin captured Jerusalem in 1187 became the assembly hall of a madrassa. The eastern half of the Templar hall was converted into the Women's Mosque of the al-Aqsa, which it remains to this day.

ACRE

Acre, or Akko in Hebrew, is on a low promontory about twelve miles north of Haifa. As the maritime gateway to Outremer throughout the Crusader period, Acre was the chief port of trade and the principal landing point for pilgrims. In 1191, four years after Jerusalem was lost to Saladin, Acre also became the capital of the truncated Kingdom of Jerusalem, and both the Templars and the Hospitallers established their headquarters here. Acre was the most powerfully defended city in

Outremer, and the Templar fortress by the sea was the strongest place in the city. But in 1291, after a long siege, Acre fell to the overwhelming Mameluke forces, which effectively marked the end of the crusading venture in the Holy Land. On the orders of the victorious Mameluke Sultan al-Ashraf Khalil, everyone remaining alive within the town was brought outside the walls and decapitated, and Acre was levelled to the ground.

Four hundred years later, however, the Ottomans began rebuilding Acre, often reusing the fallen stones, and standing their new walls and buildings on the Crusaders' foundations. This has given Acre a medieval atmosphere which, together with its striking situation looking out upon the sea, helps the visitor to imagine how the Crusader city used to be. Moreover, recent archaeological work has uncovered much of the

The Templars' secret tunnel which ran beneath the streets
of Crusader Acre was discovered only in 1994

Frankish past, in particular the Crusader Underground City and the Templar Tunnel.

You can start by walking along the Sea Wall Promenade, which for the most part follows the line of the Crusader walls. At the southwest corner of the walls where they jut out into the sea is a lighthouse, and just north of it is an area of quarried rock, now underwater, which was the site of the Templar fortress. The fortress was destroyed by the Mamelukes in 1291 and what stone blocks remained were put towards building the eighteenth-century sea walls. Just opposite this spot is the entrance to the Templar Tunnel, discovered only in 1994. The bottom part of the tunnel is cut from the bedrock, while the upper part is a barrel vault built of hewn stone. The section of the tunnel that runs westwards under the sea to the Templar fortress is not accessible, but you can follow the tunnel for a thousand feet eastwards under the old Pisan quarter to where it emerges at the Khan al-Shuna, the Grain Inn, which stands on twelfth century foundations.

Built against the northern land walls is the eighteenth-century Ottoman citadel, the largest building in Acre, which was built over the remains of the twelfth- and thirteenth-century Hospitaller headquarters which have been excavated and cleared by archaeologists. What stands revealed is the Crusader Underground City, an immense and majestic complex of halls, storerooms, hospice and crypt arranged in four wings around a courtyard. Vast as the complex is, this is only a single level of what was once a four-storey building. It is the largest surviving Crusader structure in Israel, and yet according to contemporary accounts the now vanished Templar fortress was far grander.

Syria

Tortosa of the Crusaders, known today as Tartus, was an important pilgrimage port and a strategic gateway between the Mediterranean and the Syrian interior. Tartus stands at the seaward end of the Homs Gap, which cuts through the Jebel al-Sariya, the coastal mountain range, while at the eastern end of the gap lies the important city of Homs and beyond that Damascus, which together with Cairo in Egypt was the mustering place of Muslim forces directed against the Franks of Outremer. In defence against this threat the Templars fortified Tortosa, whose cathedral stands as the finest survival of Crusader religious architecture outside Jerusalem, and in the mountains they built Chastel Blanc, or Safita as it is known today, which together with the nearby Hospitaller castle of Krak des Chevaliers gave the Crusaders complete control over the one important route between the interior of Syria and the sea. In 1291, the year when Outremer was overwhelmed by the final Mameluke assault, the Templars at Tortosa hung on two months longer than the defenders at Acre, and they clung on to their offshore island of Arwad for yet eleven years more.

TARTUS (TORTOSA)

The old quarter of Tartus, Tortosa of the Templars, is built within the remains of the Crusader citadel. A good section of its sea wall runs along the Mediterranean, while on the landward sides the citadel is encircled by an inner and outer wall. Much of these land walls survive, though they can be difficult to follow because houses have been built into the arches and bastions and are fixed against the walls themselves. The citadel occupied less than a quarter of the Crusader city and that too was surrounded by a wall, almost entirely vanished now, its southern end marked by a free-standing square tower about 500 yards to the south of the citadel and just opposite the little harbour where you can catch a launch to the island of Arwad.

Tortosa was originally in the hands of the Count of Tripoli (Trablus down the coast in northern Lebanon) who placed it in the care of the Templars following its brief occupation by Nur al-Din in 1152. The knights held out against Saladin's siege in 1188 by bolting themselves inside the keep, which rises just behind the sea wall. Entering through an opening in the sea wall you thread your way through the tangle of streets and jumble of habitations that fill the citadel enclosure. A little square with a leafy café opens up immediately behind the remains of the Templars' keep. On the north side of the square are the traces of a thirteenth-century Templar banqueting hall, while to the northeast are the remains of their chapel.

But what is especially worth seeing is the Cathedral of Our Lady of Tortosa, which lies 300 yards to the southeast, beyond the citadel walls but within what was the line of the Templars' city walls. If in doubt you can ask for the *kanisa*, church, or the *mathaf*, museum, which is what the cathedral has become, though during the centuries following the withdrawal of the Crusaders from the Holy Land it served as a mosque, a stables and an Ottoman barracks. A chapel, reputedly the first dedicated to the Virgin, is known to have been built here in the third century, long before the Roman Empire officially tolerated Christianity. When two

The fortress-like Cathedral of Our Lady at Tortosa was built to last by the Templars, after an attack by Saladin in 1188

centuries later the chapel was felled by an earthquake, the disaster was proclaimed a miracle, for the altar had survived. The Count of Tripoli built upon this history when he began construction of the cathedral in 1123 to house the miraculous altar and receive the prayers of pilgrims. But the church you see today was largely rebuilt by the Templars after they withstood Saladin's attack on Tortosa in 1188 when he destroyed most of the city, including much of the cathedral.

You enter Our Lady of Tortosa from the west, where the cathedral presents a blank wall pierced only by a small door, above which is a triangular arrangement of windows with slightly pointed arches marking the transition from the Romanesque to the Gothic. The impression is more of a fortress than a church, and you notice the vestiges of corner towers that would have served a defensive purpose. Not that it was of any help to eighteen-year-old Raymond, heir to the thrones of Antioch and Tripoli, who in 1213 was stabbed to death outside this door by two Assassins.

When you step inside you discover a medieval French cathedral, the most graceful religious building of the Crusaders in Syria. It is bare of Christian ornament, and its empty volume swallows the whispers of occasional visitors. Undazzled by detail, your eyes follow the trajectories of massive arches which soar from acanthus capitals, and you are impressed with the sense that Our Lady of Tortosa was built by men who meant to stay in the Holy Land forever.

SAFITA (CHASTEL BLANC)

Safita is approached through ascending terraces of orchards and olive groves. The town of stone-built houses painted white and pink, now an attractive summer mountain resort, has grown up around the castle the Templars called Chastel Blanc, an outpost of Tortosa against Assassin territory to the northeast and contributing towards the defence of the Homs Gap. The encircling walls of the fortress are gone but their pattern remains evident in the layout of streets and houses; what remains is the massive hilltop keep, visible against the sky for miles in every direction.

As Chastel Blanc was a Templar fortress it should come as no surprise that on entering the keep you discover that the ground floor was built as a church. Its high and dimly lit vaulted nave is rounded off by an apse at the east end with a sacristy on each side. The church was never turned into a mosque nor deconsecrated, and it now serves the Greek Orthodox community which moved here in the nineteenth century after being squeezed out of the Hauran in southern Syria by the Druze. A staircase to the right of the doorway takes you up to the first floor, which served as an armoury and housed the garrison. A further staircase leads to the open terrace at the top of the tower, in part still crenellated, with panoramic views of the town and the surrounding landscape, ranging as far as Krak des Chevaliers along the horizon to the southeast and a glimpse of the Mediterranean to the west.

The keep of Chastel Blanc, the Templars' castle at Safita, was an outpost against the Assassins, whose castle at Masyaf was close by

KRAK DES CHEVALIERS

Krak des Chevaliers, known in Arabic as Qalaat al-Husn, was a Hospitaller castle, not a Templar one, but it is mentioned here because it was part of that network of defences in the southern Jebel al-Sariya and along the Syrian coast that was the shared responsibility of the two military orders. Krak is also almost entirely undamaged and is a superb example of the concentric system, with one defensive wall set within the other, each one higher than the one before, which allowed for successive stages of retreat if need be, the defenders always having the advantage of dominating the attackers from a greater height. Situated on a mountain ridge within sight of Safita and overlooking the Homs Gap, the castle was built and expanded in phases by the Hospitallers from 1144 onwards. Its control of this strategic corridor and its forward position, so close to Homs and Hama and nearly intersecting the interior route between Damascus and Aleppo, caused one Saracen chronicler to describe it as 'a bone stuck in the very throat of the Muslims'. Yet despite repeated attempts against it, Krak held firm, and even Saladin, after his great victory over the Kingdom of Jerusalem at Hattin in 1187, took one look at its defences and marched away.

After climbing up a dark vaulted switchback ramp and passing through a portcullis you enter the court, a narrow and economical space faced on one side with an elegant loggia, where the light sifts through fine stone tracery reminiscent of Rheims. 'Grace, wisdom and beauty you may enjoy', runs the Latin inscription cut into the stone, 'but beware pride which alone can tarnish all the rest.' Beyond the loggia is a great dining hall and behind that a huge nave-like chamber, at one time filled with kitchens and bakeries, granaries and storage jars, for siege was always expected and the major castles were stocked with provisions to last up to five years. Opposite the loggia is a barrel-vaulted twelfth-century chapel built in the Romanesque style and later converted to a mosque.

The best place to appreciate the magnificence of Krak's position is from the Warden's Tower where a spiral staircase rises to a graceful and voluminous chamber, the Grand Master's apartment. Below you, like

The Hospitaller castle of Krak des Chevalier overlooking the Homs Gap was part of a defensive system which included the Templars' Chastel Blanc and their fortified city of Tartus

some giant nautilus, swirl the concentric circles of the castle's defences, the vast structure seeming to sail like a battleship high above rolling waves of orchards and wheat fields, a bountiful landscape as familiar as Provence.

Krak was not taken; it was given away. In the last years of Outremer, Krak and Safita and the other mountain castles became isolated, vulnerable and undermanned outposts facing the gathering storm of an overwhelming Mameluke enemy. Finally, after Krak had been in Christian hands for 161 years, and after a month's siege, the Hospitaller knights accepted Sultan Baybars' offer of safe passage and in 1271 rode to Tortosa of the Templars and the sea for the last time.

Arwad (Ruad)

Known to the Templars as Ruad, Arwad lies two miles off the coast of Syria, opposite Tartus. A fishing town almost completely covers the little island. There are no streets, only twisting lanes with narrowing passages, and in their midst the Crusader castle from where the Templars from Tortosa clung to a view of Christendom's lost prize for eleven years longer, until 1302.

One of an endless series of launches from Tartus lands you at the island's harbour where fishermen mend their nets near restaurants and cafés which serve the constant stream of daytrippers. Behind these are the walls of a small Muslim castle, and by this is the market, which twists back into the town. Follow this to higher ground towards the west side of the island and you come to the Crusader fortress, probably thirteenth century, with massive round corner towers. This was the last outpost of the Templars; now it is the local museum. Next to its gate is a carved relief of a lion chained to a palm, a declaration made in vain that the Crusaders were forever attached to Outremer.

Europe

The Templars in the West

By the time of their downfall in 1307 the Templars had built up a network of at least 870 castles and preceptories (that is houses and estates) throughout almost every European country which adhered to the Roman Catholic faith. But overwhelmingly their principal properties were in France, with lesser numbers in the Iberian peninsula (Spain and Portugal) and Britain. Today the situation is reversed. The most numerous Templar survivals are in Britain, Spain and Portugal, but owing to the destruction of the Templars by King Philip IV there is almost nothing to see in France.

Nevertheless it is still possible to follow the drama of events in France. Wandering round the Temple quarter in Paris, where the Templar leaders were arrested at dawn, and going to the spot along the Seine where the last Grand Master, James of Molay, was bound to a stake and burnt to death, works powerfully on the imagination and helps bring the climactic history of the order alive. In Spain and Portugal, countries which the Templars helped liberate from Muslim occupation, the order was protected and continued in new guises. For this reason several magnificent Templar castles and churches have survived there more or less intact. Much can be seen in Britain, too, where Templars were treated lightly and their properties largely returned to the noble families which had donated them to the order.

France

Perhaps no country in the West is more associated with the Templars than France. Their dramatic rise and fall was played out in such places as Troyes, Paris and Chinon. But the assault on the Templars by the French crown was so vicious and complete that very little remains to be seen. The ghosts of the Templars still inhabit certain quarters of Paris, however, and you can walk in their footsteps today.

PARIS: THE TEMPLE

The Paris Temple was in the area known today as the Marais, which is on the Right Bank just west of the Bastille. The Marais is one of the most atmospheric parts of Paris; it was left largely untouched by Baron Haussmann, the nineteenth-century planner whose love of the straight line and the grand vista led him to demolish great swathes of the old city to create the long broad boulevards lined by six- to seven-storey buildings with uniform grey facades and mansard roofs that are the architectural hallmark of Paris today. Instead the Marais is a warren of enchanting narrow streets which preserve magnificent Renaissance mansions built round intimate courtyards and humbler but no less appealing seventeenth- and eighteenth-century streets of stucco facades and slatted shutters. Yet the area was nothing more than a riverside swamp (*marais*) until the Knights Templar drained the land in the 1140s and built their headquarters in its northern part, then outside the city walls, in what is now called the Quartier du Temple.

Now nothing remains of the Paris Temple except the name itself. But the rues du Temple, Bretagne, Picardie and Beranger more or less define

The Templars' quarter in Paris survived for centuries after their fall, as evidenced by this plan of 1734. During the French Revolution, Louis XVI and Marie Antoinette were imprisoned in the Templar keep

the place occupied by the Templars' French headquarters, which was a considerable compound fortified with walls and towers to which they added, in the late thirteenth century, a powerfully built keep which was nearly twice as high as the White Tower, the keep at the heart of the Tower of London. The Templar keep in Paris was the main strongroom for the Templar bank, which was also, in effect, the treasury of the kings of France.

The close relationship between the French crown and the Templars probably explains why King Philip IV's officials were able to walk right in to the Temple at dawn on Friday 13 October 1307. Their action was so sudden, and the shock and surprise so complete, that there was no resistance. The keep, which had been the Templars' stronghold, immediately became their prison, and the two thousand or so Templars arrested simultaneously throughout France were also brought here for incarceration, examination and torture.

After the abolition of the Templars, the Paris Temple became the abode of artisans and debtors eager to avoid official regulations by living outside the city walls. But a new wall built in 1357 brought the Temple within the embrace of the growing city where it remained standing for four and a half centuries more. During the French Revolution King Louis XVI was imprisoned in the Templar keep and it was from

A late fourteenth-century illustration of the burning of James of Molay and Geoffrey of Charney on the Isle de Javiaux in the Seine

there in January 1793 that he was led out to the guillotine in what is now the Place de la Concorde. In 1808 the keep was demolished by Napoleon, who was eager to eradicate anything that might become a focus of sympathy for the royal family.

Ile des Javiaux: the Burning of the Last Templars

On the evening of 18 March 1314 James of Molay, the Templar Grand Master, and Geoffrey of Charney, the Templar's master of Normandy, were burnt at the stake on the Ile de Javiaux in the Seine. It is said that as James of Molay was bound to the stake he asked to be allowed to face the Cathedral of Notre Dame. You can revisit the scene, but you must make allowances for changes in the river. Medieval maps of Paris show four islands in the Seine. The westernmost is the Ile de la Cité with the Cathedral of Notre Dame. The next two islands to the east are shown as uninhabited; they have since joined together to form the Ile St Louis. The easternmost island of the four, which is also shown as uninhabited, is the Ile des Javiaux – but there is no island there today. Instead the island has become attached to the north bank of the Seine, and what was once the river channel to the north is now the Boulevard Morland. Along the Quai Henri IV, which follows the outline of what was the southern side of the Ile des Javiaux, there is a plaque which reads: *A cet endroit Jacques de Molay dernier grand maitre de l'ordre du Temple été brulé le 18 Mars 1314* – 'On this spot James of Molay, the last Grand Master of the Order of the Temple, was burned on 18 March 1314'. The Cathedral of Notre Dame still forms part of the view.

Spain

In Spain, as discussed earlier, the Templars were protected by King Jaime II of Aragon and reformed as the Order of Montessa, retaining most of their former properties and playing a role in defending the frontier against the remaining Muslim kingdoms of Andalusia.

There are, therefore, a number of well-preserved Templar sites in Spain, including the castles at Peñíscola near Valencia and Miravet in Catalonia. However, it is the Templars' church at Segovia and their castle at Ponferrada that perhaps best illustrate the order's presence and their architecture in Spain.

SEGOVIA: CHURCH OF VERA CRUZ

Segovia, about fifty miles north of Madrid, is a small medieval city built on a rocky ridge. It is famous for its Roman aqueduct, its late Gothic cathedral and the Alcazar, a fortified palace of the Spanish kings which was built upon the remains of an earlier Arab fortress. But across the river in a striking position in open countryside and looking back at the walled medieval city and its Alcazar is Segovia's finest ancient church, the Iglesia Vera Cruz, the Church of the True Cross. Patterned on the Rotunda of the Church of the Holy Sepulchre in Jerusalem, it was built

The Templar round Church of the True Cross outside Segovia

by the Templars in the early thirteenth century and is still impressive despite the alteration of its appearance caused by the addition of a later tower. On the outside the church is twelve-sided but the nave within is circular, and at its centre is a two-storey chamber where a chapel on its upper floor contained a piece of the True Cross (now removed to the nearby village church at Zamarramala).

PONFERRADA: THE TEMPLAR CASTLE

During the twelfth century the Christian rulers of the various Spanish kingdoms made extremely generous donations to the military orders. The Templars and the Hospitallers received estates in the north and castles in central Spain with the intention that they should defend the invasion routes used by the Muslim armies. One of these kingdoms was Leon, which later divided, one part joining Castile, the other joining Portugal. As part of this policy of bestowing lands on the military orders, in 1178 Ferdinand II of Leon donated Ponferrada to the Templars so that they could protect the pilgrimage route across northern Spain to Santiago de Compostela.

The cathedral at Compostela was said to hold the remains of Jesus' cousin, Saint James the Apostle, a belief that sprang up not long after the Great Mosque at Cordoba in southern Spain was said to hold a bone from the body of the Prophet Mohammed. Soon Saint James was being identified with the Reconquista and was seen fighting alongside the Christians at forty battles against the occupying Arabs. The pilgrimage to the saint's relics at Compostela quickly caught the imagination of Christian Europe, and at the height of its popularity in the eleventh and twelfth centuries the city was receiving over half a million pilgrims a year. After Jerusalem and Rome, Compostela was regarded as the third holiest site in Christendom, and completion of a pilgrimage to the relics ensured the remission of half one's time in Purgatory.

The Castillo de los Templarios is one of the most beautiful examples of military architecture in Spain. It had been a mud and pebble Roman castro which the Templars built up into an enormous castle built on an irregular square plan with powerful stone walls and crenellated ramparts linking twelve large towers. By guaranteeing the security of pilgrims against local brigands and Muslim incursions, the Templars ensured that Ponferrada and the region enjoyed the benefits of the passing trade, including commercial development and population growth. The castle rises above the river Sil and dominates the city's historic quarter. The approach is over a drawbridge spanning a moat; you then enter through a double arch flanked by two towers. A vast courtyard lies within, off which are various chambers including an armoury and stables, and on the far side a massive keep where the Templar master of Castille had his quarters. Recently restored, the castle has been declared a World Heritage Site by UNESCO.

Portugal

Portugal came into existence as a separate kingdom during the centuries of Christian resistance against the Muslim forces that had occupied the Iberian peninsula, a resistance in which the Templars played an important part. As in Spain, the Portuguese monarchy refused to turn against the Templars when the French king Philip IV found it politically and financially convenient to destroy them, and instead the new Order of Christ was founded. The finest Templar monuments are found in central Portugal, close to one another at Tomar and Almourol. There are, in addition and outside the direct orbit of this book, superb monuments from the Order of Christ at Sagres, where Henry the Navigator made his base, and at Belém, outside of Lisbon.

TOMAR

After the Christian reconquest of central Portugal from the Muslims, a vast part of the frontier region was given to the Knights Templar by the Portuguese king. Tomar, to the northeast of present-day Lisbon, was founded in 1160 on the site of an ancient Roman city when the Templar Grand Master of Portugal, Gualdim Pais, laid the first stone of the castle and monastery that would become the headquarters of the order in the country. The Templar presence at Tomar protected Christian settlers from the north against Arab incursions, and in 1190 they saved the entire country from being overrun by Abu Yusef al-Mansur, the Almohad caliph of Morocco. Al-Mansur had already ravaged southern Portugal by the time he laid siege to Tomar where he faced a vastly out-numbered garrison of Templars, yet they broke the back of al-Mansur's attack and drove him back to Morocco.

Thankful to the Templars for helping to establish and defend the new kingdom of Portugal, King Diniz resisted French and Papal pressure to suppress the order and hand over its possessions to the Church. Instead, in 1319 he transferred Templar property and personnel to the newly created Order of Christ, which for a while was centred at Castro Marim in the Algarve but after 1356 returned to Tomar. Prince Henry the Navigator, who was made Grand Master of the Order of Christ in 1418,

renovated and enlarged the Convento do Cristo (as the Templars' castle with its round church was called) and designed the geometrical pattern of streets seen in Tomar today, even as he was using Templar resources to send his ships on bold voyages into the Atlantic and down the coast of Africa, his caravels powered before the winds by sails painted with the Templar cross.

Convento do Cristo

Built as a Templar stronghold in 1160, the Convento do Cristo sits impressively on a hill overlooking the river Nabão and the town. The castle has an outer wall and a citadel with a keep inside. The keep is one of the oldest in Portugal; the idea was introduced to the country by the Templars, as was the use of round

A statue of a Knight of Christ with his Templar shield at the Convento do Cristo at Tomar

towers in the outer walls, which were less susceptible to mining than square towers and improved the defensive lines of fire. When Tomar was founded, most of its inhabitants lived in houses enclosed within the protective outer walls of the castle. As Grand Master of the Order of Christ, Prince Henry the Navigator had his palace here; its remains can be seen immediately to the right when entering the castle walls.

The famous round church within the castle was built in the second half of the twelfth century and like several other Templar churches across Europe it was modelled after the Rotunda of the Church of the Holy Sepulchre in Jerusalem. From the outside it is a sixteen–sided structure, with strong buttresses, round windows and a bell tower. Inside the church is circular and has a central octagonal structure, connected by arches to a surrounding ambulatory. After Prince Henry the Navigator became Grand Master of the Order of Christ he had a Gothic nave added to the round church, so that the rotunda became the apse of the enlarged church. The Convent of Christ of Tomar is one of Portugal's most important historical and artistic monuments and is a UNESCO World Heritage Site.

Church of Santa Maria do Olival

On the eastern side of Tomar is the Templar church of Santa Maria do Olival. Twenty-two Portuguese Templar masters were buried in the church, among them Gauldim Pais, master from 1157 to 1195 and the founder of the castle and the city of Tomar. He made a name for himself during the conquest of Santarem in 1147, followed by Lisbon in 1149, before heading off to Outremer where he took part in the siege of Gaza in 1153. The original inscribed slab still covers the recess in the wall containing Pais' ashes. His bravery in his tireless struggle against the Muslim invader made him the epitome of a Knight Templar, and his memory continues to be cherished in Portugal.

The church passed into the hands of the successor to the Templars, the Order of Christ, and during the age of discoveries when Portugal was building up a great empire overseas, Santa Maria do Olival served as the mother church of all the churches of Africa, Asia and the

Americas. The interior of the church is very simple. Its three naves are covered by a wooden roof supported by pointed arches rising from columns lacking capitals. The main chapel of the apse is covered by a Gothic ribbed vault. Above the church entrance is a window in the form of an open rose, while a window above the apse is in the form of the Signum Salmonis, that is the Seal of Solomon.

ALMOUROL

About twelve miles south of Tomar is the remarkable castle of Almourol rising from a small rocky island in the middle of the Tagus river. An older castle stood on this site when the area passed to the control of the Knights Templar during the Reconquista, but by 1171 they had rebuilt what they found, introducing innovations from their experience in Outremer, including the ten round towers set along the outer walls and the three-storey keep, just as at Tomar.

The castle on its island has a fairy-tale quality, as though conjured up by some medieval magician. Arriving at the island by boat, you can climb up through the trees to the well-preserved castle and keep.

The Templar castle of Almourol surveys the Tagus river

Britain

Place names such as Temple, Temple Hirst, Temple Bruer, Temple Balsall, Templecombe, Temple Ewell and Strood Temple Manor are scattered across England, and Scotland too, testimony to the way the story of the Knights Templar is woven into the living fabric of Britain. And that is not to mention the many other places without Temple in their name but which nevertheless have powerful Templar associations.

For example, in London the Church of All Hallows by the Tower, right by the Tower of London, has an altar in its crypt that the Templars are said to have brought from their last foothold in the Holy Land at Athlit, south of Haifa. Saint Mary the Virgin at Shipley in West Sussex is the village parish church, but its strong Romanesque design, the high spacious nave and chancel and the massive central tower mark it as a Templar edifice. The manor and land were among the earliest endowments to the order, and the church was built soon after, in about 1140. The Templars also made their presence felt at the shrine of Saint Thomas Cantilupe in Hereford Cathedral. Saint Thomas, the last Englishman to be canonised before the Reformation, died in 1282. He was bishop of Hereford but also provincial Grand Master of the Knights Templar, and fourteen Templars are carved round the base of his tomb. The Old Temple Kirk in the village of Temple in Midlothian, Scotland, is Gothic in style and might be late twelfth-century Templar work, though more probably it was built later by the Hospitallers. Nevertheless the village of Temple, not far from Edinburgh, was certainly the headquarters of the Knights Templar in Scotland, and if in fact nothing tangible remains from their time, the place can justly lay claim to genuine historical associations. In contrast, associations of a speculative kind have attached themselves to nearby Rosslyn Chapel, just a few miles' walk away, which, since featuring in Dan Brown's *The Da Vinci Code*, has become one of the most visited sites in Scotland.

More is said about Rosslyn Chapel below, but of indisputable historical interest there is nothing to beat Temple Church in London and Cressing Temple in the county of Essex.

LONDON: THE TEMPLE CHURCH

The Temple Church is the oldest building in the Inns of Court, a quiet backwater of London south of Fleet Street, unless you are part of Britain's industrious legal profession for whom this is the mother hive. Rather like Oxford and Cambridge colleges, the Inns are divided into distinct institutions: Inner Temple, Middle Temple, Lincoln's Inn and Gray's Inn. The first two get their names from the Knights Templar whose headquarters were at this spot.

Hugh of Payns, the first Grand Master of the Templars, established the first Templar house in London in 1128, on the site of present-day Southampton House in Holborn. This became known as the Old Temple when the Templars moved to a larger site to the south between Fleet Street and the River Thames. The new site originally included much of what is now Lincoln's Inn, and the knights were probably responsible for establishing New Street (now Chancery Lane), which led from Holborn down to their new quarters.

Following their custom, the Templars built a round church patterned on the Holy Sepulchre in Jerusalem. An inscription on the Round (as the rotunda is called) recorded that it was consecrated by Heraclius, Patriarch of Jerusalem, on 10 February 1185, in honour of the Blessed Virgin Mary. It is thought that King Henry II was also present on that day, inaugurating a long association between the kings of England and the Temple.

Among the other buildings erected by the Templars were dormitories, chambers, storehouses, stables and two dining halls, one of them in the consecrated central portion and connected to the church by a cloister. King John was one of several kings to stay here, and during his visit in 1215 he received a deputation of barons demanding a charter of liberties; and when Magna Carta was signed later in the year, the master of the Temple was one of the witnesses. Taking advantage of their special privileges, the Templars made their sanctuary a safe place for depositing treasure, and during the thirteenth century the New Temple became a busy financial centre. The first lawyers came to live in the Temple at this time as legal advisors to the order of the Knights Templar, which was one of the foremost international organisations of the age. The Templars thrived, adding to their round church a fine nave, which was consecrated in the presence of King Henry III in 1240.

After the dissolution of the Knights Templar the Pope granted their estates to the Knights Hospitaller, but King Edward II of England seized the New Temple for the Crown. Nevertheless the consecrated portion was conceded to the Hospitallers and the rest was sold to them later. But the Hospitallers do not seem to have occupied the Temple personally; instead it was let and served a source of revenue, and by the 1340s it had become tenanted by lawyers. These formed themselves into two legal societies, one using the hall next to the cloisters (the inner inn), the other using the unconsecrated buildings between the inner portion and the Outer Temple. The Temple Church became the chapel of those two societies. In 1540 King Henry VIII abolished the Hospitallers in England and confiscated their property, which the Crown continues to let to the Inner and Middle Temple. Likewise it is for the sovereign to provide a priest for the church, who to this day bears the title of Master of the Temple.

The symbolism of the Round was all-important. Jerusalem lay at the centre of all medieval maps and was the hub of the Crusaders' world. The most sacred place in this most sacred city was the Church of the Holy Sepulchre with its Rotunda built over the site believed to be the burial place of Jesus Christ. The Church of the Holy Sepulchre was the goal of every pilgrim, whose protection was the Templars' care, just as the church itself, of all buildings on earth, had to be defended from its enemies. By building round churches throughout Europe, the Templars recreated the sanctity of this most holy place. To be buried in such a place was devoutly to be desired, for to be buried in the Round was as though one was buried in Jerusalem itself. Among the knights buried in the Round was the most powerful man of his generation: William the Marshal, Earl of Pembroke, advisor to King John, regent to Henry III, and one of the instigators of Magna Carta in 1215. His sons' effigies lie around his own.

There are nine marble effigies in all as well as a stone coffin set into the floor. William, who is depicted at rest, took the cross and went crusading in the Holy Land from 1183 to 1186 where he vowed to join the Templars, a vow he fullfilled on his death-bed in 1219. But William's sons, who never took the cross, are shown with their eyes wide open, and drawing their swords from their scabbards. They are all portrayed in their early thirties, the age at which Jesus died and at which, it is said, the dead will rise on his return.

The effigies are not memorials of what has long since been and gone; they speak of what is yet to come. The Templars wore white robes with red crosses, and in the Book of *Revelation 7:14* the martyrs of Christ, clad in white robes washed in the blood of the Lamb, are those who will be called to life at the 'first resurrection'. For a millennium they will reign

The effigies of Templar knights are set into the stone floor of the circular Temple Church in London

with Christ, and at its end Satan will lead all the nations of the earth against 'the beloved city' (*Revelation 20:9*) – Jerusalem, site of the final battle. And so these knights have good reason to draw their swords, for by being buried in the Round they are already buried 'in Jerusalem', and in Jerusalem they shall rise again. Here in the Temple Church, in this replica of the Holy Sepulchre itself, the knights are waiting for their call to life, to arms and to the last climactic defence of their most sacred place on earth.

The Second World War inflicted considerable damage on the Temple area. In 1941 at the height of the Blitz, Temple Church was hit by German bombs. War and time account for the austere appearance of the church today, for much has been rebuilt but without the original decorations. The walls of the Round were once painted with lozenges and bands of colour and the grotesque heads were painted too. The famous stone knights were also damaged in the bombing, but they still have an eerie presence.

CRESSING TEMPLE, ESSEX

Cressing Temple is the oldest Templar holding outside London and the largest and most important in the county of Essex. The property lies along the high road between London and Colchester and was donated to the Templars in 1137 by Queen Matilda, wife of King Stephen of

The Barley Barn at Cressing Temple is the oldest timber-framed barn in the world

England and niece of Baldwin, the first king of Jerusalem. Unlike other Templar sites, which are built of stone, the monuments at Cressing Temple are two vast barns of wood, magnificent structures which dominate the landscape; the timbered interiors are of cathedral-like dimensions. The Wheat Barn and the Barley Barn, built between 1206 and 1256, are the two finest Templar-built barns in Europe while the Barley Barn is the oldest timber-framed barn in the world.

Cressing Temple, originally over 14,000 acres in extent, occupied a fertile site with good transport links by road and river, and by establishing a market here the Templars developed their holding as a considerable agricultural enterprise worked by over 160 tenant farmers, its surplus providing a profit which went towards paying for the order's activities in Outremer. The property would have been in the charge of a preceptor accompanied by two or three knights or sergeants, together with a chaplain, a bailiff and numerous household servants. In 1309 the estate was recorded as possessing a mansion house with associated buildings including a bakehouse, a brewhouse, a dairy, a granary and a smithy, as well as gardens, a dovecote, a chapel with cemetery, a watermill and a windmill. After the suppression of the order in 1312, Cressing Temple was given to the Knights Hospitaller.

ROSSLYN CHAPEL, SCOTLAND

Rosslyn Chapel, at Roslin, seven miles south of Edinburgh, has been co-opted into every alternative history of Britain, and among the claims made for the chapel are that it has associations with the Holy Grail, the Templars and the Freemasons.

Originally named the Collegiate Chapel of Saint Matthew, Rosslyn was designed by William St Clair (also spelt Sinclair), 1st Earl of Caithness, whose ancestors were Norman nobles. Construction of the chapel, which was built on the pattern of the choir in Glasgow Cathedral, began in 1456. The original intention was for it to be part of a much larger church, for the fashion in Scotland was to build ambitious private churches able to support a resident clerical community. But the grandiose scheme was never completed, and after William's death in

The Prentice Pillar at Rosslyn Chapel

about 1491, it fell to his son to roof over the chapel and see the interior carving and decoration to its conclusion.

Dan Brown in *The Da Vinci Code* synthesises much that has been written about Rosslyn in the alternative histories. For example, he claims that Rosslyn was built on the site of an ancient Mithraic temple, and that it is 'an exact architectural blueprint of Solomon's Temple in Jerusalem' – this despite the fact that the chapel follows the pattern of the choir in Glasgow Cathedral. He also claims that it stands on a north-south meridian that runs through Glastonbury, on a Rose Line from which the chapel gets its name. In fact Rosslyn's longitude is W3:08:41, while Glastonbury's is W2:42:52, centred on the Abbey, or W2:41:41 centred on the ancient Tor. And like any good Scots kirk, Rosslyn's name refers simply to it location, 'ross' meaning promontory or headland, and 'lyn' meaning pool or stream.

Brown also attempts to link the chapel with the Templars. Though Rosslyn does lie only four miles to the northwest of Temple, the Knights Templar headquarters in Scotland, the chapel was built well over a century after the dissolution of the Templars. As for any link between the Sinclairs and the order, the one thing that can be said for certain is that a descendant of William Sinclair testified *against* the Templars during their trial at Edinburgh's Holyrood Palace in 1309.

Nevertheless, Rosslyn Chapel is an extraordinary place to visit. The exterior is alive with exaggeratedly decorated stone buttresses, arches, finials and canopies, and the interior stonework is if anything even more exotic, every surface covered in richly allegorical sculpture that draws heavily on biblical and medieval Christian symbolism – the Seven Deadly Sins, the Dance of Death and so on – and also on figurative naturalistic work and pagan mythological images – look out for the numerous Green Men.

The most remarkable of all the thousands of pieces of virtuoso stonework is the twisted Prentice Pillar, which stands at a corner of the Lady Chapel, to the right of the main altar, with entwined dragons at its foot. Local legend has it that the column was created by an apprentice subsequently murdered by his master in a jealous rage. Dan Brown's idea that a second facing pillar is an 'exact replica' of Boaz, the pillar that the Bible places on the left of the entrance to Solomon's Temple, is pure invention. There is a second column at Rosslyn dubbed the Mason's Pillar, but the name developed out of a local legend to do with stone-carving and has nothing to do with Freemasons. Nor is there a 'massive subterranean chamber' lurking beneath the chapel, as Dan Brown claims, though high-tech efforts to find one are unceasing.

In 2005 a modern-day descendant, Dr Andrew Sinclair, denounced *The Da Vinci Code*. 'The book is preposterous,' he said, 'its message pernicious, its history a bungle and a muddle. What it says about the Grail and Rosslyn is absolute invention.' But as every good conspiracy theorist knows, he would say that.

Part 7
Templarism

ROBERT TAYLOR

ELIZABETH TAYLOR

JOAN FONTAINE

GEORGE SANDERS

EMLYN WILLIAMS

↑ *Sir Walter Scott cast the Templars as the villains in* Ivanhoe *and Hollywood has continued the tradition, as in this 1952 film version of the novel, and onwards to the historically confused* Kingdom of Heaven *in 2005*

Born Again Templars

Templars in Popular Culture

When Anthony Burgess reviewed *The Holy Blood and the Holy Grail* – the book that put the Templars at the heart of a millennium of conspiracies – he said, 'I can only see this as a marvellous theme for a novel.' How prescient he was. A small army of novelists, from Umberto Eco to Dan Brown, have taken the book's pseudo-history of the Knights Templar for their plots. The Templars have become screen regulars, too, and are keeping up with the times with starring roles in medieval-themed computer games.

Not that adopting the Templars in fiction is entirely a modern phenomenon. The literary trail starts in the thirteenth century with Wolfram von Eschenbach's epic poem *Parzival* (which reworks Chrétien de Troyes' unfinished Grail romance *Perceval*) in which a group of knights known as Templeisen guard the Grail.

Rise of the Templar Literary Phenomenon

The writer who really put the Templars on the modern literary map was Sir Walter Scott, whose first foray into medieval fiction, *Ivanhoe* (1819), featured Sir Brian de Bois-Gilbert, a lustful Grand Master of the Templars, as its chief villain. King Richard the Lionheart – and the Templars – intrigued Scott so much that he returned to the patch in *The Talisman* (1825). His creation was so successful that it even spawned parody, in American novelist Herman Melville's *Typee* (1846) and, in more extended form, *The Paradise of Bachelors* (1855). In this tale of a dinner at Temple Bar, Melville enjoys musing on the 'moral blight that tainted at last this sacred brotherhood' and turned them into hypocrites and rakes.

The Templars then went quiet for a few decades – leaving aside a namecheck in Leslie Charteris' hero Simon Templar – until the 1950s, when Maurice Druon wrote a series of seven historical novels, *The Accursed Kings*. These start with James of Molay's burning in 1314 and his supposed curse on the Capetian dynasty. In the 1970s Druon's novels were made into an acclaimed mini-series in France. Something was obviously stirring. In 1972 Ishmael Reed made a Templar knight, Hinkle von Hampton, the villain in his post-modernist satire *Mumbo Jumbo* and Pierre Barbet wrote *Baphomet's Meteor*, a bizarre sci-fi take on the legend in which the Templars are manipulated by aliens. The best novel to date about the order, William Watson's sadly neglected *The Last of the Templars*, also appeared.

The publication of *The Holy Blood and the Holy Grail* (1982) introduced the order's puzzling legend to a wider audience. That same year Lawrence Durrell's *Constance*, the third volume in his *Avignon Quintet*, honoured the Templars as secret Gnostics – which is why, he suggests, James of Molay was burned at the stake on Pope Clement V's orders. Before their destruction, imagines Durrell, the Templars buried a secret treasure near Avignon, a treasure coveted by Hitler, who hopes it will inspire his Nazi 'black chivalry'. Umberto Eco, that astute student of popular culture, spoofed the Templar obsession and popularised it in his international bestseller *Foucault's Pendulum* (1988), memorably noting that you could always tell a lunatic because 'sooner or later he brings up the Templars'.

However, with Spielberg's film *Indiana Jones and the Last Crusade* (1989), an order that had officially died out seven hundred years ago suddenly came to feel like part of the zeitgeist. In the next decade, Katherine Kurtz, an American novelist (who claims to be a 'Templar at heart') launched a series of heroic Templar fantasy novels; British writer Michael Jecks penned various Cadfael-esque murder mysteries starring a Templar called Sir Baldwin; and Swedish author Jan Guillou entered the fray with a trilogy about a Swedish Templar. The pace was hotting up, and as *The Da Vinci Code* (2003) became one of the bestselling books ever, the Templars entered the book charts centre stage, with Raymond Khoury's *The Last Templar* (2005) and Steve Berry's *The Templar Legacy* (2006).

Templar Plots

The blockbuster Templar plot draws loosely on history and myth. Here are some of the more crucial ingredients.

✠ **James of Molay (Jacques de Molay) is a hero.** Steven Berry, in *The Templar Legacy*, dares to suggest that the last Grand Master broke under torture, although, to compensate, he says it is James of Molay's image on the Turin Shroud. But most of the time, Molay is so brave and far-sighted that it is a mystery how he failed to handle King Philip.

✠ **The Templars have secret knowledge.** What they know varies but it is often suggested that in the Holy Land they became acquainted with some profound, esoteric wisdom after hobnobbing with their Muslim opponents. For example, a Templar killing of an Assassin envoy becomes a thread with which the most elaborate fantasies can be spun.

✠ **The Templars criss-cross the globe.** Scotland, Paris, New York, Israel, the Languedoc, Turin, Copenhagen – no place on earth is safe as these complex plots unravel as surrogate travelogues.

✠ **A modern-day Templar geek is usually a villain,** just like Sir Leigh Teabing in *The Da Vinci Code* and the less eccentrically monikered Vance Williams in Khoury's *The Last Templar*.

✠ **Popes are devious** and none more so than Leo X (1475–1521), who is forever quoted as saying, 'It has served us well, this myth of Christ.' In fact this remark was put into the Pope's mouth by John Bale (1495–1563), a rabidly anti-Catholic propagandist.

✠ **Never hesitate to draw on the theories of** *The Holy Blood and the Holy Grail* – but in appendices and bibliographies designed to suggest that a fiction is grounded in fact, don't credit this (nonsensical) book.

✠ **Heresy and Satanism make good copy** – especially the Templars' supposed worship of an Anti-christ called Baphomet.

✠ **The Templars still exist.** And they are behind everything.

TEMPLAR NOVELS

Templar novels are beginning to outweigh historical accounts of the period. Here's the pick of the crop, from Scott to the present.

Sir Walter Scott *Ivanhoe* (1819) and *The Talisman* (1825)

The Scottish novelist was obviously fascinated by the Templars – they provide the pantomime villains in these two famous novels – but not so fascinated that he looked much beyond the charges used to justify the order's suppression. So in *The Talisman* the Grand Master presides over an order accused of heresy, suspected of being in league with the devil, and so arrogant that it would risk the downfall of Western civilisation to preserve itself. Scott even finds something sinister in the Grand Master's abacus, 'a mystic staff of office, the peculiar form of which has given rise to such singular conjectures and commentaries, leading to suspicions that this celebrated fraternity of Christian knights were embodied under the foulest symbols of paganism'. Some traditions suggest that the Templar abacus was modelled on the staff carried by Moses' brother Aaron, which hardly makes it pagan, even if it later became associated with Freemasonry.

Willing to glorify any calumny against the Templars, Scott has these reckless knights entering into a rash alliance with the Austrians against King Richard I and Saladin in *The Talisman*. In reality Richard was as obsessed by the Crusades as the Templars, which may be why he confirmed the order's land holdings in England and granted them a kind of diplomatic immunity from English law.

Scott's most iconic Templar villain is hard-hearted Sir Brian de Bois-Gilbert, who, the novelist hints, personifies the order. Ivanhoe's father Cedric describes him as 'valiant as the bravest of his order but stained with their usual vices, pride, arrogance, cruelty and voluptuousness'. Bois-Gilbert may have about as much in common with the real Templars as the Arthur in Disney's *The Sword in the Stone* has with the historical King Arthur. But he has, through sheer charisma – and a wonderful portrayal by George Sanders in the 1952 movie – become the most famous fictional Knight Templar of them all.

Maurice Druon *The Accursed Kings* (1955-77)

A Prix Goncourt-winning novelist, a minister of culture under Georges Pompidou, and the co-author of an anthem sung by the French resistance, Maurice Druon's life is almost as interesting as his fiction. In the 1950s he began a series of novels, *Les Rois Maudits* (*The Accursed Kings*), on the story of James of Molay's supposed curse – flung at King Philip as he burnt at the stake. At the heart of Druon's saga is a real historical puzzle. When Molay burned, Philip was in good health and had three grown sons. Yet within twenty-five years, lack of male issue forced the Capetian dynasty to hand the throne to their Valois cousins.

Druon's seven novels – *The Iron King, The Strangled Queen, The Poisoned Crown, The Royal Succession, The She-Wolf of France, The Lily and the Lion, When a King Loses France* – span six tumultuous decades in French history, starting with Philip being refused a loan by the Templars and ending with the Valois dynasty. Although the series is named in honour of Molay's curse, the plot is driven, in part, by another real story of the era: the campaign by Robert III of Artois, related through marriage to the first Valois king, to reclaim land from his aunt. Robert's pursuit of this grievance led to exile and war.

Druon takes care to achieve a level of historical accuracy but nonetheless bends the facts to suit his story. The dissolution of the Templars is a spur of the moment enterprise, not the fruit of meticulous planning. Philip does get his hands on Templar gold, but, when the Pope dies, becomes obsessed by James of Molay's curse and, in the second novel, wastes away to death. Nonetheless, these first two novels are of genuine interest to any Templar aficionado.

Pierre Barbet *Baphomet's Meteor* (1972)

As the Templars have long existed in an alternative dimension, between fact and fiction, it was smart of pseudonymous French sci-fi author Pierre Barbet to write a fictional alternative history in which Baphomet, the mysterious head the knights were accused of worshipping, is a stranded extraterrestrial who gives the Templars the scientific expertise and atomic weaponry they need to take over the world and develop the technology he needs to repair his spaceship. Alas, Baphomet has not allowed for human deviousness.

The mysteries of Christianity were obviously of lifelong interest to Barbet, who was a doctor and wrote *A Doctor at Calvary*, one of the definitive medical accounts of the crucifixion.

William Watson
Last Of The Templars (1979)

If you only read one Templar novel, try this. Watson brings a novelist's insight into his historically scrupulous account of the Templars' precipitous decline from the fall of Acre in 1291 to the burning of James of Molay in 1314. For once the Templars are not mystics, seers or heretics blackmailing the Church but the soldiers and bankers of historical record. Watson's clever, dreamlike narrative offers a cogent analysis of the factors that doomed the order: the rise of nationalism, the order's arrogance, the greed of King Philip, Papal acquiescence and, most of all, the loss of the Holy Land and the end of the Crusades, which left the Templars, without a mission, suddenly superfluous.

Beltran, the last of the order, is a soldier-monk whose personal allegiance lies with Thibaud Gaudin, the penultimate Grand Master, who effectively dies from the strain of trying to reverse the decline in the Templars' fortunes. Watson convincingly records the milestones on the order's road to nowhere. While most novelists describe Molay's death as a ceremony accompanied by pomp and circumstance, Watson presents the burning as a hurried, slightly disorganised spectacle, unforgettably noting, 'The Grand Master has become a cinder.'

Watson sees the brutal, unpredictable reality behind the noble stereotypes of conflict in the Holy Land and handles his historical cast – especially King Philip, his unscrupulous aide William of Nogaret and Pope Clement – with aplomb, even offering an intriguing explanation for the fact that all three were dead by Christmas 1314. *Last of the Templars* is worth reading both for its insight into the order and as a brilliant historical novel.

Umberto Eco *Foucault's Pendulum* (1988)

In Eco's second novel – following his hugely successful medieval whodunit, *The Name of the Rose* – three Italian intellectuals jokingly prepare The Plan, a ludicrously comprehensive plot which will explain everything – the Templars, the Rosicrucians, the Count of St Germain (an eighteenth-century con man who claimed to be immortal), the Merovingians, Jesus, the Nazis. A plot that anticipates, in some ways, the central premise of *The Da Vinci Code*.

In Eco's book, the Templars, according to a history written by a sinister colonel, were guardians of a secret treasure and ought to have taken over the world in 1944 but were mysteriously foiled. From this, Eco spins all manner of conceits with such enthusiasm that, at times, you can feel as if you are listening to a monologue by a very erudite pub bore. But you can forgive him a lot for inventing a secret society drolly known as the Synarchic Knights of Templar Rebirth.

Jan Guillou *The Crusades Trilogy* (1998–2000)

Swedish author Guillou's novels are characterised by macho, politically correct heroes. In this trilogy set in the twelfth century, Swedish knight Arn Magnusson arrives in the Holy Land, condemned to serve twenty years as a Knight Templar for a youthful indiscretion, with the usual preconceptions about infidel Muslims being a brutish and uncivilised lot. But he soon casts off those prejudices and becomes a pro-Muslim multiculturalist who only fights for the Christians out of a sense of duty. Guillou blends fact, legend and fiction to make his point, even having his hero pardoned by Saladin because he once saved the great Muslim leader's life from robbers.

Guillou has a sure feel for the nuanced relationship between the Templars and their royal allies in the Holy Land and for the detail of historical battle. He blames the destruction of the Christian armies and the fall of Jerusalem on certain non-Templar military leaders and the King of Jerusalem. His Templars are brave, noble, well trained and ruthless; it is the incompetence that surrounds them that dooms their cause. A Templar spin doctor could not have put it better. Guillou does a similarly eloquent PR job for Saladin.

Dan Brown *The Da Vinci Code* (2003)

Everyone loves a conspiracy. Brown is so convinced this is true, he tells us twice. The assumption being that our obsession with a nothing-is-as-it-seems version of history might blind us to the way this compelling story edits, stretches and wilfully misunderstands the facts. Any reader who took Brown's guidance on the Templars literally would conclude that they were founded by a mysterious order called the Priory of Sion, busied themselves by ensuring that motifs of the vagina, womb and clitoris were incorporated into many medieval cathedrals, and worshipped their own fertility god. Alas and alack, the Priory – which Brown seems to think was a real entity – was the fanciful invention of one Pierre Plantard, a French forger who came up with the idea in 1956, elaborated and reinforced his claims with a series of further forgeries, then finally admitted under oath that he had made the whole thing up – but of course if you are a true conspiracy theorist you know what that means! Apart from possibly those knights who jousted in drag at Acre in 1286 – and the chronicler does not say that there were any Templars among them – there is no evidence that the Templars ever made any attempt to get in touch with their feminine side. In fact, their rule warned: 'The company of woman is a dangerous thing.'

The novel's central anti-clerical message means that the downfall of the Templars is attributed not to King Philip IV but to 'Machiavellian' Pope Clement V, who, fed up with being blackmailed about the secret of the Grail, unleashed an 'ingeniously planned sting operation' on the innocent order and saw to it that the tortured knights' ashes were 'tossed unceremoniously into the Tiber'. This would have been some toss as Clement V never stepped foot in Italy, never mind Rome.

Kate Mosse *Labyrinth* (2005)

Labyrinth reads like one of those books where the author is more worried about achieving the desired blockbuster pagination (700 pages) than how the story is told. But after 250 pages, the narrative begins to gather momentum as the threads of her parallel lives – Cathar Alaïs and modern-day volunteer archaeologist Alice Tanner – intersect compellingly. Mosse takes many themes associated with the Templars – the Grail, the Cathars, the implication of secret knowledge from the East – but only mentions the order in passing as she builds to a finale in which the Grail is revealed as a chalice, something that enables initiates to live for 800 years and 'the love that is handed down from generation to generation'.

When she researched the novel, Mosse writes, she felt sure there would be a role for the Templars but decided 'the connections people like to make between the Albigensian heresy and the Knights Templar are based on nothing more than historical coincidence'. On her website *www.mosselabyrinth.co.uk* she has published her notes on the man she refers to as 'the great Jacques de Molay' and speculates that the Knights Templar may have been the 'fair-headed people using the power of the covenant' who, in Ethiopian tradition, raised the massive obelisk at Axum. While many rumours and legends link the Templars to Ethiopia (usually in connection with the Ark of the Covenant), the obelisk is 1600–1700 years old. So not historical nor a coincidence.

Julia Navarro *The Brotherhood of the Holy Shroud* (2006)

This is one of the best Templar-inspired novels, Navarro alternating between a modern-day investigation into a mutilated body at Turin Cathedral and a well-told, and in large part nicely conceived, secret history of the Shroud. In this, the Templars – and a ruthless secret brotherhood from the biblical town of Edessa – are the antagonists.

The Templars are portrayed, as one of the investigators says, 'as supermen who can do anything' whose most sacred mission, once they have blackmailed the Byzantine emperor to hand it over, is to protect the Shroud. They manage to smuggle it out of Acre just before the Holy Land falls in 1291, but their annus horribilis, 1307, forces the order into desperate measures. One of the plotters trying to get his hands on the Shroud is said to be a direct descendant of Geoffrey of Charney, who burned with James of Molay. This makes possible sense as the widow of a man called Charney, who may have been the nephew of Geoffrey of Charney, put the Shroud on display in 1357. Navarro suggests that the Templars survived – initially in such places as Portugal, where, as she correctly notes, the order was simply nationalised, and in Scotland – and are so powerful today that they can, with impunity, organise the assassination of policemen who get too close to their secret.

Navarro tantalises readers with the idea that 'there was a figure to whom the Templars prayed throughout the world though His name was not Baphomet'. In secret chapel meetings, she suggests they worshipped 'a painting, an image of a strange figure, an idol'. Wisely, she does not elucidate, so the reader can take their pick from the usual suspects: Sophia the Greek goddess of wisdom, the Prophet Mohammed, the mummified head of Jesus, an Egyptian cat or the head of a Sufi martyr.

Raymond Khoury *The Last Templar* (2005)

Khoury used to write for BBC TV's superior spy drama *Spooks* and he kicks off his bestselling novel with a stunning conceit, as four horsemen dressed as Templars storm the opening of an exhibition of Vatican artefacts in New York. As FBI agent Sean Reilly and archaeologist Tess Chaykin investigate, they discover a secret that has lain buried for a thousand years.

As a page turner, Khoury's 'deadly game of cat and mouse across three continents' is as compelling as Dan Brown's novels. Like Brown and Berry, he finds the idea that the Templars' real treasure was gold, money or the medieval equivalent of traveller's cheques just too mundane. So he has a Templar ship called *Falcon Temple* setting sail on the order of the Grand Master days before the fall of Acre with a mysterious chest that contains the writings of 'a man the entire world knew as Jesus Christ'. This seems to conflate two historical events: the real removal of the Templar treasure from the Holy Land and the activities of a disgraced Templar sergeant called Roger of Flor who made a fortune by ferrying the desperate and wealthy out of Acre in his galley called the *Falcon*. Khoury also mentions the legend of the Templars' maritime escape, specifically the fleet of eighteen galleys that sailed out of La Rochelle the night before the Templars were arrested in 1307, never to be seen again.

For Khoury's Templars, the treasure is a sideshow. Their real purpose is to unite the three religions that held sway in medieval times – Christianity, Judaism and Islam – by exposing the fraud at the heart of the resurrection myth and humbling the arrogant clergy. It is at this point that fiction and history finally part company for good. But this final implausibility does not spoil the fun.

Steve Berry *The Templar Legacy* (2006)

This blockbuster never quite recovers from having a hero named Cotton ('it's a long story,' he says whenever someone asks, which they do tediously often) and an evil Templar mastermind called Raymond de Roquefort who wants to bring Christianity to its knees and restore the Templars to their former power by publishing a secret gospel which proves that Jesus never physically came back from the dead.

In interviews, Berry talks as if the Templars are old chums so it would be intriguing to discover where he gets some of his ideas from. He often quotes the Templar Rule in the novel, suggesting that it forbade knights from washing, though nobody who comes into contact with his Templars seems deterred by body odours. And his imagination goes into overdrive when it comes to James of Molay's burning. He has King Philip watching dispassionately, though the historical sources seem pretty clear that he was not present, and then a crack squad of Templars swimming across the Seine to fetch the Master's burnt bones back in their mouths. That said, Berry gets quite a lot of stuff right. Like the battle cry ('Beauséant') and the fact, recently confirmed, that the Templars were absolved by Clement V of the charges brought against them.

The novel's most original suggestion is that James of Molay's image, not Christ's, is mysteriously preserved on the Turin Shroud. The order is linked with the Shroud and the famous carbon-dating does suggest that the portion of tested cloth comes from the thirteenth to fourteenth centuries, the Templar era. Berry says he got the idea from *The Second Messiah* by Christopher Knight and Robert Lomas, two Freemasons turned amateur historians. The book suggests that James of Molay was tortured and crucified in a parody of Christ's agony by Philip's henchman William of Nogaret, a theory Berry draws on in some truly excruciating scenes. But historians find a conflict of evidence about whether James of Molay confessed with or without torture, let alone that he underwent a kind of crucifixion.

Robyn Young *The Brethren Trilogy* (2006–08)

The rise of the Mamelukes and their mounting pressure against the Crusader states during the last decades of the thirteenth century provides the setting for Robyn Young's Brethren trilogy. *Brethren* is the first volume of the trilogy, and the plot turns on a mysterious book that goes missing from the order's vaults which holds the key to a secret group of knights. The locations run from the filthy backstreets of medieval London and Paris to the shimmering light and burning heat of Syria and Palestine where the Mameluke Sultan Baybars is renewing the struggle against the Christians. Also there are girls, and love. The second volume, *Crusade*, brings the reader to Acre where 'a ruthless cabal of Western merchants, profiteering from slaves and armaments, has devised a shocking plan to reignite hostilities in the Holy Land'. Also there are girls, and love. *Requiem*, the final volume, covers the downfall of the Templars at the hands of Philip IV of France. And there are girls, and love. The tragedy of the Crusades, and of the Templars, we are led to understand, was that nobody listened to the Brethren, that secret group of social workers operating within the heart of the Knights Templar who might have made everything nice. The trilogy's lashings of love interest ensures that where historical fiction fails, as it does throughout, Mills and Boon rushes to the breach.

THE TEMPLARS IN MOVIES

For decades, Hollywood's perception of the Templars began and ended with George Sanders' suave villainy as Sir Brian de Bois-Gilbert in *Ivanhoe* (1952). Apart from perennial inferior remakes of Scott's saga, the Templars did not get much of a look-in until the 1970s when Spanish director Amando de Ossorio brought the order back to life as zombies in his *Blind Dead* movies.

And then came George Lucas. There is a theory that the Jedi knights in *Star Wars* (1977) are thinly disguised Templars and that their massacre (in 2005's *Revenge of the Sith*) is a reference to the destruc-

tion of the order in 1307. There are rumours that in the original script the knights were known as Jedi Templar. The Jedi, like the Templars, were warrior monks whose behaviour was governed by a code. And the Templars – through their supposed association with the Holy Grail and the Ark of the Covenant – are often credited with mysterious, even supernatural powers which, some *Star Wars* aficionados insist, resembles the Force that the Jedi knights must master.

More easily identifiable Templar and Grail myths came to the fore in two Steven Spielberg blockbusters that Lucas produced: *Raiders of the Lost Ark* (1981) and *Indiana Jones and the*

Last Crusade (1989). And these created something of a genre, being followed by the confused Dolph Lundgren thriller *The Minion* (1998), the entertaining Indiana Jones clone *National Treasure* (2001), the baffling *Revelation* (2001), Christophe Gans' horror movie, *Brotherhood of the Wolf* (2001), and Ridley Scott's sword and sandal epic, *Kingdom of Heaven* (2005). Not to mention the movie version of *The Da Vinci Code* (2006).

The *Blind Dead* movies (1971–75)

The *Blind Dead* series kicked off with *Tombs of the Blind Dead* (1971) in which the Templars – known only as Knights of the East but identifiable from their garb – are brought back from the dead as blind mummies. Slow, creepy and bizarre – the zombie-Templars are blind so they hunt by sound – the film was successful enough for Ossorio to make three more: *Return of the Blind Dead* (1973), *The Ghost Galleon* (1974) and *Night of the Seagulls* (1975). The series inspired a New York punk band called The Templars.

The *Indiana Jones* Trilogy (1981–89)

'All of a sudden, whoosh, it was gone.' That remark by one of the US intelligence officers who recruits Indiana Jones to save the Ark from the Nazis pretty much sums up what we know about the fate of the Ark of the Covenant in *Raiders of the Lost Ark* (1981). The Ark was supposed to make armies invincible – hence Hitler's interest – though it mysteriously failed to prevent the occupation of Jerusalem by the Babylonians and, in Spielberg's version of history, by the Egyptians too. This first film in Steven Spielberg's series bases its plot on the historically nonsensical proposition that the Ark was taken to Egypt by Pharaoh Shishak, which if true would have made it impossible for the Templars to have made off with it two thousand years later, as some would have us believe.

The third film in the series, *Indiana Jones and the Last Crusade* (1989), has a suggestively Templar theme and features a scene in which the weary Templar-like guardian of the Holy Grail looks forward with quiet relief to ending his 800-year watch. Jones (Harrison Ford) and his father (Sean Connery) combine to prevent the chalice falling into Nazi hands. Even though the sets are full of eight-pointed stars and talk of chivalrous knights abounds, the Templars are not mentioned once. Instead we get a secret military order called the Knights of the Cruciform Sword.

But the story does capture the Grail's mythic significance. When the heroes and the villains find the cave where the knight keeps watch over the hidden treasure and the Holy Grail, the knight warns them to choose wisely. The shallow, mercenary villain picks the blingiest goblet and dies. Indy, who has no real interest in the Grail but knows his father is obsessed by it, drinks from a plain wooden cup – the kind of cup a carpenter might have, he suggests – and it heals his troubled relationship with his father. In spirit, the denouement is consistent with Eschenbach's poem *Parzival* – a vague source for this movie – which suggests that you have to be truly selfless to be worthy of the Grail.

The Minion (1998)

The budget for this film was $12 million. A pity they did not spend a cent on research. Dolph Lundgren is a butt-kicking Templar monk with a spiked leather glove whose sacred duty it is to do what the Templars have always done and stop a key that has kept the Anti-christ imprisoned for thousands of years from falling into the wrong hands. The laughs start as soon as Françoise Robertson's Native American archaeologist stares at some skeletons in a hidden chamber in New York and decides the Templar garb they are wearing was made in Ireland in the sixth century. Although ostensibly a Templar, Lundgren fails to point out that she is six hundred years out. The idea that the order was founded in the twelfth century, we are told later, is merely conventional wisdom. There are rumours, we are assured, that the Templars may have started a thousand years before and, the film suggests, it may even have been started by Saint Peter. After such revelations, we barely pause to wonder how a bunch of warrior monks in Jerusalem come to be wearing Irish weave and ended up in New York. It is those Templars, you see. They can do anything.

National Treasure (2001)

Michael Baigent and Richard Leigh, two thirds of the trinity behind *The Holy Blood and the Holy Grail*, suggested in their book *The Temple and the Lodge* that the Knights Templar survived their dissolution by hiding in Scotland and centuries later, as Freemasons, plotted the independence of the United States. The seductive idea of a Templar-mason continuum was first floated in France in the 1740s, by Scottish-born Freemason Andrew Michael Ramsay, and provides the slender hook for this *Indiana Jones*-style adventure in which Nicolas Cage – and eventually his dotty dad Jon Voight – seek the lost Templar treasure with the aid of a map some Templars thoughtfully drew, in invisible ink, on the back of the Declaration of Independence. The clues seem inordinately complex, as if a Templar Einstein had conceived them for other Einsteins to crack. And there is no credible reason for the treasure to be in America at all – other than box-office takings. The film also goes into the business of unfinished pyramids and all-seeing eyes as found on American dollars being masonic symbols.

Revelation (2001)

A sacred artefact from the time of Christ, missing for centuries, suddenly turns up in the back of a camper van and becomes the focus for a struggle between good (billionaire Terence Stamp, his son James D'Arcy and alchemist Natasha Wightman) and evil, personified by a 2000-year-old demonic Grand Master (Udo Kier) who is suffering from post-traumatic stress disorder after watching Christ's crucifixion. The artefact is a wooden box, containing the first coded reference to Christ on the cross, which has since had all kinds of arcane graffiti carved on it. The Templars protected the box and its explosive secret but Kier is desperate to get hold of it, crack the code and use it to clone Jesus. Badly acted and scripted, exhibiting a heroic disregard for continuity, this movie draws on *The Holy Blood and the Holy Grail*'s heretical proposition about Jesus and Mary Magdalene and the idea of a secret order that links Christ, the Merovingian kings and Sir Isaac Newton, but it adds a few more bizarre scenarios and throws in some occult lore to achieve a truly magnificent incoherence.

Brotherhood of the Wolf (2001)

Gans' unusual horror movie is silly but compelling. A rogue branch of the Templars – the brotherhood of the film's title – have been sent to France by the Pope to scare Louis XV. They take a rather lateral view of their brief, deciding the best way to frighten the monarch is to let a beast, wearing Templar armour, feast on the women and children in a small town.

Kingdom of Heaven (2005)

Making a film about the Crusades at the time of the war in Iraq was bound to be politically sensitive. So in pursuit of an acceptable and simplistic message – that the Christian West is not always good and the Muslim East is not all bad – director Ridley Scott revises history wholesale, or rather makes it up.

To be fair, he might have been unduly influenced by the novels of his namesake, Walter Scott. His Saladin (charismatically played by the Syrian actor Ghassan Massoud), who is wise, benevolent and omnipotent, owes more to

Scott's portrayal of him in *The Talisman* than to the historical character. And the film's war-crazed Templars are partly descended from the Templar baddie in *Ivanhoe*. Both Guy of Lusignan, the king of Jerusalem, and Rainald of Chatillon, who are presented as unmitigated villains, are also presented as Templars, which in reality they were not. The real Templar in the film, the Grand Master Gerard of Ridefort, is presented in the worst possible terms, exceeding the most hostile accounts given of him in the more biased chronicles of the time.

Time and again the point is made that religion is a bad thing, or at least Christianity is, and so the only really good Franks in the film are absurdly anachronistic liberal humanists and agnostics like Jeremy Irons' Tiberias (in effect Count Raymond III of Tripoli, who was also lord of Tiberias), and Orlando Bloom's Balian. This may help explain why Bloom has all the charisma and martial presence of a petulant office supply manager complaining about missing paperclips. Fortunately the Muslims in the film are permitted their devout convictions and come across as far more real if no less sanguinary people. Apart from some generalities – there was such a place as Jerusalem and it fell to Saladin – there is nothing that bears much relation to historical fact.

TEMPLARS ON TV

The Knights Templar have only intermittently fascinated programme makers. Until Raymond Khoury finally adapts his own novel *The Last Templar* for television, the order's greatest contribution to TV drama must be the first dramatisation of Maurice Druon's *The Accursed Kings* novels made for French television in 1972 and shown with subtitles on the BBC. The original series was as acclaimed in France as *I Claudius* was in Britain. Remaking it was always going to be risky but thanks to the presence of such big names as Gerard Depardieu (who shone as James of Molay) and Jeanne Moreau, and decent effects using computer-generated imagery, the 2005 remake was not bad.

In Britain and America the Templars have inspired more documentarists than dramatists. In the acclaimed eco-thriller *Edge of Darkness* (1985), Troy Kennedy Martin worked the Templars into the drama's back story, suggesting that two of the protagonists, Grogan and Jedburgh, were a Templar and a Teutonic knight in previous lives. Martin admitted to being fascinated by the secret myth of the Templars and in his story their descendants are plotting to take humanity – or at least the order's soldier-scholars – to another planet.

Another rare exception to the general indifference of television to the subject is *The Last Knight* (2000), an episode in the US fantasy/adventure series *Relic Hunter*, in which Tia Carrere's globetrotting professor and Christien Anholt's linguist investigate a medallion that may have belonged to James of Molay and search for his famed invincible sword. The medallion's inscription reads, in part, 'Pierre Chevalier', which, Carrere says, happens to be a painting in the Louvre. By finding the abbey in the picture, they discover a secret Templar burial ground and James of Molay's disappointingly unmagical sword. They are told by a French confidant that 'the Templars were the rock stars of their times', a notion that rather spoils the historical background.

TEMPLARS ROCK

The knights who guard the Grail in Richard Wagner's *Parsifal* (1882) were never actually identified as Templars by the composer, though he did suggest their costumes should resemble those worn by the order's knights. If you judge the knights purely by their costumes, you would have to say this magnificent, influential and controversial opera is probably the best musical work associated with the order.

But Wagner is not the only classical composer to touch on Templar themes. Sir Arthur Sullivan (*Ivanhoe*), Otto Nicolai (*Il Templario*), Heinrich Marschner (*Der Templer und die Jüdin*), and Michael William Balfe (*Il Talismano*) have all written operas inspired by Sir Walter Scott's Templar sagas, *Ivanhoe* and *The Talisman*.

The Templars have also had a marginal influence on pop and rock music. Amando de Ossorio's *Blind Dead* movies inspired a New York punk band called The Templars. Formed in 1991, this multi-racial skinhead band drew on punk, glam rock and rock and roll, named their studios Acre, and adopted Templar surnames. Their first album *The Return of Jacques de Molay* was released in 1994 on Dim Records. Other Templar-themed releases followed, alluding to the battle at the Horns of Hattin, Ossorio's movies and Outremer. Drummer Phil Rigaud says the band's name was 'an homage to the warriors of the past'. Their song 'The Templars' manages to compress the order's history into four surprisingly conventional rhyming verses.

In 1997, the epic German heavy metal band Grave Digger released a concept album devoted to the order, called *Knights of the Cross*. The album, the second in a medieval trilogy, included such tracks as 'Baphomet', 'The Curse of Jacques', 'Monks of War' and 'Keepers of the Holy Grail', not to mention 'Battle of Bannockburn', their allusion to the Baigent and Leigh theory that a band of Templars helped the Scots achieve independence.

The Templars' curious appeal to European heavy-metal bands was confirmed when, from the late 1990s onwards, Swedish band HammerFall released tracks like 'Templars Of Steel' and 'The Templar Flame', and released a concert DVD called *The Templar Renegade Crusades*. The band's official website (*www.hammerfall.net*) even has a forum called The Templar Area.

TEMPLAR GAMING

As you might expect, the Templars have appeared in many of the medieval-themed video games. *Medieval Total War* allows players to build up divisions of Templar knights and do battle with Turks and Almohads across Europe and the Middle East. It is surprisingly instructive. And

most recently, the Templars have been given rather more sinister walk-on parts in *Assassin's Creed* (pictured), a game which conjures a graphically rich reconstruction of the Crusader era and in good Templar fiction style introduces a kind of *Matrix* dimension to the plot. There is clearly pop culture life in the order yet.

Further Reading

There is a huge volume of work on the Templars – from serious scholarship to pseudo-academic alternative history. The reviews following are a selection of the most important and the most interesting, along with digressions into related areas such as the Crusades and medieval heresy. Templar-related fiction is covered in the previous chapter.

History of the Templars

The New Knighthood: A History of the Order of the Temple, Malcolm Barber, Cambridge University Press (UK) 1994, (US) 1995. Barber is *the* academic authority on the Templars and this is his definitive work. Lucidly separating myth from history, he offers a full and detailed account of the order, its origins, heyday and suppression, and flourishing afterlife in the popular imagination. However, like all other books reviewed in this section, it was written before the discovery of the Chinon Parchment.

The Trial of the Templars, Malcolm Barber, Cambridge University Press (UK and US) 1993. The motivations of the participants and the long-term repercussions of the trial of the Templars have been the subject of intense and unresolved controversy, which still has resonances in our own time. In this classic account, Barber discusses the trial in the context of the Crusades, heresy, the Papacy and the French monarchy.

The Templars: Selected Sources, Malcolm Barber and Keith Bate, translators, Manchester University Press (UK and US) 2002. A collection of translated contemporary sources that document the origins of the Knights Templar and the circumstances of their suppression and dissolution. It offers a valuable insight into the lives of those who joined, supported and attacked the order and examines the varied facets of its activities during the twelfth and thirteenth centuries.

The Murdered Magicians, Peter Partner, Oxford University Press (UK and US) 1982. On the one hand an historical account of the Templars, on the other an argument that they were transformed by fairy-tale and myth from dull and obedient servants of the Church into enlightened magicians of freedom and knowledge.

The Templars, Piers Paul Reid, Weidenfeld and Nicolson (UK) 1999, Da Capo Press (US) 2006. A highly readable and sympathetic account of the Templars that draws on sound historical scholarship while delivering a dramatic and driving narrative.

The Knights Templar: A New History, Helen Nicholson, Sutton Publishing (UK) 2001, (US) 2004. This history of the Templars brings in new material from France, Spain, Portugal and elsewhere, much of which English-speaking readers will not have seen before. The book also has the virtue of being highly illustrated with many pictures of Templar sites across Europe and the Middle East.

The Chinon Chart: Papal Absolution to the Last Templar, Master Jacques de Molay, Barbara Frale, *Journal of Medieval History,* Volume 30, Number 2, Amsterdam 2004. Frale's discovery of the Chinon chart or parchment in the Vatican Secret Archives in 2001 was little short of a revolution for Templar studies and it is no exaggeration to say that everything written about the end of the Knights Templar before this publication has to be rewritten in its light.

Medieval Pilgrimages

To Be a Pilgrim: The Medieval Pilgrimage Experience, Sarah Hopper, Sutton Publishing (UK and US) 2002. This introductory survey of pilgrimage looks at the reasons for its popularity and explores the medieval pilgrimage experience. The book is illustrated throughout with images from medieval art, surviving artefacts such as pilgrim's badges, maps of the routes taken and photographs of the sites and shrines visited.

History of the Crusades

A History of the Crusades, three volumes, Steven Runciman, Penguin (UK) 1990, (US) 1987. Runciman succeeds in his magisterial work to enthral the layman as much as he satisfies the historian with the excitement of battle, the interplay of personalities and ambitions, and the effect of the Crusades on European history. The first volume takes the story through the First Crusade to the establishment of the Kingdom of Jerusalem, while the second and third volumes describe the Frankish years of glory in Outremer followed by their defeats and the undermining of the Crusaders' ideals.

The Crusades Through Arab Eyes, Amin Maalouf, Saqi Books (UK) 2001, Schocken (US) 1989. An interesting sifting of material – though almost everything in this account can be found in Runciman's *History of the Crusades*, and Arab writers were in fact never as interested in the Crusades as writers in Outremer or the West.

The Chronicles of the Crusades, Jean de Joinville and Geoffroy de Villehardouin, Penguin (UK and US) 1970. Both accounts are by French soldiers who fought in the holy wars, Villehardouin in the Fourth Crusade and its infamous conquest of Constantinople, and – relevant to the history of the Templars – Joinville in the Seventh Crusade when King Louis of France (the future St Louis) so miserably failed in his invasion of Egypt and cost so many Templar lives.

The Atlas of the Crusades, Jonathan Riley-Smith, editor, Times Books (UK), Facts on File (US), 1990. More than 120 maps accompanied by linking narrative, contemporary accounts and illustrations follow the military campaigns in detail and provide reconstructions of Crusader cities and castles and cross-sections of such buildings as the Church of the Holy Sepulchre.

Crusader Castles

Crusader Castles, Hugh Kennedy, Cambridge University Press (UK and US) 2001. An outstanding study of both Crusader and Muslim castles in the Holy Land, and in particular those castles built by the military orders. The work concludes with comments on the impact of the Crusader experience on castle-building back in the West. An appendix gives detailed coverage of the construction of the Templar castle at Saphet.

Jerusalem and the Temple Mount

A History of Jerusalem, Karen Armstrong, HarperCollins (UK) 1996, Ballentine Books (US) 1997. The way Armstrong uncovers layer after layer of the city's history is fascinating and informative, though it does suffer from an anti-Jewish and anti-Christian bias.

Below the Temple Mount in Jerusalem: A Sourcebook on the Cisterns, Subterranean Chambers and Conduits of the Haram Al-Sharif, Shimon Gibson and David M. Jacobson, British Archaeological Reports (UK), 1996. Since archaeological research is forbidden on the Temple Mount, the only source for what lies below are the reports, from ancient times to the early twentieth century, gathered here and meticulously analysed.

The Temple of Jerusalem, Simon Goldhill, Profile Books (UK) 2004, Harvard University Press (US) 2005. Part archaeology, and part religious and political history, this is a readable and informed account of the history of the Temple, from its founding to present times.

History of the Middle East

A History of the Arab Peoples, Albert Hourani, Faber (UK) 1991, Belknap Press (US) 2003. A useful general history of the Arab world which gives scant attention to the Crusades – testimony to how little they actually mattered in the larger world view of Arab imperialism.

The Middle East in the Middle Ages, Robert Irwin, Croom Helm (UK) 1986, ACLS History E-Book Project (US) 1999. The only serious study of the Mameluke period, and from that perspective covering the final decades, from 1250 to 1291, of the Crusader presence in Outremer.

Templar Locations in Britain

In Search of the Knights Templar: A Guide to the Sites in Britain, Simon Brighton, Weidenfield & Nicolson (UK and US) 2006. Much of the story of the Templars can be read from their material traces, which form an intimate part of the British landscape. This well-illustrated book is a complete guide to the surprising number of Templar churches, castles, estates and other survivals round the country.

The Holy Grail

Arthurian Romances, Chrétien de Troyes, Penguin Classics (UK and US) 1991. Where the Grail began. The medieval Grail myth was invented by the twelfth-century French writer of courtly romance, Chrétien de Troyes, but he died leaving his story hanging in the air, and it has been tantalising people ever since.

The Holy Grail: Imagination and Belief, Richard Barber, Allen Lane/Penguin (UK) 2004, Harvard University Press (US) 2005. This serious, fascinating and reliable compendium of theology, literary criticism and cultural history adds up to the true biography of a medieval myth.

The Cathars, Dualism and Other Heresies

The Cathars: Dualist Heretics in Languedoc in the High Middle Ages, Malcolm Barber, Longman (UK and US) 2000. Medieval heresy, orthodoxy and the Crusades are the subjects of this book, which also examines the social and political history of Languedoc and the rise of the Capetian dynasty. The Cathars infiltrated the highest ranks of society and posed a major threat not only to the Catholic Church but to secular authorities as well. This is a fascinating study of the development of radical religious belief and its violent suppression.

Montaillou, Emanuel Le Roy Ladurie, Penguin Books (UK) 1980, (US) 1990. The history of a small medieval village in the French Pyrenees, the last to actively support the Cathar heresy, told from a thoroughly human perspective.

The Other God: Dualist Religions from Antiquity to the Cathar Heresy, Yuri Stoyanov, Yale University Press (UK and US) 2000. A comprehensive history of religious dualism, the doctrine that man and cosmos are constant battlegrounds for the forces of good and evil and their supernatural protagonists, from late Egyptian religion to the crusade against dualism in medieval Europe.

Freemasons

King Solomon's Temple in the Masonic Tradition, Alex Horne, The Aquarian Press (UK) 1972, Wilshire Book Company (US) 1974. Using biblical and non-biblical sources, this work examines the position held by the Temple of Solomon in the allegorical, symbolical and spiritual background to the legends and practise of Freemasonry.

The Freemasons: A History of the World's Most Powerful Secret Society, Jasper Ridley, Constable and Robinson (UK) 2000, Arcade Publishing (US) 2001. Neither a Freemason nor a conspiracy theorist, Ridley is a veteran historian and biographer who provides a balanced and thoughtful account.

Revolutionary Brotherhood, Steven C. Bullock, University of North Carolina Press (UK and US) 1996. The introduction of Freemasonry from Britain to America in the 1730s and its role in establishing the new republic.

The Rosslyn Hoax?, Robert L.D. Cooper, Lewis Masonic (UK) 2006. Cooper is curator at the Grand Lodge of Scotland Library, and his many works include books on Scottish heritage, Freemasonry, a biography of the Sinclair (St Clair) family and a history of Rosslyn Chapel. Using original documents, he explores the fabrications and wishful thinking that lie behind the claims of a Templar connection with the Freemasons and with Rosslyn, the Sinclairs and Scotland.

Alternative History

The Holy Blood and the Holy Grail, Michael Baigent, Richard Leigh and Henry Lincoln, Arrow Books (UK and US) 1982. This was the book that brought together and often invented the elements – the Grail as the bloodline of Jesus, Mary Magdalene as his wife, the Templars and the Cathars – that powered Dan Brown's *The Da Vinci Code*. Two entire chapters, and many other scattered pages, are devoted to misrepresenting and manufacturing Templar history.

The Temple and the Lodge, Michael Baigent and Richard Leigh, Arcade Publishing (UK) 1991, Arrow (US) 2006. Building on their earlier success, the authors here link the Templars to the Freemasons via the Grail, the Scots Guards, Robert the Bruce, the French royal family, the Rosicrucians and the British Royal Society – and from these to the founders of the United States.

The Templar Revelation, Lynn Picknett and Clive Prince, Corgi (UK), Touchstone (US), 1998. The Leonardo da Vinci element in Dan Brown's *The Da Vinci Code* came straight out of this book, which also finds new and curious links between Mary Magdalene, the Freemasons, the Cathars and the Templars.

The Hiram Key, Christopher Knight and Robert Lomas, Arrow Books (UK and US) 1997. The Temple of Solomon, Hiram, the ancient Egyptians, Gnostics, Jesus, the Freemasons and, yes, the Templars all come together here to explain why 'the last four thousand years are never going to look the same again'.

Websites

There are myriad sites on the Web dealing with the Templars and the Crusades, as well as with such subjects as Gnosticism, the Ark of the Covenant and the Holy Grail. Here are some of the more useful and interesting ones.

Ancient and Medieval History Resources

The Online Reference Book for Medieval Studies
the-orb.net

The Crusades, the Templars, Islam, you name it: there is a wealth of serious sources available on this online reference site. Search for Templars, for example, and among other things you get an encylopedia entry by Malcolm Barber, the world's leading authority on the order, which in turn refers you to such subjects as the Latin Rule of 1129 and St Bernard's treatise *De Laude Novae Militiae*. The ORB is an academic site, written and maintained by medieval scholars for the benefit of their fellow instructors and serious students. All articles have been judged by at least two peer reviewers. Authors are held to high standards of accuracy, currency and relevance to the field of medieval studies.

The Internet Medieval Sourcebook
www.fordham.edu/halsall/sbook.html
This is a subsection of the Online Reference Book for Medieval Studies and will direct you to original sources for Pope Urban II's speech at Clermont launching the First Crusade, William of Tyre's account of the foundation of the Knights Templar, Ernoul's chronicle covering the battle of Hattin, the *Itinerarium Peregrinorium et Gesta Regis Ricardi* on how Richard the Lionheart made peace with Saladin, and Ludolph of Suchem's account of the fall of Acre in 1291. There are also such sources as the Cathar Gospel of John the Evangelist, Al-Makrisi's account of the Crusade of St Louis, and Benjamin of Tudela's twelfth-century account of his travels to Jerusalem and beyond.

Internet Ancient History Sourcebook
www.fordham.edu/halsall/ancient/asbook.html
Also a subsection of ORB, this website provides original sources for ancient history, including ancient Israel, the Graeco-Roman world and early Christianity.

Internet Jewish History Sourcebook
www.fordham.edu/halsall/jewish/jewishsbook.html
The ORB subsection providing sources for Jewish history.

Internet Islamic History Sourcebook
www.fordham.edu/halsall/islam/islamsbook.html
The ORB subsection providing sources for Islamic history.

Islamic Historiography
www.theatlantic.com/doc/199901/koran
'What is the Koran?' by Toby Lester, executive editor of Atlantic Unbound.
www.opendemocracy.net/faith-europe_islam/mohammed_3866.jsp
'What do we actually know about Mohammed?' by Patricia Crone, professor of Islamic History, Princeton University.
www.islamic-awareness.org
Information on Islam and rebuttal of critical arguments.

The Crusades

Crusades Encylopedia
www.crusades-encyclopedia.com
Established by Andrew Host, an American academic specialising in the Crusades, this website is a hobby with a serious purpose: to serve as a trustworthy tool

in providing reliable online material for students or enthusiasts of the period. It provides hundreds of primary and secondary sources on the Crusades, sections on such subjects as women and the Crusades, and on Islam, Judaism and the Crusades, as well as an extensive bibliography and links to each of the Crusades, to the Reconquista, to the military orders and to the Templars in particular.

The Templars

Jacob's Ford (Chastellet Castle) archaeological site
ateret.huji.ac.il
This site illustrates the continuing archaeological excavation of the Templar castle of Chastellet at Vadum Jacob, that is Jacob's Ford in northern Israel, which guarded the route across the Jordan river from Damascus. The castle was attacked by Saladin, eight hundred of its defenders were killed and their bodies were thrown into a ditch. These Templar bones and the remains of the castle itself provide new insights into the Crusader past.

Templar History magazine
www.templarhistory.com
This website of the leading magazine aimed at Templar enthusiasts contains numerous articles on Templar history, personalities, battles, locations, the myths that have grown up around the order, and so on, plus images, the text of original documents and an introduction to the literature about the Templars. Not to miss a trick, it also sells Templar shirts, hats and mugs.

Templar Globe
templars.wordpress.com
The Templar Globe announces itself as the bulletin of the International Chancellery of the Ordo Supremus Militaris Templi Hierosolymitani Universalis; in fact it appears to be a one-man blog, assisted by outside contributions, devoted loosely to things Templar. Its entries are in English, French, Spanish and Portuguese, and are generally accompanied by excellent illustrations, photographs and even videos.

Skull and Crossbones
www.skullandcrossbones.org
From an orthodox account of the Templars, this site branches out into fanciful and entertaining speculations, such as that the Templar fleet escaped the clutches of Philip IV, sailed for Scotland where the Templars helped Robert the Bruce win the battle of Bannockburn, and centuries later turned to piracy in the Caribbean. There are speculations too on Solomon's Temple and the exact position it would have occupied on today's Temple Mount, and articles on such varied topics as Saladin, the Dead Sea Scrolls, Prince Henry the Navigator, Athlit, the last Templar outpost on the mainland of Outremer, and descendants of the Templars now supposedly living in the backwoods of Tennessee.

The Chinon Parchment

The Chinon Parchment at the Vatican Secret Archives
asv.vatican.va/en/visit/doc/inform.htm
This site displays the original Chinon Parchment recently found in the Vatican Secret Archives and allows you to zoom in on every detail. The parchment gave Papal absolution to Grand Master James of Molay and other leading members of the Templars, clearing them of heresy, blasphemy and the other calumnies heaped upon them by King Philip IV of France.

The Chinon Parchment in Translation
www.inrebus.com/chinon.html
The Chinon Parchment, written in Latin, is here translated into English.

Jerusalem

Jerusalem Virtual Library
www.jerusalem-library.org
A cooperative venture between Al-Quds University and the Hebrew University of Jerusalem, this site provides online access to documents, maps, plans, inscriptions, illustrations and photographs illuminating the history of Jerusalem.

The Jerusalem Archaeological Park
www.archpark.org.il
Maps, plans, photographs and virtual reconstructions provide a vivid introduction to the archaeology of Jerusalem.

Undiscovered Jerusalem

www.gebus.com/index_eng.htm

An illustrated presentation of Jerusalem curiosities, including secret excavations beneath the Temple Mount, controversies over the Church of the Holy Sepulchre, the whereabouts of the True Cross, and a madness known as the Jerusalem Syndrome that overcomes a proportion of visitors to the city, usually Protestant Americans, who imagine themselves to be Mary Magdalene, John the Baptist or Jesus Christ.

The Ark of the Covenant

History of the Ark of the Covenant

www.arkstory.com/arkstory.html

Speculations on what happened to the Ark of the Covenant, with numerous links.

The Holy Grail

The Camelot Project

www.lib.rochester.edu/camelot

This educational website features the history of the Grail legend as told through art and literature. It is part of a project which looks at the Arthurian legend.

Gnosticism, Catharism and the Occult

The Gnostic Society

www.gnosis.org

Website of the Los Angeles-based Gnostic Society, with endless information on Gnosticism including translations and photographs of ancient Gnostic documents.

Gnosticism and Its Successors
www.bopsecrets.org/rexroth/essays/gnosticism.htm
An essay on Gnosticism and its successors, including Catharism and the modern-day taste for the occult, by the eminent American critic Kenneth Rexroth.

Freemasons

Pietre-Stones: Review of Freemasonry
www.freemasons-freemasonry.com
The premier educational source for Freemasons in all things to do with Freemasonry, including history, research papers, books, conferences, news and links – in five languages.

Index

The use of surnames has changed over time. Prior to the fifteenth century, individuals were known by their first name with a modifier. This index follows accepted practise in filing these individuals under their first name. So, for example, James of Molay goes under J for James and not M for Molay.

Names of fictitious characters are given in inverted commas, with the source in brackets e.g. Baltran (*Last of the Templars*).

The Templars:
a chronology

C1209 BC ✠ Date of the first non-biblical reference to Israel, contained on a stele of the Egyptian Pharaoh Merneptah. This approximates the traditional date, c1200 BC, for the arrival of the Jews in the Promised Land after their Exodus from Egypt.

C993 BC ✠ David conquers Jerusalem and makes it his capital; he brings the Ark of the Covenant to the city.

C958–C951 BC ✠ Solomon builds the Temple in Jerusalem; the Ark of the Covenant is placed in its holy of holies.

586 BC ✠ Assyrians capture Jerusalem and destroy the city and Solomon's Temple. The Ark of the Covenant is destroyed or lost at or before this time.

520 BC ✠ Work begins on the construction of the Second Temple in Jerusalem.

63 BC ✠ Palestine (as the Romans call it) becomes part of the Roman Empire.

20 BC–64 AD ✠ Construction of Herod's Temple.

C30 AD ✠ Crucifixion of Jesus of Nazareth in Jerusalem.

70 AD ✠ The Roman emperor Titus puts down the Jewish Revolt and destroys Jerusalem and Herod's Temple.

135 AD ✠ After the Second Jewish Revolt the Roman emperor Hadrian obliterates all trace of the Temple and builds a temple of Jupiter on the site.

C140 AD ✠ Valentinus teaches Gnosticism, which flourishes throughout the second and third centuries.

313 AD ✠ Edict of Toleration legalises Christianity throughout the Roman Empire.

326–28 AD ✠ Helena, mother of the emperor Constantine the Great, makes a pilgrimage to the Holy Land and discovers the True Cross and the Holy Sepulchre.

335 AD ✠ Dedication of the Church of the Holy Sepulchre.

622 AD ✠ Mohammed, the founder of Islam, flees his opponents in Mecca and establishes himself in Medina; this flight, hegira, marks the beginning of the Muslim calendar.

632 AD ✠ Death of Mohammed, by which time he has conquered all Arabia and brought it under the sway of Islam.

633 AD ✠ Mohammed's successor the caliph Umar declares a jihad against the Byzantine Empire.

633–37 AD ✠ Arab Muslim armies invade Syria, Iraq and Palestine.

638 AD ✠ Jerusalem is conquered by an Arab army under the caliph Umar.

710 AD ✠ The Arabs invade Spain.

732 AD ✠ Arab army defeated at Poitiers in France by Charles Martel.

750 AD ✠ Umayyad dynasty overthrown by the Abbasid dynasty which transfers the capital of the Arab Empire from Damascus to Baghdad.

938 AD ✠ Jerusalem's Muslims attack the city's majority Christian population during Palm Sunday procession and set fire to the Church of the Holy Sepulchre.

969 AD ✠ Fatimids invade Egypt and found Cairo.

1004 ✠ The Fatimid caliph Hakim launches a ferocious persecution of Christians throughout Egypt and Palestine.

1009 ✠ A turning point in Western attitudes towards the Muslim East comes when the Church of the Holy Sepulchre is destroyed on the orders of the caliph Hakim.

1014 ✠ By this year over 40,000 churches have been destroyed as a result of anti-Christian pogroms incited by Hakim.

1055 ✠ Seljuk Turks take Baghdad.

1056 ✠ Muslims forbid Christian pilgrims to enter Jerusalem.

1063 ✠ The papacy gives its blessing to a Crusade against the Muslim occupation of Spain.

1064 ✠ Hundreds of unarmed Christian pilgrims are murdered within sight of Jerusalem.

1071–80 ✠ Seljuk Turks occupy Asia Minor, Syria and Palestine.

1074 ✠ The Byzantine Emperor appeals to the Pope for help but without result.

1085 ✠ Christians capture Toledo from the Muslims in Spain.

1095 ✠ Again the Byzantines appeal to the West for help. Pope Urban II calls for a Crusade to defend the Byzantine Empire against the Seljuk Turks and to liberate Jerusalem.

1099 ✠ Jerusalem is captured from the Fatimids by the First Crusade.

1113 ✠ Foundation of the Knights Hospitaller.

1119 ✠ A large party of unarmed pilgrims is attacked by Muslims and many hundreds are killed while on their way from Jerusalem to the River Jordan (Easter). Foundation of the Knights Templar (Christmas Day) to defend pilgrims and the Holy Land.

1120 ✠ At the Council of Nablus (January), the Templars are accepted in the East. Probably during this year Templars are headquartered in al-Aqsa mosque on the Temple Mount in Jerusalem.

1127 ✠ Hugh of Payns, the first Templar Grand Master, meets Bernard of Clairvaux.

1129 ✠ Council of Troyes. Establishment of the Latin Rule of the Templars.

C1131 ✠ *In Praise of the New Knighthood* written by Bernard of Clairvaux.

1130s–1140s ✠ The Templars given grants of land and put in charge of castles by the emerging kingdom of Portugal as part of its struggle to repel the Muslim occupation of the Iberian peninsula.

C1136 ✠ The Templars are put in charge of Baghras castle to defend the Amanus Pass north of Antioch.

1139 ✠ The papal bull Omne Datum Optimum establishes the Templars as an independent and permanent order within the Catholic Church, answerable only to the Pope.

1140s ✠ Templars build the Paris Temple, which becomes the headquarters of their international financial empire.

1144 ✠ The County of Edessa falls to Zengi, marking the start of the Muslim reaction against the Crusaders.

1148–49 ✠ The Second Crusade.

1149–50 ✠ Gaza is granted to the Templars.

C1152 ✠ The Templars are given Chastel Blanc (Safita) and Tartus.

1153 ✠ Ascalon falls to the Franks.

1164–1167 ✠ King of Jerusalem's Egyptian campaigns supported by the Templars.

1171 ✠ Saladin puts an end to Fatimid rule and founds the Ayyubid dynasty in Egypt and Syria.

1173 ✠ The Templars murder the Assassin envoy.

1176 ✠ The Assassins threaten Saladin.

1181 ✠ Chretien des Troyes begins his romance, *Perceval, The Story of the Grail*.

1185 ✠ Temple Church in London is consecrated by Patriarch Heraclius of Jerusalem.

1187 ✠ The battles of the Springs of Cresson (1 May) and of Hattin (4 July). Jerusalem falls to Saladin (2 October).

1189–92 ✠ The Third Crusade.

1191 ✠ The Templars establish new headquarters at Acre.

1191–92 ✠ The Templars occupy and briefly own Cyprus.

1202–04 ✠ The Fourth Crusade. It is diverted by the Venetians to the Byzantine capital, Constantinople, which it captures (1204).

1208 ✠ Albigensian Crusade launched against the Cathars.

1218 ✠ Templars build a new fortress at Athlit.

1218–21 ✠ The Fifth Crusade.

1228–29 ✠ Crusade of Frederick II; he regains Jerusalem by treaty.

1236 ✠ The Christians capture Cordoba in Spain.

1244 ✠ Fall of the Cathar stronghold at Montsegur. Loss of Jerusalem. Battle of La Forbie.

1248–54 ✠ Crusade of St Louis.

1250–60 ✠ Emergence of a Mameluke sultanate in Egypt and Syria.

1266 ✠ The Mamelukes take the Templar castle of Saphet (Safad).

1268 ✠ The Mamelukes take Beaufort castle from the Templars.

1271 ✠ The Templars abandon Safita (Chastel Blanc) and the Hospitallers abandon Krak des Chevaliers to the Mamelukes.

1271–72 ✠ Crusade of Edward of England; he agrees a ten-year truce with the Mamelukes.

1291 ✠ Fall of Acre to the Mamelukes (May); the Templars evacuate Tortosa and Athlit (August).

1300–01 ✠ Templars attack the Egyptian coast; attempt to retake Outremer fails.

1302 ✠ Loss of Ruad off the Syrian coast and the massacre of the Templar garrison.

1307 ✠ Arrest of the Templars in France (October).

1308 ✠ James of Molay and other Templar leaders meet secretly with papal emissaries at Chinon and are absolved.

1310 ✠ Burning of fifty-four Templars as relapsed heretics near Paris.

1312 ✠ The papacy abolishes the Templars and transfers their property to the Knights Hospitaller.

1314 ✠ James of Molay, the last Grand Master, and Geoffrey of Charney are burnt to death in Paris (March). Pope Clement V dies (April). Robert the Bruce wins the battle of Bannockburn (June). Philip IV of France dies (November).

1319 ✠ Establishment of the Knights of Christ, successors to the Templars in Portugal.

1418 ✠ Prince Henry the Navigator becomes Grand Master of the Knights of Christ.

1456 ✠ Construction of Rosslyn Chapel.

1487 ✠ Publication of *Malleus Maleficarum*, the witchfinders' handbook.

1492 ✠ Christopher Columbus discovers America. The Christians capture Granada and drive the Muslims out of Spain.

1497 ✠ Vasco da Gama, a member of the Knights of Christ, finds the sea route round Africa to India.

C.1550 ✠ Origins of the Freemasons in England and Scotland.

1571 ✠ Destruction of the Templar archive in Cyprus by the Ottomans.

1687 ✠ Publication of *Principia Mathematica* by
Sir Isaac Newton.

1717 ✠ Foundation of the Freemasons' Grand Lodge in London.

1736 or 1737 ✠ Ramsay's Oration declares that Freemasons are the descendants of the Crusaders.

c1760 ✠ George Frederick Johnson states that Freemasons are the direct heirs of the Templars.

1776 ✠ American Declaration of Independence.

1789 ✠ Outbreak of the French Revolution.

1793 ✠ Louis XVI goes to the guillotine; 'James of Molay is avenged!'

1797 ✠ Augustin Barruel blames the Templars and Freemasons for the French Revolution.

1843 ✠ Scottish masonic order of Knights Templar invents the myth of the Templars at Bannockburn.

1844 ✠ James Smith, founder of the Mormons, is killed by a mob.

2001 ✠ Discovery of the Chinon Parchment in the Vatican Secret Archives.

Picture credits

Chapter openings, Corbis; p.18, Corbis; p.35, Corbis; p.43, Corbis; p.46, Corbis; p.73, Bettmann/Corbis; p.79, Stefano Bianchetti/Corbis; p.88, Bettmann/Corbis; p.100, Bettmann/Corbis; p.103, Alamy; p.115, Corbis; p.120, Alamy; p.139, Alamy; p.143, Alamy; p.147, Alamy; p.183, Bettmann/Corbis; p.189, British Library; p.196, Alamy; p.202, Alamy; p.206, Corbis; p.208, Alamy; p.210, Alamy; p.212, Hulton-Deutsch Collection/Corbis; p.218, Alamy; p.222, Alamy; p.240, Alamy; p.243, Alamy; p.247, Alamy; p.249, Alamy; p.254, British Library; p.260, Corbis; p.263, Bridgeman; p.266, Hulton Archive/Getty Images; p.268, Alamy; p.278, Bettmann/Corbis; p.289, Reuters/Corbis; p.292, Hanan Isachar/Corbis; p.298, Alamy; p.301, Alamy; p.305, Alamy; p.310, British Library; p.312, Alamy; p.315, Alamy; p.317, Alamy; p.321, Alamy; p.322, Alamy; p.328, Alamy; p.340, Alamy

A note on names

The names of all persons in this book have been rendered into English forms, so Hugues de Payns, one of the founders of the Templars, is Hugh of Payns; Jacques de Molay, the last Grand Master of the Templars, is James of Molay; and Guillaume de Nogaret, the persecutor of the Templars, is William of Nogaret. Similarly Salah al-Din Yusuf ibn Ayyub is simply Saladin.